KT-143-405

AS-Level
Geography

This book is packed with thorough notes and detailed case studies
covering everything you need to know for AQA AS-Level Geography
(including all the optional topics for Unit 1).

It's also got plenty of stuff to help you prepare for the exams.
There are warm-up and exam-style practice questions for every topic,
plus an Exam Skills section full of notes on the graph, map and statistical skills
you need for the Unit 2 exam.

And of course, we've done our best to make the whole thing vaguely entertaining for you.

Complete Revision and Practice
Exam Board: AQA

Published by CGP

Editors:
Ellen Bowness, Charlotte Burrows, Adam Moorhouse.

Contributors:
Margaret Collinson, Kevin Cooper, Chris Critchlow, Michael F. Dean, Paddy Gannon,
Thomas Leverage (M. A.), Helen Nurton, Sophie Watkins, Dennis Watts, Eileen Worthington BSc hons.

Proofreaders:
Katie Braid, Rosie Gillham

ISBN: 978 1 84762 417 8

With thanks to Laura Jakubowski for the copyright research.

Groovy website: www.cgpbooks.co.uk
Jolly bits of clipart from CorelDRAW®
Printed by Elanders Ltd, Newcastle upon Tyne.

Based on the classic CGP style created by Richard Parsons.

Photocopying – it's dull, grey and sometimes a bit naughty. Luckily, it's dead cheap, easy and quick to
order more copies of this book from CGP – just call us on 0870 750 1242. Phew!

Text, design, layout and original illustrations © Coordination Group Publications Ltd. (CGP) 2009
All rights reserved.

Contents

The Hydrological Cycle

What better way to start off a lovely new geography book than with some nice rivers...

Drainage Basins are Local Open Systems

Water doesn't **come into** or **leave** planet Earth — it's continuously **cycled** between the **oceans** and the **atmosphere**, returning to the ocean when it falls as **rain** (or other forms of **precipitation**, e.g. snow). This is known as the **global hydrological cycle**. The global hydrological cycle is a **closed system** — there are no **inputs** or **outputs**. There are also **local** hydrological cycles, e.g. **drainage basin hydrological cycles**:

1)   A river's **drainage basin** is the area **surrounding** the river where the rain falling on the land **flows** into that river. This area is also called the river's **catchment**.

2)   The **boundary** of a drainage basin is the **watershed** — any precipitation falling **beyond** the watershed enters a **different drainage basin**.

3)   Drainage basins are **open systems** with **inputs** and **outputs**.

4)   Water comes **into** the system as **precipitation** and **leaves** via **evaporation**, **transpiration** and **river discharge**.

Drainage basin of River A | Drainage basin of River B
Rain falling this side of the watershed will flow into this river. | Rain falling this side of the watershed will flow into this river.
watershed

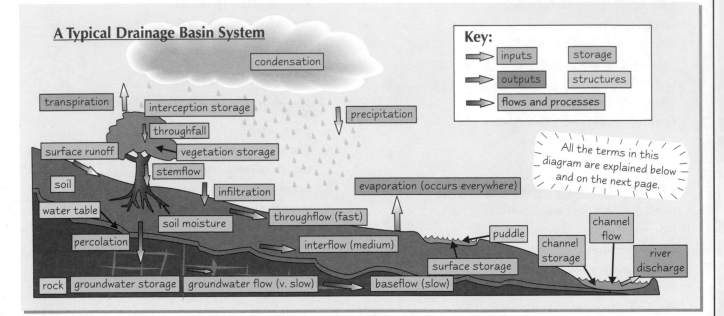

A Typical Drainage Basin System

Key:
→ inputs   storage
→ outputs   structures
→ flows and processes

condensation
transpiration
interception storage
throughfall
precipitation
surface runoff
vegetation storage
stemflow
soil
infiltration
evaporation (occurs everywhere)
water table
soil moisture
throughflow (fast)
percolation
interflow (medium)
puddle
channel flow
channel storage
river discharge
surface storage
rock | groundwater storage | groundwater flow (v. slow) | baseflow (slow)

All the terms in this diagram are explained below and on the next page.

You Need to *Learn* All This *Drainage Basin Terminology*

Inputs — Water Coming into the System

Precipitation includes **all** the ways moisture **comes out** of the atmosphere.
Precipitation is mainly **rain**, but don't forget the other types like **snow**, **hail**, **dew** and **frost**.

Storage — Water Stored in the System

1)   **Interception** is when some precipitation **lands on vegetation** or other structures, like **buildings** and **concrete** or **tarmac** surfaces, before it reaches the soil. Interception creates a **significant store** of water in **wooded areas**. **Interception storage** is only **temporary** because the collected water **evaporates** quickly.

2)   **Vegetation storage** is water that's been **taken up** by **plants**. It's all the water **contained** in plants at any one time.

3)   **Surface storage** includes water in **puddles (depression storage)**, **ponds** and **lakes**.

4)   **Groundwater storage** is water stored in the ground, either in the **soil** (**soil moisture**) or in **rocks**. The **water table** is the top surface of the **zone of saturation** — the zone of **soil** or **rock** where **all** the **pores** in the soil or rock are **full of water**. **Porous rocks** (rocks with lots of **holes** in them) that hold water are called **aquifers**.

5)   **Channel storage** is so obvious that it's often overlooked — it's the **water** held in a **river** or **stream channel**.

The Hydrological Cycle

Flows and Processes — Water Moving from One Place to Another

1) **Surface runoff** (also called **overland flow**) is water **flowing over** the **land**. It can flow over the **whole surface** or in **little channels**. Surface runoff is common in **arid areas** where **torrential rain** falls on **hard baked** land.

2) **Throughfall** is water **dripping** from one **leaf** (or other plant part) to **another**.

3) **Stemflow** is water running down a plant **stem** or a **tree trunk**.

4) **Throughflow** is water moving slowly **downhill** through the **soil**. Throughflow is **faster** through **"pipes"** — things like **cracks** in the **soil**, or **animal burrows**.

5) **Infiltration** is water **soaking** into the soil. **Infiltration rates** are influenced by **soil type**, **soil structure** and how much water's **already in** the soil. In a heavy **storm**, water **can't** infiltrate fast enough, so it **flows** over the surface.

6) **Percolation** is water **seeping down** through soil **into the water table**.

7) **Groundwater flow** is water flowing **slowly below** the **water table** through **permeable rock**. Water flows **slowly** through most rocks, but rocks that are **highly permeable** with lots of **joints** (gaps that water can get through) can have **faster** groundwater flow, e.g. limestone.

8) **Baseflow** is groundwater flow that **feeds** into rivers through river **banks** and river **beds**.

9) **Interflow** is water flowing **downhill** through **permeable rock above** the water table.

10) **Channel flow** is the water flowing in the **river** or **stream** itself. This is also called the **river's discharge**.

Outputs — Water Leaving the System

1) **Evaporation** is water turning into **water vapour** — **turning** from a **liquid** to a **gas**.

2) **Transpiration** is **evaporation** from **plant leaves** — plants and trees **take up** water through their roots and **transport** it to their **leaves** where it evaporates into the atmosphere.

3) **Evapotranspiration** is the process of evaporation and transpiration **together**.

4) **River discharge**, or **river flow**, is another **output**.

Potential evapotranspiration (**PET**) is the amount of water that **could** be lost by evapotranspiration. **Actual evapotranspiration** is what **actually** happens. For example, in a **desert** potential evapotranspiration is **high** (because **heat increases** the amount of **evaporation**) but actual transpiration is **low** (because there **isn't** that much moisture in the first place).

The *Water Balance* Shows the Balance Between *Inputs* and *Outputs*

Water balance is worked out from **inputs** (precipitation) and **outputs** (channel discharge and evapotranspiration). The water balance affects how much water is **stored** in the basin. The general water balance in the **UK** shows **seasonal patterns**:

1) In **wet seasons**, precipitation **exceeds** evapotranspiration. This creates a **water surplus**. The **ground stores fill** with water so there's **more surface runoff** and **higher discharge**, so **river levels rise**.

2) In **drier seasons**, precipitation is **lower than** evapotranspiration. **Ground stores** are **depleted** as some water is **used** (e.g. by plants and humans) and some flows into the **river channel**, but **isn't** replaced by precipitation.

3) So, at the **end** of a dry season, there's a **deficit** (**shortage**) of water in the ground. The ground stores are **recharged** in the next **wet season** (i.e. autumn).

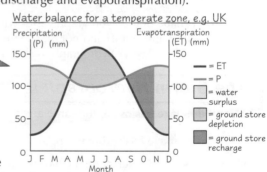

Water balance for a temperate zone, e.g. UK

- = ET
- = P
- = water surplus
- = ground store depletion
- = ground store recharge

Practice Questions

Q1 List five ways in which water is stored in the hydrological cycle.

Q2 Water vapour evaporates from the leaves of plants. What is this process called?

Exam Question

Q1 Describe how the water balance of the UK changes with the seasons. [4 marks]

My grandad has issues with water flow...

There are loads of words that you need to remember on these pages. It might seem like a pain, but if you learn them all now it'll mean the rest of the section will make a lot more sense. And you thought geography was just about colouring in maps...

River Discharge

Phew, I'm glad those last two pages are over — too many definitions for my liking.
None on this page thankfully... OK, when I said none, I actually meant a few.

River Discharge is the Volume of Water Flowing in a River

River discharge is simply the **volume** of water (in cubic metres, **m³**) that **flows** in a river **per second**. Unsurprisingly, it's measured in **cubic metres per second** (**m³/s**) — this is a bit of a mouthful, so geographers usually just shorten it to **cumecs**. River discharge is **affected** by:

1) **Precipitation** — the **more** precipitation, the **higher the discharge**.
2) **Hot weather** — the **higher** the temperature, the **lower the discharge** because the rate of **evaporation** is **higher**.
3) **Removal of water** from the river (**abstraction**) — also **reduces the discharge**.

Nelly was an abstraction master when she had a thirst on.

Hydrographs Show River Discharge Over a Period of Time

Hydrographs are graphs of river **discharge** over **time**. They show how the **volume of water** flowing at a certain point in a river **changes** over a **period of time**. **Storm hydrographs** show river discharge around the time of a **storm event**. They only cover a relatively **short time period** (hours or days, rather than weeks or months).

(1) **Peak discharge** — this is the **highest** point on the graph, when the **river discharge** is at its **greatest**.

(2) **Lag time** — this is the delay between **peak rainfall** and **peak discharge**. This delay happens because it takes **time** for the rainwater to **flow** into the river. A **shorter** lag time can **increase peak discharge** because more water reaches the river during a **shorter period of time**.

(3) **Rising limb** — this is the part of the graph **up to** peak discharge. The river discharge **increases** as rainwater flows into the river.

(4) **Falling limb** — this is the part of the graph **after** peak discharge. **Discharge** is **decreasing** because **less water** is flowing into the river. A **shallow** falling limb shows water is flowing in from **stores** long after it's **stopped raining**.

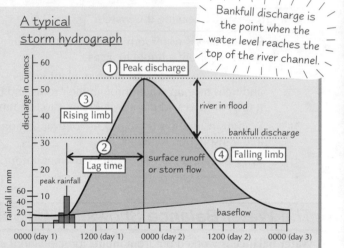

Bankfull discharge is the point when the water level reaches the top of the river channel.

The **exact shape** of the hydrograph varies with each **river drainage basin** and each individual **storm event** (see below). A basin with **rapid runoff** and not much **storage** capacity gives a hydrograph with a **short lag time** and **high peak discharge**. This is called a "**flashy**" hydrograph — the graph has **steep**, roughly **symmetrical** rising and falling limbs.

The Storm Hydrograph is Affected by Physical Factors

Not all **drainage basins** are the **same** and the **weather** tends to vary too — these **physical factors** affect the storm hydrograph:

1) **Drainage basin characteristics** — the **physical features** of the drainage basin affect **lag time** and **peak discharge**.

- **Larger drainage basins** can catch **more precipitation**, so they have a **higher peak discharge** compared to smaller basins. But **smaller basins** generally have **shorter lag times** because precipitation has **less distance** to travel, so reaches the main channel **quicker**.
- **Steep-sided** drainage basins have **shorter lag times** than shallower basins — water flows **more quickly** downhill into the river on steep slopes. This can also **increase peak discharge**.
- **Circular** basins are more likely to have a **flashy** hydrograph than **long, narrow** basins. This is because all points on the **watershed** are roughly the **same distance** from the point of discharge **measurement**. This means lots of water will reach the measuring point at the **same time**, **increasing peak discharge**.
- Basins with **lots of streams** (high **drainage density**) drain **quickly**, so have **shorter lag times**.

2) The **amount** of water **already present** in the drainage basin ("**antecedent moisture**") — affects **lag time**.

- If the ground's already **waterlogged** (the soil can't **absorb** any more water) then **infiltration** is **reduced** and **surface runoff increases**. Surface runoff is much **faster** than **throughflow** or **baseflow**, so rainwater reaches the river **more quickly, reducing lag time**.

River Discharge

3) **Rock type** — affects **lag time** and **peak discharge**.

- **Impermeable rocks** don't **store** water or let water **flow** through them. This **reduces infiltration** and **increases surface runoff, reducing lag time**. **Peak discharge** also **increases** as **more water** reaches the river in a shorter period.

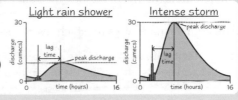

See pages 2-3 for definitions.

4) **Soil type** — affects **lag time** and **peak discharge**.

- **Sandy soils** allow a lot of **infiltration**, but **clay soils** have very **low infiltration rates**. Low infiltration rates **increase surface runoff, reducing lag time** and **increasing peak discharge**.

5) **Vegetation** — affects **lag time** and **peak discharge**.

- Vegetation **intercepts** precipitation and **slows its movement** to the river channel, **increasing lag time**. Interception is **highest** when there's **lots of vegetation** and **deciduous trees** have their **leaves**.
- The **more vegetation** there is in a basin, the **more water** is **lost** (through **transpiration** and **evaporation** directly from the vegetation) before it reaches the river channel, **reducing peak discharge**.

6) **Precipitation** — affects **peak discharge**.

- **Intense storms** will generate **more precipitation** and so **greater peak discharges** than **light rain showers**.
- The **type** of precipitation also affects **lag time** — e.g. snow that's fallen in a **winter storm** can melt (**meltwater**) and flow into the river in **spring**, giving a **very long lag time**.

7) **Temperature** — affects **lag time** and **peak discharge**.

- **Hot, dry** conditions and **cold, freezing** conditions both result in **hard ground**. This **reduces** infiltration and **increases surface runoff** – reducing **lag time** and increasing **peak discharge**.
- **High temperatures** can **increase evapotranspiration**, so **less water** reaches the river channel, reducing **peak discharge**.

Human Activity Also Affects the Hydrograph

1) In **urban areas**, much of the **soil** is covered with man-made **impermeable** materials like **concrete**. Water **can't infiltrate** into the soil, which **increases surface runoff**, so water flows **more quickly** into the river. This makes the **lag time short** and **increases peak discharge**.

2) Man-made **drainage systems** affect the hydrograph in a similar way. Water flows down **drains** into the river before it can **evaporate** or **infiltrate** into the soil, causing a **shorter lag time** and **increased peak discharge**.

Practice Questions

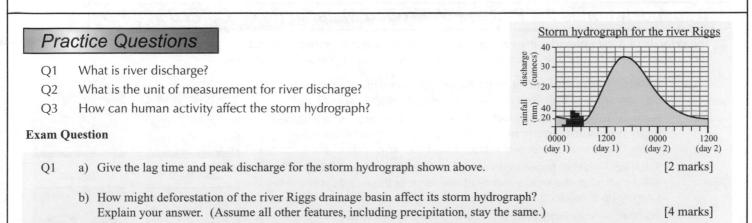

Q1 What is river discharge?

Q2 What is the unit of measurement for river discharge?

Q3 How can human activity affect the storm hydrograph?

Exam Question

Q1 a) Give the lag time and peak discharge for the storm hydrograph shown above. [2 marks]

b) How might deforestation of the river Riggs drainage basin affect its storm hydrograph? Explain your answer. (Assume all other features, including precipitation, stay the same.) [4 marks]

I ain't saying she's a gold digger, but she loves her flashy hydrographs...

Storm hydrographs can look quite confusing, but they're not so bad once you've got your head round them. If you can explain how and why all the physical factors and human activities affect river discharge and lag time then you've nailed it, good and proper.

River Processes

I could try and come up with an amusing introduction to erosion, but I'm only four pages into this section and rivers are really starting to wear me down.

Erosion Can Affect the Length, Depth and Width of a River

The **energy** of a river flowing **downhill** causes **erosion**. The **bed** (the **bottom** of the river channel) and **banks** (the **sides** of the river channel) of a river can be **eroded** — making the river **longer**, **deeper** and **wider**:

Headward erosion

Valley head

Banks

River

Key
→ Direction of water flow
→ Direction of erosion

Headward erosion makes the river **longer**. It happens near a river's **source** as **throughflow** and **surface runoff** causes **erosion** at the point the water **enters** the river channel (the **valley head**).

Vertical erosion

River | Banks

Vertical erosion deepens river channels. It happens in the **upper stages** of a river.

Lateral erosion

River | Banks

Lateral erosion makes the river **wider**. It happens in the **middle** and **lower** stages of a river.

There are **five** main ways in which river erosion happens:

1) **Hydraulic action** — the **pressure** of the **water** breaks **rock particles** away from the bed and banks. It's strongest in **rapids** and **waterfalls** (see p. 10), and during **floods**.

2) **Abrasion (corrasion)** — eroded pieces of rock in the water **scrape** and **rub** against the bed and banks, **removing material**. **Most erosion** of river beds and banks happens by abrasion.

3) **Attrition** — eroded rocks **smash** into each other and break into **smaller** fragments. Their edges also get **rounded off** as they rub together. Attrition **doesn't erode** the bed and banks — it just makes the particles of rock in the river **smaller** and **more rounded**.

The more eroded material a river carries, the more erosion it can cause by abrasion.

4) **Cavitation** — **air bubbles** in turbulent stretches of water **implode** causing **shockwaves** that **break** pieces of rock off the banks and bed.

5) **Corrosion (solution)** — the dissolving of rock by **chemical processes**. **Carbon dioxide** dissolves in water to form a **weak acid**, which reacts with rocks like **limestone** and **chalk**, breaking them down.

Transportation is the Process of Eroded Material Being Carried in a River

The **velocity** of a river provides the **energy** needed for it to **transport eroded material**. The eroded material carried in a river is called its **load**, and it can be carried in **four** ways:

1) **Solution** — substances that can **dissolve** are carried along **in** the water. E.g. **limestone** is dissolved into river water that's slightly **acidic**.

2) **Suspension** — very **fine** material, like **silt** and **clay** particles, is whipped up by **turbulence** (**erratic swirling** of water) and carried along in the water. **Most** eroded material is transported this way.

3) **Saltation** — **larger particles**, like **pebbles** or **gravel**, are too heavy to be carried in suspension. Instead, the **force** of the water causes them to **bounce** along the river bed.

4) **Traction** — **very large** particles, e.g. **boulders**, are **pushed** along the river bed by the force of the water.

Material transported by **traction** or **saltation** is called the river's **bedload**.

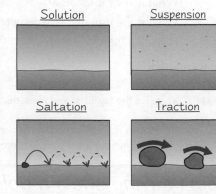

Solution   Suspension

Saltation   Traction

River Processes

Deposition is the Process of Dropping Eroded Material

Deposition happens when the river **loses energy**. When it **slows down**, it loses energy and **drops** some of its load. The speed and energy of a river can be reduced in many ways:

1) **Reduced rainfall** causes **lower discharge**, which means the river **slows down** and has **less energy**.

2) **Increased evaporation** or **abstraction** (taking water out of a river for human use) also causes **lower discharge**.

3) **Friction**, e.g. in **shallow** areas of the river and **close to the banks**, reduces the **speed** of the river, reducing its **energy**.

4) When the river is forced to **slow down**, e.g. before a **narrow section** of the channel, it **loses energy**.

5) A lot of energy is **lost** when the river meets the **sea** (the sea **absorbs** the energy).

The Capacity of a River is the Total Amount of Material It Can Carry

1) The **capacity** is the **total load** (measured in volume, weight or mass) that a river can **transport** at a given point.

2) The load of a river can be **divided** into **different categories** according to **particle size**. The particle sizes range from fine **silt** and **clay** (less than 0.1 mm in diameter) to **big boulders**.

3) The **competence** describes the **maximum particle size** that a river is capable of **transporting** at a given point.

The Hjulström Curve Shows the Link Between River Velocity and Competence

The **competence** of a river is affected by the amount of **energy** it has, which is related to its **velocity** — generally, the greater the velocity, the greater the energy. The **Hjulström curve** shows the **relationship** between river velocity and competence. It also shows how the **processes** of **erosion**, **deposition** and **transportation** vary with river velocity:

- The **critical erosion velocity curve** on the graph shows the **minimum velocity needed** for the river to **pick up** (erode) and **transport** particles of **different sizes** (in suspension or as bedload). It takes a **higher velocity** to **erode** material than it does to just **transport** material.

- The **mean settling velocity curve** shows the velocities at which particles of **different sizes** are **deposited**, i.e. it shows the **competence** of the river at different velocities.

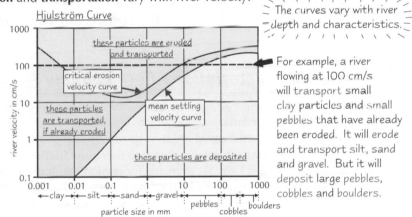

The curves vary with river depth and characteristics.

For example, a river flowing at 100 cm/s will transport small clay particles and small pebbles that have already been eroded. It will erode and transport silt, sand and gravel. But it will deposit large pebbles, cobbles and boulders.

The graph also shows that particles of **sand** (between 0.1 and 1 mm in diameter) can be **eroded** at **lower velocities** than **finer particles** such as **silt** and **clay**. This is because **silt** and **clay** particles **stick together more** than sand, which means they're **harder** to dislodge, so it requires **more energy** (greater velocity) to erode them.

Practice Questions

Q1 Name the four ways a river can transport its load.

Q2 Briefly describe two reasons why a river drops its load.

Q3 What is meant by the competence of a river?

Exam Questions

Q1 Describe the five main ways in which river erosion can happen. [5 marks]

Q2 Outline how the critical erosion velocity curve on a Hjulström graph varies with particle size. [6 marks]

Hjulström curve — sounds more like something you'd find in IKEA®...

OK, apart from that scary-looking diagram, this is all pretty simple. Bits of river beds and banks get knocked and scraped into the water (erosion). The river carries the material along while it's got enough speed and energy (transportation) and then drops it when it slows down (deposition). The faster the river is going, the more energy it has, so the more stuff it can carry. Not too bad...

The Long Profile and Channel Characteristics

The long profile — well, it's long and, erm, a profile. And that's all I have to say about that. Well, not quite...

The **Long Profile** Shows the **River's Gradient** from Its **Source** to the **Sea**

1) A **long profile** shows you how the **gradient** of the river channel **changes** from the river's **source** to its mouth by showing the **height of the river bed** above the **base level** for the whole length of the river.

2) The **base level** is the **lowest point** that the river **can erode to** — usually **sea level** (or the level of a **lake** or **reservoir**).

3) The **total amount** of erosion and deposition along the **full course** of a river are **balanced**. But the **rates** of **erosion** and **deposition change** along the course of a river. This can result in the formation of **landforms** such as **waterfalls** (where the rate of **erosion** is **higher** than the rate of **deposition** — see p. 10), which make the profile **uneven**.

4) Because the **total** amount of erosion and deposition is **balanced**, the rate of erosion of landforms like waterfalls is **equal** to the rate of deposition elsewhere along the river. This means that **over time** the long profile will **change** from being uneven to a **smooth curve**. This is called a **graded profile** (but it hardly ever happens).

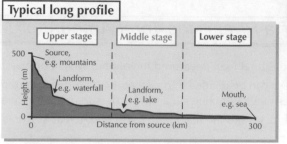

Typical long profile

Upper stage | Middle stage | Lower stage

Source, e.g. mountains

Landform, e.g. waterfall

Landform, e.g. lake

Mouth, e.g. sea

Height (m)

Distance from source (km)

Graded profile

Erosion has 'smoothed out' the waterfall.

Deposition has 'filled in' the lake.

Height

Distance from source

Royal profile

A river's course can be split into **three stages** — **upper** (near the source), **middle**, and **lower** (near the mouth). The **energy** of a river **varies** in each stage:

1) In the **upper stage**, the **gradient** is **steep** and the river is **high** above sea level, which gives it lots of **potential energy** (energy that can be **converted** into **other forms**, e.g. kinetic).

2) As the gradient **decreases** towards the **middle stage**, potential energy is converted to **kinetic energy** (movement) — the river **gains velocity**.

3) In the **lower stage**, the river has **little** potential energy, but **lots** of kinetic energy — it flows **faster**.

Channel Characteristics Affect **Velocity** and **Discharge**

The **velocity** (kinetic energy) and **discharge** of a river **increase** as you go **downstream** from source to mouth. Discharge **increases** as **tributaries** (smaller streams and rivers) and **more surface runoff** join the main channel. **River velocity** is influenced by gradient (see above), **discharge** and **channel characteristics** — the **shape** and **roughness**.

1) Most of a river's kinetic energy is used to **overcome friction** — the rest causes **erosion**. The **more energy** a river has available for **erosion** and **transportation**, the **more efficient** it is. An efficient river will have a **high velocity**, **high discharge** and **little friction**.

2) **Efficiency** is measured by **hydraulic radius**. The **larger** its hydraulic radius the **more efficient** a river is.

- The **hydraulic radius** is the channel's **cross-section area divided** by the **length** of its **wetted perimeter** (the **total length** of the **banks** and river **bed** that are in contact with the water).
- **Contact** between the water and the wetted perimeter creates **friction**, which **increases energy loss** and **slows the river down**.
- A **larger hydraulic radius** means that a **smaller proportion** of water is in contact with the wetted perimeter. So **friction is lower**, which **reduces energy loss**, increasing **velocity** and **discharge**.
- **Smooth, narrow, deep** channels (like channel **A**) have a **larger hydraulic radius** and so are **more efficient** than **shallow, broader** ones (like channel **B**).

A
Banks 5 m
Bed 5 m
Wetted perimeter = 15 m
Cross-section area = 25 m²
Hydraulic radius = 1.7

B
Banks 2 m
Bed 7 m
Wetted perimeter = 11 m
Cross-section area = 14 m²
Hydraulic radius = 1.3

3) **Channel roughness** also affects the efficiency. **Protruding banks** and **large, angular boulders** on the river bed **increase the wetted perimeter** and cause **more friction**. This **reduces** efficiency, velocity and discharge.

4) As channel roughness **increases**, so does **turbulence** (erratic swirling of the water in the main flow). Turbulent flow is **more effective** at **picking up** particles from the river bed than smooth flow — so turbulence causes **greater erosion**.

5) Channel roughness is **greatest** in the **upper stages** of the river. So although the **gradient** is steep, the river **loses** a lot of energy to **friction**, so discharge and velocity are **lowest** here during **normal conditions**.

6) In the **lower stages**, the banks and bed of the river are **smooth**, so there's much **less friction**. This means **less energy** is lost, so discharge and velocity are the **highest** in this stage.

The Long Profile and Channel Characteristics

River Processes Change as the River Flows from Source to Mouth

Upper stage	Middle stage	Lower stage
EROSION Mainly **vertical** and by **abrasion** (there's also some **hydraulic action**). Erosion occurs when there are **high-energy conditions** (i.e. when **velocity** and **discharge** are high after heavy rain or ice melt). The **rough channel** causes **turbulence** and the **large, angular bedload** is dragged along the **river bed**, causing **intense** downwards (**vertical**) **erosion**.	**EROSION** Mainly **lateral** and by **abrasion**. **Attrition** of **larger particles** in this stage means that sediment **particle size decreases** from source to mouth.	**EROSION** Although **velocity** and **discharge** are **highest** in this stage, there's **less erosion** because **turbulence is lower** and **sediment particle size is reduced** (reducing abrasion). Some **lateral erosion** occurs during the **formation of meanders**.
TRANSPORTATION Mainly **large particles** such as **boulders** carried by **traction** or **saltation** during high-energy conditions.	**TRANSPORTATION** More material carried in **suspension** as particle size **decreases**. Some larger particles moved by **saltation**.	**TRANSPORTATION** Mainly **smaller particles** such as **silt** and **clay** carried by **suspension**, or substances carried **in solution**.
DEPOSITION Little deposition — mainly **largest particles** deposited in the **river bed** as energy levels drop.	**DEPOSITION** **Sand** and **gravel** are deposited across the **flood plain** as the river floods and **friction** reduces the river's energy.	**DEPOSITION** **Smaller particles** such as **sand, silt** and **clay** are deposited on the **flood plain** when the river **floods** and in the **river mouth** as the **sea absorbs river energy**.

There's more about these processes on page 6.

The Cross Profile Shows the Shape of the River Channel and Valley

The **cross profile** of a river shows you what a **cross-section** of the **river channel** or the **river valley** looks like. The **valley** cross profile changes during the **different stages** of a river's **long profile**.

1) **Upper stage** valleys are **steep V shapes**. **Vertical** erosion creates **narrow** valley floors and **steeply sloped** sides.
2) **Middle stage** valleys are **wider**, caused by **lateral erosion**. **Deposition** creates a **flood plain** on the valley floor.
3) **Lower stage** valleys are **wide** with **gently sloping** sides. There's a much **wider flood plain** caused by **deposition**.

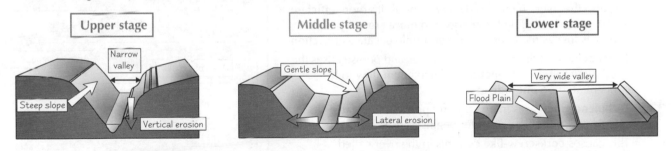

Practice Questions

Q1 What does the long profile of a river show?

Q2 Describe the features of a lower stage river valley.

Exam Questions

Q1 What does the hydraulic radius tell you about a river, and how is it calculated? [3 marks]

Q2 Outline how the processes of erosion, transportation and deposition change along a river's long profile. [6 marks]

It's not the length of your wetted perimeter that counts, it's the hydraulic radius...

Phew, there's quite a lot of terms to learn on these pages: wetted perimeter, hydraulic radius, efficiency, roughness and turbulence. Learn what they all mean and how they affect velocity, discharge, erosion, transportation and deposition during the river's stages.

River Landforms

Hurrah! After a few pretty dull pages, you get to learn about all kinds of brilliant river landforms.

> *Fluvial just means it's caused by rivers and streams.*

Waterfalls, Rapids and Potholes are Caused by Fluvial Erosion

Waterfalls

1) Waterfalls form where a band of **hard** rock meets **softer** rock. The soft rock is **eroded more** than the harder rock, causing a 'step' in the river bed.

2) The water flowing over the step **speeds up** due to the **lack of friction** as it drops over the step. This increase in speed gives the water **greater erosive power**, causing further erosion of the soft rock and **undercutting** of the harder rock.

3) As the hard rock is **undercut**, it can **collapse**. A deep **plunge pool** is carved out by **abrasion** at the foot of the waterfall as the bits of **collapsed rock** are **swirled** round by **turbulence**.

4) **Over time**, **more undercutting** causes **more collapse**. The waterfall will **retreat** (move **back up** the channel), leaving behind a **steep-sided gorge**.

Potholes

Potholes are **small circular hollows** in the river bed. They're formed by **abrasion** as turbulence swirls a river's **bedload** round in a **circular motion**, causing it to **rub** and **scrape** out holes.

Rapids

Rapids are relatively steep sections of river with **turbulent flow** where there are **several sections** of **hard rock**. They're a bit like **mini-waterfalls**.

Meanders are Formed by Combined Erosion and Deposition

Large, **sweeping curves** in a river's middle and lower stages are called **meanders**. They're formed by **erosion** and **deposition**.

1) **Meanders** form where **alternating pools** (areas of **deep** water) and **riffles** (**shallow** water) develop at **equally spaced intervals** along a stretch of river. The distance between pools is **5-6 times** the **width** of the river bed.

2) Because the river channel is **deeper** in pools it's more **efficient** (see p. 8), so it has **greater energy** and **more erosive power**. Energy is **lost** as the river flows over a riffle because of **friction**.

3) The **spacing** and **distance** between riffles and pools causes the river's flow to become **uneven** and **maximum flow** to be concentrated on **one side** of the river.

4) **Turbulence increases** in and around **pools** as the **water speeds up**, so the flow of water begins to **twist** and **coil**.

5) This causes **corkscrew-like** currents in the river called **helicoidal flow**, which **spiral** from bank to bank between pools.

6) The helicoidal flow causes more **erosion** and **deepening** of the pools. It also causes **eroded material** to be **deposited** on the **inside** of the **next bend**, where the river **loses energy**.

7) The **combination** of erosion and deposition **exaggerates** the bends until large **meanders** are formed. The combined processes also create the meanders' distinctive **asymmetric cross-section**.

8) **Oxbow lakes** are formed when the **neck** of the loop of a meander is **broken** through, often during **flooding**. **Deposition** dams off the loop, leaving an oxbow lake.

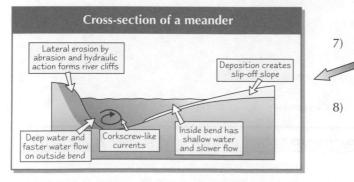

River Landforms

Braiding, Flood Plains, Levees and Deltas are Caused by Fluvial Deposition

Braiding

1) **Braiding** occurs when rivers are carrying a **vast amount** of **eroded sediment** (e.g. in meltwater).

2) If the river's **velocity drops**, or the sediment **load** becomes **too much** for the river to carry, sediment is **deposited** in the channel.

3) This causes the river to **divide** into many **small**, **winding** channels that eventually rejoin to form a single channel.

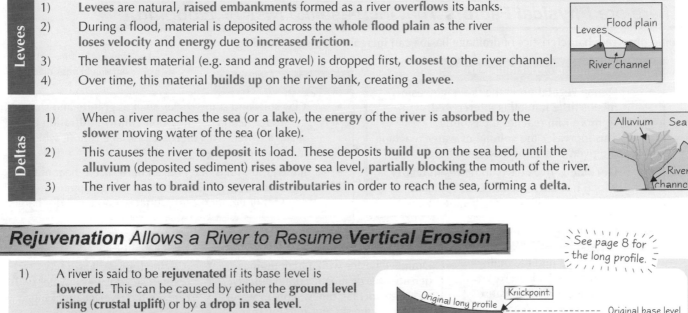

River channel

Deposited sediment

Flood plains

1) When a river **overflows** its banks and floods the flat land either side of the river (the **flood plain**), there's an **increase** in the **wetted perimeter** and **reduction** in **hydraulic radius**.

2) This **increases friction**, reducing the velocity of the river and causing fine **silt** and **sand** to be **deposited** across the flood plain.

Levees

1) **Levees** are natural, **raised embankments** formed as a river **overflows** its banks.

2) During a flood, material is deposited across the **whole flood plain** as the river **loses velocity** and **energy** due to **increased friction**.

3) The **heaviest** material (e.g. sand and gravel) is dropped first, **closest** to the river channel.

4) Over time, this material **builds up** on the river bank, creating a **levee**.

Levees — Flood plain
River channel

Deltas

1) When a river reaches the sea (or a lake), the **energy** of the **river** is **absorbed** by the **slower** moving water of the sea (or lake).

2) This causes the river to **deposit** its load. These deposits **build up** on the sea bed, until the **alluvium** (deposited sediment) **rises above** sea level, **partially blocking** the mouth of the river.

3) The river has to **braid** into several **distributaries** in order to reach the sea, forming a **delta**.

Alluvium   Sea
River channel

Rejuvenation Allows a River to Resume Vertical Erosion

See page 8 for the long profile.

1) A river is said to be **rejuvenated** if its base level is **lowered**. This can be caused by either the **ground level rising** (**crustal uplift**) or by a **drop in sea level**.

2) The drop in base level gives the river greater **potential energy**, increasing its **vertical erosion** potential.

3) The **long profile** of the river is **extended** and a **knickpoint** (a sharp change in gradient, often a **waterfall**) will form and mark the junction between the **original** long profile and the new one.

Original long profile — Knickpoint — Original base level
New long profile — New base level
Source   Mouth

There are distinctive **landforms** associated with rejuvenation:

1) **River terraces** are former **flood plains** which have been left **above** the level of **present-day** flooding following increased **vertical erosion**.

2) **Incised meanders** are formed when a river keeps its meandering course as **vertical erosion** increases. The result is a **deep**, **winding valley** with **steep sides**. The river is left **far below** the level of the **former flood plain**.

Practice Questions

Q1 Briefly describe how waterfalls are formed.

Q2 Name two river landforms associated with rejuvenated rivers.

Exam Question

Q1 Describe the formation of levees. [4 marks]

Drove my Chevy to the levee — but the levee was just an old riverbank...

Don't be too rapid in going over the stuff on these pages — you'll only end up in deep water. But don't spend forever meandering around the facts. Slip off and take a break if you need to and come back rejuvenated. That's the best way to nick points in the exam.

Causes and Impacts of Flooding

Right... time to learn what causes rivers to go wild (but not in a good way, unless you're a kayaker) and what happens when they do.

Prolonged Rainfall and Heavy Rainfall are the Main Causes of Flooding

1) **Flooding** occurs when the **discharge** of a river is **so high** that the **river spills over** its **banks** onto the **flood plain**.

2) A **major cause** of flooding is **prolonged rainfall**. After a **long period** of **rain**, the **ground** becomes **saturated** (it **can't absorb** any more water). Any further rainfall **can't infiltrate**, which **increases surface runoff**, which **increases discharge**.

3) **Heavy rainfall** (e.g. the rain you get with **thunderstorms**) can lead to **rapid surface runoff** if the rainfall is **too intense** for **infiltration** to occur. This can lead to a **sharp rise** in **river discharge** called a **flash flood**.

4) **Melting snow** and **ice** also lead to a **huge increase** in a river's **discharge**. For example, **melting snow** in the **Himalayas** contributes to the **annual summer flooding** of the **River Ganges** in **Bangladesh**.

If you don't know what any of these terms mean see pages 2-3.

There are Physical Factors That Increase the Risk of Flooding...

Some **physical characteristics** of **drainage basins** can **increase** the **risk** of flooding:

Lag time is the time between peak rainfall and peak discharge.

Sparse vegetation or deciduous trees

- **Sparse vegetation** in the drainage basin means **little rainfall** is **intercepted**, so **more rain** reaches the **ground**. This **increases the volume of water** reaching the river, which **increases discharge**.

- **Deciduous trees** have **no leaves** in **winter**, which has the **same effect** as sparse vegetation — little rainfall is intercepted.

Impermeable ground

- **Clay soils** and some **rocks**, such as **granite** and **shale**, are **impermeable** — they **don't allow infiltration** of surface water. This **increases surface runoff**, which **increases discharge**.

- If the ground has been **baked hard** by the heat of the summer, or it's **frozen**, the **same thing happens** — water **can't infiltrate**, increasing surface runoff and discharge.

Circular drainage basins

Water draining into the main river channel will **all arrive** in a **short space of time** because all points in the basin are a similar distance from the river. This **increases discharge**.

High drainage density

Drainage basins with a **high drainage density** (lots of streams) drain **quickly**, so have **short lag times**. Lots of water flows from the streams into the main river in a **short space of time**, **increasing discharge**.

Steep slopes

If the **drainage basin** has **steep-sided valleys**, water will reach the **river channel** much **faster** because water flows **more quickly** on steeper slopes. This **increases discharge**.

...and Human Factors

Humans often make flooding more **frequent** and more **severe** by **changing things** in the **drainage basin**:

A lot of these factors are the same as those that reduce lag time and increase the peak discharge on a flood hydrograph — see pages 4-5.

Urbanisation

- **Urban areas** have **large areas** of **impermeable tarmac** and **concrete**, so when it rains **surface runoff** is **very rapid**.

- **Gutters** and **drains** quickly take **runoff** to **rivers**.

- Both of these things **reduce lag time** and so **increase discharge**.

Deforestation

- **Clearing trees** and plants **reduces interception** and **evapotranspiration**. This **increases** the **volume of water** that reaches the channel, which **increases discharge**.

- Deforestation leaves the soil **loose**. The soil is **eroded** by rainwater and **carried** to the **river**, which **raises the river bed**. This **reduces** the **channel capacity**, so it takes **less water** for the river to **flood**.

Flood management strategies

Flood management strategies (see pages 16-17) can actually end up making **flooding worse**. For example, if **dams fail** they release a **huge volume** of **water all at once** — giving a huge **increase** in **discharge**.

Agriculture

Overgrazing leaves areas with **less vegetation**, so has the same effect as deforestation (see above). **Overgrazing** and **ploughing** also **increase soil erosion**.

Climate change

Climate change could cause an **increase** in **rainfall** and **more storms** in some areas, which could **increase flooding**.

Causes and Impacts of Flooding

Flooding Affects People, the Economy and the Environment

Here are some of the **possible** impacts:

Social impacts

1) **People** and **animals** can be **killed**.
2) **Floodwater** is often **contaminated** with **sewage**, which can lead to a **lack** of **clean drinking water**.
3) **Contaminated water** can also put people at **risk** of **diseases** (e.g. **diarrhoea** and **dysentery**)
4) **Possessions** can be **damaged** by floodwater or **lost** (washed away).
5) People can be made **homeless** as their **properties** are **inundated** or **damaged**.

Economic impacts

1) **Businesses** often have to shut down as premises are **inundated** and **power supplies** are affected.
2) **Rescue work** and **repairs** are usually **costly**. **Insurance premiums** go **up** after floods.
3) **Unemployment levels** often **rise** as **businesses shut down** because they can't recover from the flooding.
4) **Public transport, roads** and **bridges** can be **destroyed**.
5) **Crops** can be **destroyed**. This can lead to a **rise** in the **price** of **food**.

Environmental impacts

1) **Floodwater contaminated** with sewage and rubbish can **pollute rivers**.
2) **River banks** are **eroded**.

Positive impacts include:

1) **River sediment** is **deposited** on the **flood plain**. This makes the land **more fertile**.
2) **Wetlands** can be created, e.g. **marshes** and **ponds**, which are **habitats** for many species.

The **social** impact is usually **higher** in **poorer countries** because flood defences are poorer, people are less able to evacuate, sanitation systems aren't as good and buildings are of a poorer quality. The **absolute economic** impact is usually **higher** in **richer countries** as they have more high value buildings and infrastructure. However, the **relative economic** impact is usually **higher** in **poorer countries** — the buildings and crops that are damaged are worth less money, but this affects the economy more because they have less money to recover from it (e.g. to rebuild homes).

Flood Frequency Can be Calculated

1) Floods of a **very large size** (**magnitude**) don't happen very often — they're **not very frequent**.
2) **Small floods** happen more often — they're **more frequent**.
3) Large floods usually occur due to **unusually** heavy or prolonged rainfall.
4) By keeping **records** over many **years**, people can **predict how often** a flood of a certain magnitude may **occur** — this is called the **flood return interval** (**RI**).

> For example, if a **2 m** high flood occurred along a river in **1701, 1806** and **1899** — then the **return interval** of a 2 m high flood is about **100 years**.

5) A **small flood** may have an **RI** of **one** or **two years**, whereas a **huge flood** may have an **RI** of **100 years** or more.

There are exceptions to this rule — large floods occur frequently when they're caused by annual snow melt or annual monsoons, e.g. a large flood happens in Bangladesh every year.

Henry made sure he was definitely prepared for the flood this time.

Practice Questions

Q1 Why is prolonged rainfall a major cause of flooding?

Q2 Name two human activities that increase the risk of flooding.

Q3 Briefly describe the possible social impacts of flooding.

Q4 Briefly describe the possible economic impacts of flooding.

Q5 What is a flood return interval?

Exam Questions

Q1 Outline the physical characteristics of a drainage basin that would have a high risk of flooding. [6 marks]

Q2 Explain two ways in which urbanisation increases the risk of flooding. [5 marks]

If only the "getting wet" part of flooding were the worst part...

It's normal for rivers to flood occasionally, but us humans have made it more of a problem. You need to learn all the causes and impacts of flooding — use boring old list-making to help you. List the causes under two headings (natural and human) and the impacts under three headings (social, economic and environmental). Colour them nice and prettily. Oh yeah — then learn 'em.

Causes and Impacts of Flooding — Case Studies

Just to make learning case studies more difficult, the causes and impacts of flooding are different in different places. Flooding in poorer areas tends to have a much bigger impact on people's lives and health than flooding in wealthier areas...

Case Study 1 — Flooding of South Asia, 2007

Parts of **South Asia** flood **most years**, usually in **late summer**. This is **because**:

1) **South Asia** has a **monsoon climate** — **80%** of **rain** falls in just **four months**.

2) Much of **South Asia** is **low-lying land**, particularly **Bangladesh** where **90%** of **land** is **less** than **10 m above sea level**.

3) **Melting snow** and **ice** from the **Himalayas** in the **late summer** months **increase** the **Brahmaputra River discharge**.

In **July** and **August 2007**, the **flooding** was **particularly severe** in **Bangladesh** and **India**.

Physical factors were the main cause...
1) The **monsoon** came **suddenly** after a **very dry, early summer**.
2) There was **heavy rainfall** — **Assam** had a **record 169.5 mm** in **24 hours** on **22nd July**, and **900 mm** in total for **July**.
3) The **long duration** of **heavy rainfall** completely **saturated** the **soil**, **increasing surface runoff** and **increasing discharge**.
4) The **peak discharges** of the **River Ganges** and **Brahmaputra** coincided, which **increased the river discharge downstream**.

...but **human activities** made the **flooding worse**
1) **Deforestation** in **Nepal** and the **Himalayas** meant less rainfall was intercepted, which **increased discharge**.
2) The **growth** of **urban areas**, due to **migration**, also **increased surface runoff**.
3) **Collapse** of old **earth dams** in **Madhya Pradesh**, **India**, caused **further flooding**.

The Flooding Had Major Impacts, Especially on People

SOCIAL IMPACTS

1) **Over 2000 people died**. The **death toll** was **high** for many reasons, e.g. many people were **reluctant** to **evacuate** (as they'd have to leave their **land** and **livestock unattended**) and many **children drowned** because they **couldn't swim**. **Poor transport links** meant evacuation was **slow**.

2) As **wells** became **polluted** with **sewage**, there was a **lack** of **clean drinking water**. **Over 100 000 people** caught **water-borne diseases** (e.g. dysentery and diarrhoea).

3) An estimated **25 million people** were made **homeless**.

4) **112 000 houses** were **destroyed** in **India**, as **porous mud bricks** became **saturated** by **floodwater**.

5) **Dhaka** (Bangladesh's capital) was **inundated**, especially the **poorer districts** and **shanty towns** near the river.

6) Children **lost out** on **education** as **4000 schools** were **affected** and **44 schools** were totally **destroyed**.

ECONOMIC IMPACTS

1) The **cost** of the **flood** was estimated at **US$ 1 billion**, including damage to **crops** and **property**.

2) **Factories** were **closed** around **Dhaka**, due to **flood damage** and **loss** of **raw materials** (e.g. **rice**). Many of the **poorest workers** became **unemployed**.

3) There was **widespread loss** of **livestock** (e.g. **cattle**). Since **80%** of **Bangladeshis rely** on **agriculture**, many **lost** their **livelihoods**.

4) **550 000 hectares** of **land couldn't** be **planted** with **rice** at **peak time**, because of **flooded fields**. A **lower rice crop** meant the **world price** of **basmati rice rose** by **10%**.

5) **10 000 km** of **roads** were **destroyed**. Landslides blocked roads in the **highlands** of **Nepal** and **Assam**.

6) **Debt increased**, both **individually** (e.g. farmers borrowed money for food and seeds) and **nationally** (e.g. governments imported food and medicine).

ENVIRONMENTAL IMPACTS

1) The flood deposited **fertile silt** on the **flood plain**.

2) **Rivers** were **polluted** with **sewage**.

Human Factors Made the Impacts Worse

1) **Bangladesh** is a **poor country** so there **aren't** many **flood defences** or **flood warning systems** in place.

2) **Low incomes, few savings** and **little insurance** limited people's **ability** to **recover** after the flood.

3) **Corrupt officials diverted aid money** away from the people most in need.

Causes and Impacts of Flooding — Case Studies

Case Study 2 — Flooding of Carlisle, Cumbria, 2005

The **River Eden** runs through **North Cumbria** and reaches the sea near **Carlisle**.

1) The **drainage basin** of the River Eden is **very large** so it **catches** a **large volume** of **rainfall**, leading to a **high river discharge**.

2) Some parts of the basin have **steep sides**, so water runs **quickly** down to the **river**.

3) There are **many streams** that **drain quickly** into the river, making the **lag time short**.

On **8th January 2005**, the **River Eden** flooded **Carlisle**.
The **flood return interval** (RI) of such a large flood is about **200 years**.

Physical factors were the main cause...

1) There was **heavy rainfall on the 6th** January, for **36 hours**. **200 mm** of **rainfall** was recorded, which was the **equivalent of four months** rain.

2) Rain fell on **saturated ground** so the water **didn't soak** into the ground but **ran straight off** into the **river**.

3) This caused a **very high peak discharge** (**over 1520 cumecs**), compared to an **average discharge of 52 cumecs**.

...but human activities made the flooding worse

1) Carlisle is a **large built-up area**, with **impermeable concrete** and **tarmac surfaces**, and **little soil** or **vegetation**. This meant there was **little infiltration** of rainfall and **high surface runoff**, which **increased discharge**.

2) **Drains** and **sewerage systems overflowed** in some areas — becoming a **source** of **flooding** themselves. **25%** of the **flooding problems** were associated with **overflowing drains**.

The Flooding Had Major Impacts, Particularly on Carlisle's Economy

SOCIAL IMPACTS

1) **Three people died** in the floods.

2) **Over 3000 people** were made **homeless** for up to a **year** and thousands of **personal possessions** were damaged. Living in **temporary accommodation** disrupted lives in many ways, e.g. **travel arrangements** were **disrupted**, people were **separated** from **community networks** and friends, and they had **problems receiving post**.

3) Children **lost out on education** as **four schools** were **severely flooded**. **Newman Catholic School** didn't re-open until **Easter**.

4) There was an **increase** in **stress-related illnesses** following the floods.

ENVIRONMENTAL IMPACTS

1) The flooding **increased river bank erosion** in some areas.

2) **Rivers** were **polluted** with rubbish and sewage.

ECONOMIC IMPACTS

1) It took about a **year** to **repair** the **damage** to homes and repairs **cost over £100 million**.

2) **350 businesses** had to **shut down** as there was **no electricity, telephone service** or **transport**. Trade activities from Carlisle **railway** station were **suspended**.

3) **United Biscuits**, the **largest employer** in Carlisle, was **flooded** with **3 m** of water that caused **over £5 million damage**. **33** out of 1100 employees **lost their jobs**.

4) **70 000 addresses** had **no power**. The **sewage works, police station, fire station** and **council offices** were **severely flooded**.

5) **80 buses** (most of the public transport fleet) were **destroyed**. Many **roads** and **bridges** were **damaged**, e.g. **Warwick Road**.

Practice Questions

Q1 Briefly describe the physical reasons why the 2007 floods in South Asia were particularly severe.

Q2 Briefly describe the economic impacts of the 2005 Carlisle flood.

Exam Question

Q1 Using two named examples, compare the impacts of flooding in poorer and wealthier countries. [10 marks]

Rain, rain, go away — come again another day but not all at once in one big downpour...

Flooding can cause havoc, and it takes a lot of time and money to get things back to normal again. And it's not just the sheer amount of water — don't forget the knock-on effects, like contaminated water supplies, landslides, job losses, food price rises...

Flood Management Strategies

Flooding can cause major disasters, so unsurprisingly people try to stop it happening. There are various ways of doing this, but as usual there are various problems associated with each way.

There's **Not Enough Money** to **Protect Everywhere** from **Flooding**

1) The aim of flood management is to **protect homes**, **businesses** and the **environment** from **flooding**.

2) This is because flooding can have severe **social**, **economic** and **environmental impacts** (see p. 13).

3) It's **tricky** trying to **manage flooding** though — there **isn't enough money** available to **protect everywhere**.

4) Choosing **which** places are protected (and **how** they're protected) is done using **cost-benefit analysis**.

5) **Large settlements** and **important industrial sites** (e.g. power plants) are **more likely** to be protected than small settlements or farmland.

Flood Management Includes Hard Engineering and Soft Engineering

1 Hard Engineering Defences Involve Built Structures

Hard engineering defences are **man-made structures** that **reduce flooding**.
General disadvantages of hard engineering defences include:

1) They're **expensive** to **build** and **maintain**, and need **technical skill**. **Poorer countries** often **can't afford** these flood defences.

2) **Floods** happen **less often**, but they can be **more hazardous** if they do happen. E.g. if a **dam breaks** then a **huge** amount of water will **rapidly flood** the land.

3) **Natural processes** are **disrupted**, e.g. **crops** don't get **fertile silt** from river sediment during **low-level flooding**.

4) Some people think they're **ugly**.

Fortunately, flood defence strategies have progressed somewhat over the years.

Here are some of the **most common** types of **hard engineering defences**:

Scheme	How it works	Extra benefits	Disadvantages
Dams	Dams are huge walls built across rivers. A reservoir (artificial lake) is formed behind the dam. Flood water is caught by the dam, which prevents flooding downstream. The water is released as a steady flow throughout the year.	• Turbines are often built into the dams, which generate electricity. • Steady water release allows irrigation of land below the dam throughout the year. • People can use the reservoir for recreational activities, e.g. sailing.	• They're very expensive. • Land is flooded when a reservoir is created. This often destroys farmland and forces people to move elsewhere. • They affect wildlife, e.g. they can prevent salmon migrating upstream to breeding grounds. • They trap sediment normally carried in rivers. This can cause the dam to fail. It can also cause increased erosion downstream, as there's less protective sediment being deposited.
Channel straightening	Channel straightening is where meanders are removed by building artificial cut-throughs. This makes the water flow faster, which reduces flooding because water drains downstream more quickly and doesn't build up to a point where the river channel can't contain it any more.	It takes less time to navigate the river because it has been made shorter.	• Flooding may happen downstream instead, as flood water is carried there faster. • More erosion occurs downstream because the river flows faster. • Altering river channels disturbs wildlife habitats.
Levees	Levees are embankments built along rivers. The river can hold more water without overflowing and so it floods less often.	They allow the flood plain to be built upon.	• They're quite expensive. • There's a risk of severe flooding if the levees are breached.
Diversion spillways	Diversion spillways are channels that take water elsewhere if the water level in the river is too high. Water is normally diverted around an important area or to another river. They prevent flooding because river discharge is reduced. The spillways often have gates that can be opened, so the release of water can be controlled.		• An increase in discharge when the diverted water joins another river (or rejoins the same one) could cause flooding below that point. • If spillways are overwhelmed, water will flood areas not used to flooding, which could cause even bigger problems.

Flood Management Strategies

(2) Soft Engineering Defences Work With, Not Against, the Basin Processes

Soft engineering defences use **knowledge** of the **whole river basin** and its **processes**, to try to **work with nature**. General **advantages** are:

1) They're **cheaper** to **maintain** than hard engineering defences — this is **especially important** for **poorer countries**.
2) **Flooding** is more **predictable**, **reducing** the **risk** of an **unexpected disaster**.
3) They can **improve opportunities** for **recreation**, such as **fishing**.
4) Some people think they're **more attractive** than hard engineering schemes.

Here are some of the **most common** types of **soft engineering defences** that **reduce flooding**:

Scheme	How it works	Extra benefits	Disadvantages
Land use management	Planning restrictions prevent buildings or roads being constructed on the flood plain. Use of the flood plain is restricted to things like playing fields, allotments or parks. More water can infiltrate so there's less surface runoff, which reduces discharge and flooding.	• There are no new buildings or roads on the flood plain to be damaged, so the impact of any flooding is reduced. • It provides recreational opportunities, e.g. football fields.	• It restricts development. This is especially a problem where there's a shortage of housing. • It can't be used in areas that are already urbanised.
Wetland and river bank conservation	Wetlands store flood water and also slow it down. This reduces flooding downstream. So conserving or re-establishing wetlands gives natural protection from flooding. Planting trees and shrubs along the river bank increases interception and lag time, and reduces discharge. This also decreases flooding.	• Vegetation protects the surface soil from erosion. • The vegetation provides habitats for wildlife.	Less land is available for farming.
River restoration	River restoration involves making the river more natural, e.g. by removing man-made levees. The flood plain can then flood naturally. As the water spreads out over the flood plain the river's discharge is reduced (because less water is in the channel), which reduces flooding downstream.	• Little maintenance is needed, as the river's left in its natural state. • The river provides a better habitat for wildlife.	Local flood risk can increase, especially if nothing's done to prevent major flooding.
Alteration of urban surfaces	Building porous pavements or soakaways increases infiltration, which reduces rapid surface runoff to the river channel. This increases lag time, which reduces discharge and flooding.	Any pollutants in the water are filtered out by the soil before the water reaches the channel.	It's expensive.

Areas of trees and shrubs along river banks are called riparian buffers.

Soakaways are hollows or trenches filled with gravel.

The **impact** of **flooding** can also be **reduced**:

Scheme	How it works	Disadvantages
Weather forecasts and flood warnings	The Environment Agency monitors weather forecasts, rainfall and river discharge. They warn people about possible floods through TV, radio, newspapers and the internet. This means people can evacuate before the flood happens, saving lives. People can also move possessions and use sandbags to help reduce damage if flooding occurs.	• Some people might not be able to access the communication network. • Flash floods may happen too fast for warnings. • People may ignore warnings if they were inaccurate in the past.

Soft Engineering is More Sustainable than Hard Engineering

Hard engineering is often **expensive** and **disrupts natural processes**. Soft engineering tends to be **cheaper** and requires **much less time** and **money** to **maintain** than hard engineering. Soft engineering is designed to **integrate** with the natural **environment** and it creates areas like **wetlands**, which are important **habitats** for **wildlife**. So soft engineering's a **more sustainable management strategy** than hard engineering because it has a **lower economic cost** and **environmental impact**.

Practice Questions

Q1 What is hard engineering? Give an example of a hard engineering flood defence.
Q2 What is soft engineering? Give two advantages of using soft engineering rather than hard engineering defences.

Exam Question

Q1 Explain how flooding can be reduced without the use of major man-made structures. [8 marks]

Flood management strategies — let the ideas come flooding in...

Flood management is a pretty difficult task — whatever scheme you decide on, there are drawbacks. Also, saving your own neck often causes a flood somewhere else — usually downstream of you (which isn't a very neighbourly thing to do, really)...

Flood Management Strategies — Case Studies

Here are two beautiful case studies for you — showing you how different places manage floods in different ways.

Hard Engineering is Used on the Yangtze to Control Flooding

1) The **Yangtze River** flows through **China**. At 6380 km long, it's the **third longest** river in the world.

2) **Seasonal flooding** is **common** around the Yangtze — China has a **rainy season** that lasts from about **June** until **August** and the huge **increase** in **river discharge** during this time often causes flooding. Flooding causes **huge problems** as there's lots of **farmland** and loads of **major cities** next to the river, e.g. **Wuhan** and **Nanjing**.

3) **Five major floods** have happened over the **last century** — in 1931, 1935, 1949, 1954 and 1998.

4) The flood of **1954** covered **193 000 km²** of land and **killed 33 169 people**. Over **18 million people** had to **move**. It covered the city of **Wuhan** for **over 3 months**.

5) The flood in **1998 killed** around **3000 people** and made **14 million** people **homeless**.

6) **Flood protection** is mostly done through **hard engineering** defences.

Defences Include Dams and Levees

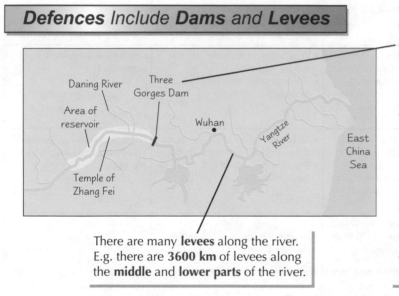

There are many **levees** along the river. E.g. there are **3600 km** of levees along the **middle** and **lower parts** of the river.

There are many **dams** on the Yangtze that reduce flooding (**46** are planned or under construction at the moment). The biggest of these is the **Three Gorges Dam**:

1) Work began on the **101 m high** Three Gorges Dam in **1994**.

2) A **reservoir** is building up behind the dam (it takes years to build up as the dam is huge). The reservoir **catches** any **flood water**, which can then be slowly released over time. The reservoir can store around **22 km³** of flood water.

3) It's also the largest **hydroelectric power station** in the world. The flow of water turns **26 turbines** built into the dam.

4) **Locks** have been built alongside the dam so **ships** can get past it.

Hard Engineering Has Reduced Flooding but Has Also Caused Problems

The construction of the **Three Gorges Dam** has had many **positive effects**, but also plenty of **negative effects**:

Positive effects

1) It's thought that the dam has **reduced major flooding** from **once every 10 years**, to once every **100 years**.

2) The turbines in the dam produce a lot of **electricity** — capacity is likely to reach **22.5 gigawatts** (enough to supply about **3%** of China's demand, which is loads).

3) The **reduction in flooding** has made it much **safer** to **navigate** up the Yangtze. **River shipping** has also **increased** as **bigger ships** can now travel up the river because the reservoir is deeper than the old river.

Negative effects

1) People have had to **relocate** as the water level in the reservoir has risen. It's thought that between **1.3** and **2 million people** in total will have to **relocate** by the time it's full — **13 cities** and **1352 villages** will be submerged.

2) The reservoir will also flood **farmland**, **657 factories**, and **1300** sites of **cultural** and **historic interest**. For example, as the water rises the **Temple of Zhang Fei** will be submerged.

3) A huge amount of **sediment** is normally carried down the Yangtze River. The dam will **trap** the sediment, which could lead to **failure** of the dam and cause **catastrophic flooding**.

4) The dam could **destroy habitats** and **endanger species**. E.g. the endangered **Siberian crane** spends the winter in wetlands below the dam, which are expected to be affected by less flooding. Fewer than 100 **baiji dolphins** are left in the Yangtze, and the dam could **reduce their food supply**.

5) The Three Gorges Dam **doesn't protect everyone** — rising water levels in the reservoir will **increase flooding** along the **tributaries** that lead into it, e.g. the **Daning River**. The increased water levels in the tributaries will also increase **erosion** of **riverbanks**, causing collapses and landslides.

Levees have also caused problems:

1) In the **1998 floods** many levees **broke**, which contributed to **devastating flooding**.

2) After this, many levees were **reinforced**. They were **effective** at **reducing flooding** in the **2002 floods** (though the floods were **less severe** than the 1998 ones).

Flood Management Strategies — Case Studies

Soft Engineering is Used in Abingdon to Control Flooding

1) **Abingdon**, a town in South-east England, was **built** on the **flood plains** of the **River Thames** and the **River Ock**.

2) **1500 properties** in Abingdon have a **1% chance** of **flooding** in a given year.

3) Abingdon has had **regular floods** over the years — in 1947, 1968, 1977, 1979, 1992, 2000 and 2007.

4) **Intense storms** in **July 2007** caused particularly bad **flash floods**. The **River Thames** and **Ock** burst their banks, flooding **660 properties** in **Abingdon**. **Increased surface runoff** in built-up areas made the flooding **even worse**.

5) **Hard engineering** defences have been considered but have been **rejected** for various reasons. E.g. a **diversion spillway** to transport Ock floodwater south of Abingdon was **too expensive**, and **flood barriers** to protect properties along the Ock would **increase flood risk downstream**. Flood protection is mostly done through **soft engineering** defences.

Defences Include Land Use Management, Flood Warnings and Soakaways

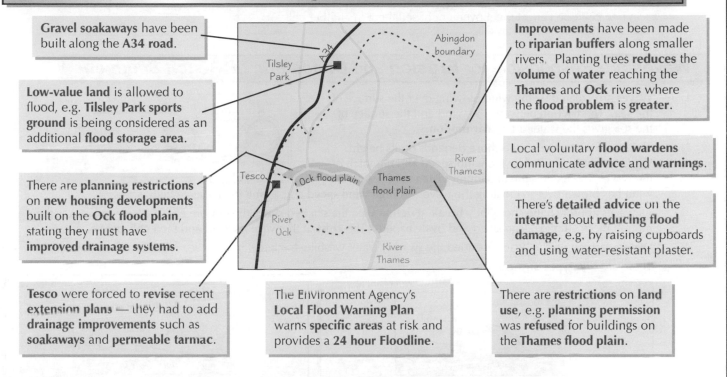

Gravel soakaways have been built along the **A34 road**.

Low-value land is allowed to flood, e.g. **Tilsley Park sports ground** is being considered as an additional **flood storage area**.

There are **planning restrictions** on **new housing developments** built on the **Ock flood plain**, stating they must have **improved drainage systems**.

Improvements have been made to **riparian buffers** along smaller rivers. Planting trees **reduces** the **volume** of **water** reaching the Thames and Ock rivers where the **flood problem** is **greater**.

Local voluntary **flood wardens** communicate **advice** and **warnings**.

There's **detailed advice** on the **internet** about **reducing flood damage**, e.g. by raising cupboards and using water-resistant plaster.

Tesco were forced to **revise** recent extension plans — they had to add **drainage improvements** such as **soakaways** and **permeable tarmac**.

The **Environment Agency's Local Flood Warning Plan** warns **specific areas** at risk and provides a **24 hour Floodline**.

There are **restrictions** on **land use**, e.g. **planning permission** was **refused** for buildings on the **Thames flood plain**.

Soft Engineering Reduces Damage but Floods Still Happen

1) It's **difficult** to **measure** the **success** of flood defences because it's hard to figure out if any reduction in flooding was because of the **success** of new defences, or because the weather conditions were **less severe**.

2) Several **flood warnings** were issued by the **Environment Agency** in early **2008**.

3) The **Ock flood plain**, which has developments on, **didn't get flooded**. The **Thames flood plain did get flooded** but it's largely **clear of development**, due to **land use management** and **planning restrictions**.

4) The **2008 floods** did **less damage** than in previous years, with **minimal cost**, **little disruption** to community services, **no lives lost** and only a **few injuries**. However, **flooding** does still happen in **Abingdon**.

Practice Questions

Q1 List the types of hard engineering used on the Yangtze.

Q2 List the types of soft engineering used around Abingdon.

Exam Question

Q1 With reference to named examples, discuss the success of different engineering approaches to flood prevention. [10 marks]

Maybe if we all get together and ask the clouds to please not rain...

You can't ask for two case studies more different than these. You need to know who's built what, where, and why — and if it's successful.

Introduction to Coastal Environments

Coastal environments are the areas where the land meets the sea. And they're almost as exciting as they sound...

Coasts are Systems — They Have Inputs, Processes and Outputs

1) **INPUTS** — **river sediment**, sediment from **cliffs** that have been **eroded** or suffered **landslides**, and sediment that has been **transported** by waves from **offshore** (out at sea).

2) **PROCESSES** — **wave action**, **tidal movement**, **erosion**, **weathering**, **transportation**, **deposition**.

3) **OUTPUTS** — sediment **washed out to sea**, or deposited **further along** the coast.

> **Coastal sediment cells** (also called **littoral cells**) are lengths of coastline that are pretty much entirely **self-contained** for the movement of sediment. Each one is a **coastal system**. So **processes** going on in **one cell** don't affect the movement of sediment in **another** cell.

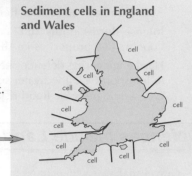

Sediment cells in England and Wales

Waves are Responsible for Erosion and Deposition of Beach Sediment

1) **Waves** are created by the **wind** blowing over the surface of the sea. The **friction** between the wind and the surface of the sea gives the water a **circular motion**.

2) The **effect of a wave** on the **shore** depends on its **height**. Wave height is affected by the **wind speed** and the **fetch** of the wave. The fetch is the **maximum distance of sea** the wind has blown over in creating the waves. A **high wind speed** and a **long fetch** create **high** waves.

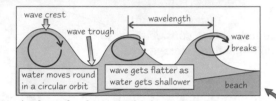

3) As waves approach the shore they **break**. **Friction** with the sea bed **slows** the bottom of the waves and makes their motion more elliptical (squashed and oval-shaped). The **crest** of the wave rises up and then **collapses**.

4) Water washing **up** the beach is called the **swash**. Water washing **back** towards the sea is called the **backwash**.

5) There are **two types** of wave:

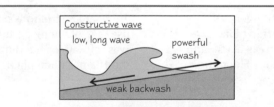

Constructive waves have a **low frequency** (only around **6-8** waves per minute). They're **low** and **long**, which gives them a more **elliptical** cross profile. The powerful swash carries material up the beach and **deposits** it.

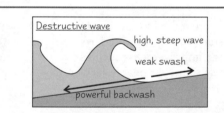

Destructive waves are **high** and **steep**, with a more **circular** cross profile. They have a **higher frequency** (**10-14** waves a minute). The strong backwash **removes** material from the beach.

6) The waves in an area are usually mainly constructive or mainly destructive.

Wave frequency is how many waves pass a point in a particular time.

Tides Affect Where Waves Break

Tides are the periodic **rise** and **fall** of the **ocean surface**. They're caused by the gravitational pull of the **Moon** and the **Sun**. Tides affect the **position** at which **waves break** on the beach (at high tide they break higher up the shore). The area of land between **maximum high tide** and **minimum low tide** is where landforms are created and destroyed.

See page 52 for more on weathering.

Sub-aerial Weathering Occurs Along the Coastline

1) **Sub-aerial weathering** describes coastal processes that are **not linked** to the action of the sea. It includes **freeze-thaw weathering** and **salt weathering**. Weathering **weakens cliffs** and makes them **more vulnerable** to **erosion**.

2) **Throughflow** (the flow of water through the cliffs) and **runoff** (the flow of water over the land) caused by **heavy rain** can also make cliffs more **unstable** and increase the likelihood of **mass movement**.

3) Mass movement is the **movement of material downhill** due to gravity. It includes **landslides**, **slumping** (a type of landslide) and **rockfalls**.

Introduction to Coastal Environments

There are **Five** Main Ways **Waves Erode** the **Coastline**

Waves don't just erode beaches — they also erode **rocks** and **cliffs**. Here are the five main ways they do it:

1) **Abrasion/corrasion** — Bits of rock and sediment transported by the waves smash and grind against rocks and cliffs, breaking bits off and smoothing surfaces.

2) **Hydraulic action** — Air in cracks in cliffs is **compressed** when waves crash in. The pressure exerted by the compressed air breaks off rock pieces.

3) **Quarrying** — The energy of a wave as it breaks against a cliff is enough to detach bits of rock.

4) **Corrosion/solution** — **Soluble rocks** (e.g. limestone, chalk) get gradually **dissolved** by the seawater.

5) **Attrition** — Bits of rock in the water smash against **each other** and break into smaller bits.

The **Rate** at Which a Stretch of Coastline is Eroded Depends on **Several Factors**

1) **The width of beach** — i.e. the distance between high and low tide marks. Beaches slow down waves, reducing their erosive power. So a wide, flat beach will protect cliffs more than narrow, steeper beaches.

2) **The breaking point of the waves** — a wave that breaks directly at the foot of a cliff transfers the most energy to the cliff and causes the most erosion. Waves that hit the cliff before they break, or break further offshore will erode much less.

3) **The aspect** — if the coastline faces the dominant wind and wave direction, erosion will be faster.

4) **The fetch of the waves** — waves with a longer fetch are much higher and steeper, and have more energy, so will cause the most erosion.

See page 25 for a case study of coastal erosion.

5) **Rock type** — hard rocks like granite are much more resistant to erosion than softer rocks, e.g. clay.

Currents Transport **Sediment**

1) A **current** is the general flow of water in one direction.

2) Currents move material **along** the coast — this is called **longshore drift**.

3) **Swash** carries sediment (e.g. shingle, pebbles) **up** the beach, **parallel** to the prevailing wind. **Backwash** carries sediment back **down** the beach, at **right angles** to the shoreline.

4) When there's an **angle** between the prevailing wind and the shoreline, a few rounds of swash and backwash move the sediment **along** the shoreline.

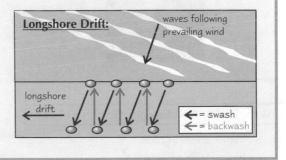

Practice Questions

Q1   Draw a table to show the main inputs, processes and outputs of a coastal system.

Q2   Sketch a diagram to show how longshore drift works.

Exam Questions

Q1   Describe the characteristics of constructive and destructive waves.   [4 marks]

Q2   Outline how cliffs are eroded along the coastline.   [6 marks]

What did the sea say to the beach — nothing, it just waved...

You really need to get your head around all the processes going on at the coast — cliffs are eroded and weathered, currents carry sediment about and constructive waves deposit it. Then there are destructive waves that annoyingly remove prime sunbathing spots.

Coastal Landforms

Get your bucket and spade ready — it's time to learn about coastal landforms. Wait a minute, where are the sandcastles...

Some **Coastal Landforms** are Caused by **Erosion**

CLIFFS AND WAVE-CUT PLATFORMS

1) **Cliffs** are a common coastal landform. Over time, cliffs **retreat** due to the action of **waves** and **weathering**.

2) Weathering and wave erosion cause a **notch** to form at the high water mark. This eventually develops into a **cave**.

3) Rock above the cave becomes **unstable** with nothing to support it, and it **collapses**.

4) **Wave-cut platforms** are **flat surfaces** left behind when a cliff is eroded.

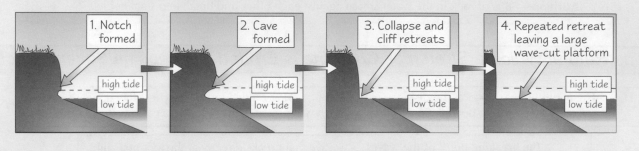

HEADLANDS AND BAYS

1) **Headlands** and **bays** form where there are **bands** of alternating **hard rock** and **soft rock** at **right angles** to the shoreline.

2) The **soft rock** is **eroded quickly**, forming a **bay**. The **harder rock** is **eroded less** and sticks out as a **headland**.

CAVES, BLOW HOLES, ARCHES AND STACKS

1) Weak areas in rock (e.g. joints) are **eroded** to form **caves**.

2) Occasionally, the roof of a cave is **weakened** along a major joint by **hydraulic pressure** and the roof **collapses** to form a **blow hole**.

3) Caves on the opposite sides of a narrow headland may eventually join up to form an **arch**.

4) When an **arch** collapses, it forms a **stack**.

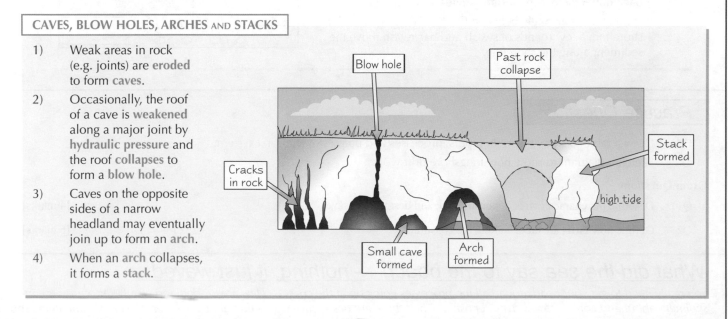

Coastal Landforms

Some **Coastal Landforms** are Caused by **Deposition**

BEACHES

1) **Beaches** are formed when **constructive** waves **deposit sediment** on the shore.

2) **Shingle** beaches are **steep** and **narrow**. They're made up of **larger** particles, which pile up at steep angles. **Sand** beaches, formed from **smaller** particles, are **wide** and **flat**.

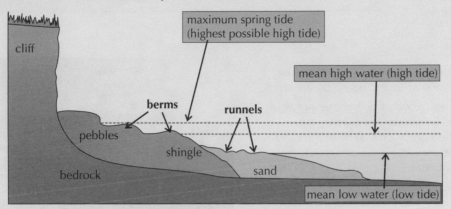

Beaches have their own **associated features**:

1) **Berms** are **ridges** of sand and pebbles (about 1-2 metres high) found at **high tide** marks. They're formed by deposition of coarse material at the limit of the **swash**.

2) **Runnels** are **grooves** in the sand running **parallel** to the shore. They're formed by **backwash** draining to the sea.

3) **Cusps** are **crescent-shaped indentations** that form on beaches of mixed sand and shingle. It's **not known** exactly how they form, but they develop in areas where waves break parallel to the beach and where there's a large **tidal range** (the difference in height between **high** and **low tides**).

SPITS

Spits tend to form where the coast suddenly **changes direction**, e.g. across river mouths.

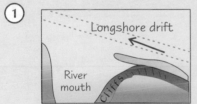

Longshore drift (see p. 21) continues to **deposit** material across the river mouth, leaving a bank of **sand** and **shingle** sticking out into the sea.

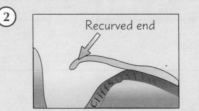

Occasional **changes** to the dominant wind and wave direction may lead to a spit having a **curved end** (the fancy name for this is a **recurved end**).

Over time, several recurved ends may be abandoned as the waves return to their **original direction**.

The area **behind** the spit is **sheltered** from the waves and often develops into **mudflats** and **salt marshes** (see p. 24).

Watch out for the spit...

Coastal Landforms

Chaz was a bit annoyed that the bar didn't go right across the river, but he was enjoying the lagoon...

BARS

1) Bars are formed when a **spit joins two headlands together**.

2) This can occur across a **bay** or across a **river mouth** (if the river isn't too strong).

3) A **lagoon** forms **behind** the bar.

SAND DUNES

1) Sand dunes are formed when **sand deposited** by longshore drift is moved up the beach by the **wind**.

2) Sand trapped by driftwood or berms (see previous page) is colonised by **plants** and **grasses**, e.g. marram grass. The vegetation **stabilises** the sand and encourages **more sand** to accumulate there, forming **embryo dunes**.

3) Over time, the oldest dunes migrate inland as newer embryo dunes are formed. These **mature dunes** can reach heights of up to 10 m.

©iStockphoto.com/Eric Gevaert

SALT MARSHES

1) Salt marshes form in areas of **sheltered water**, e.g. river estuaries or behind spits.

2) As **silt** and **mud** are **deposited** by the river or the tide, **mudflats** develop.

3) The mudflats are colonised by **vegetation** that can survive the **high salt levels** and long periods of **submergence** by the tide.

4) The plants **trap more mud** and **silt**, and gradually they create an area of marshland that remains **exposed** for longer and longer **between tides**.

©iStockphoto.com/Linda Steward

Practice Questions

Q1 Name four landforms of coastal erosion and four landforms of coastal deposition.

Q2 Describe where headlands and bays form.

Q3 Briefly describe how stacks are formed.

Q4 What are berms, runnels and cusps?

Q5 Where do salt marshes form?

Exam Questions

Q1 Describe how erosion can create a wave-cut platform. [5 marks]

Q2 Describe how spits are formed. [6 marks]

Man walks into a bar, gets his feet wet...

At AS level, the landforms you have to know are pretty much the same ones you have to know for GCSE (not much help if you didn't do GCSE, I know, but then they're not that hard to learn anyway). You just need to know more detail about the processes involved in their formation. And you thought it was going to be all excitement and glamour once you got to AS level. Sorry.

Coastal Erosion — Case Study

The Holderness coastline in East Yorkshire is the fastest eroding coastline in Europe (what a claim to fame).
If you get a case study question in the exam you need to have a bagful of juicy facts at the ready, so get learnin'.

The Average **Rate of Erosion** at Holderness is About **1.8 Metres per Year**

The Holderness coastline is **61 km long** — it stretches from Flamborough Head to Spurn Head. In some places, e.g. **Great Cowden**, the rate of erosion has been over **10 m/year** in recent years. The main **reasons** for this rapid erosion at Holderness are shown in **purple**. Some of the possible **social**, **economic** and **environmental impacts** of the erosion are also shown.

1) **Easily eroded rock type** — the cliffs are mostly made of **till** (or 'boulder clay'). Not only is till **easily eroded** through **corrasion**, but it's also prone to **slumping** when wet.

2) **Narrow beaches** — beaches slow the waves, **reducing** their **erosive power**. Narrow beaches **protect** the cliffs **less**. Beaches along the Holderness coast are narrow for two main reasons:
   - **Flamborough Head stops sediment** from the north replenishing the beaches along Holderness. It's also made of **chalk**, which dissolves when eroded rather than making sand for the beaches.
   - **Coastal defences**, e.g. at Mappleton (see p. 30 for why these lead to narrow beaches). This is a **human** cause of erosion.

3) **Powerful waves** — the waves are powerful because of:
   - The **long fetch** (all the way from the **Arctic Ocean**).
   - The coast faces the **dominant wind** and **wave direction** (from the **north-east**).

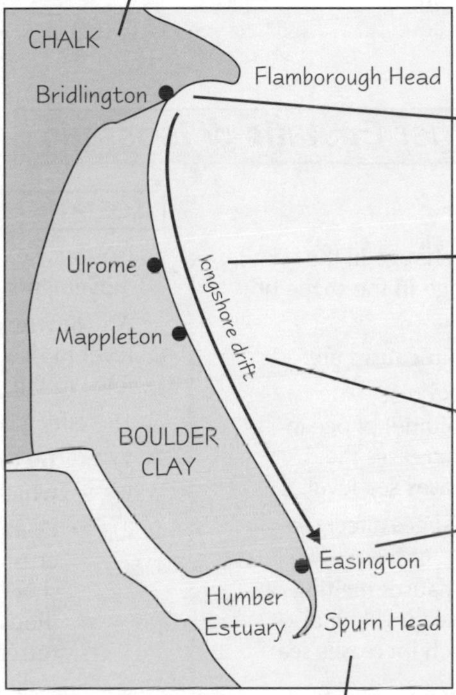

1) **Property prices** along the coast have **fallen** sharply for those houses at risk from erosion.

2) Around **30 villages** have been lost since **Roman times**.

3) **Visitor numbers** in **Bridlington** **dropped** by over **30%** between **1998** and **2006** (though this could have been due to other reasons).

4) Many **caravan parks** are at risk from erosion, e.g. **Seaside Caravan Park** at **Ulrome** is losing an average of **10 pitches a year**.

5) **£2 million** was spent at **Mappleton** in **1991** to **protect** the coast.

6) The **Gas Terminal** at **Easington** is at risk (it's only **25 m** from the cliff edge). This terminal accounts for **25%** of **Britain's gas supply**.

7) **80 000 m²** of good quality **farmland** is lost each year. This has a huge effect on **farmers' livelihoods**.

8) Some **SSSIs** (Sites of Special Scientific Interest) are threatened — e.g. **The Lagoons** near **Easington** are part of an SSSI. It has a colony of over 1% of the British breeding population of **little terns**. The lagoons are separated from the sea by a narrow strip of sand and shingle. Erosion of this would connect the lakes to the sea and 'The Lagoons' would be destroyed.

Map labels: CHALK, Flamborough Head, Bridlington, Ulrome, longshore drift, Mappleton, BOULDER CLAY, Easington, Humber Estuary, Spurn Head

Practice Questions

Q1   For a named area, briefly describe three impacts of coastal erosion.

Exam Question

Q1   With reference to one named area describe and explain the causes of coastal erosion.   [15 marks]

Like easily eroded till, I'll be gone when the morning comes...

You need to know a case study of coastal erosion as well as you know how to make beans on toast. Draw an annotated diagram to refresh your memory... toast, then butter, then beans, er... sorry, I mean label the physical causes, human causes and impacts.

Sea Level Changes

There's a fair bit to learn on these two pages. Just try and keep your head above the water...

Coastal Flooding is Now More Likely Because of Rising Sea Level

1) Sea level **varies** on a daily basis with the **tidal cycle**. **Onshore winds** and **low atmospheric pressure systems** also cause the sea surface to rise **temporarily**.

2) On a much longer time scale, global sea level is rising at almost **2 mm** each year, which is forecast to **increase** to **4 or 5 mm** a year by 2100.

3) This will increase both the **frequency** and **severity** of flooding in low-lying coastal areas.

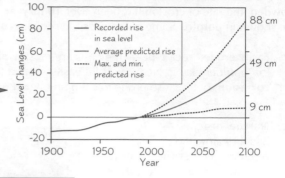

Recorded and predicted sea level change

Sea Level Changes are Either Eustatic or Isostatic

EUSTATIC

Eustatic sea level change is caused by a change in the **volume of water** in the sea, or by a change in the **shape** of the **ocean basins**.

The effects are always **global** and the main **causes** are:

1) **Tectonic movements** of the Earth's crust that alter the shape (and so the volume) of ocean basins. E.g. sea floor spreading **increases** the **volume** of the basin and so **decreases** sea level.

2) **Changes in climate**. Different changes affect sea level in different ways:

  • An **increase** in **temperature** causes **melting** of **ice sheets**, which **increases** sea level. It also causes water to **expand**, which **increases** sea level further.

  • A **decrease** in **temperature** causes more precipitation to fall as **snow**. This increases the volume of water **stored** in **glaciers** and so reduces the volume of the sea, which **decreases** sea level.

ISOSTATIC

Isostatic sea level change is caused by **vertical movements** of the land **relative** to the sea.

Any **downward** movement of the land causes sea level to **rise** locally, while **uplift of land** causes sea level to **fall**.

The effects are always **local** and the main **causes** are:

1) **Tectonic** (crustal) uplift or depression, which occurs mostly at plate boundaries.

2) **Compression** or **decompression** of the Earth's crust due to accumulation or melting of **ice sheets**. Slow uplift of land can continue for thousands of years after the weight of a **retreating glacier** has gone. **Accumulation of sediment**, mostly at the mouths of major rivers, can also cause **compression**.

3) **Subsidence** of land due to shrinkage after **abstraction of groundwater**, e.g. drainage of marshland.

Sea Level Rise Can Have a Variety of Impacts

1) **More frequent** and **more severe coastal flooding**.
    Flooding of low-lying areas has increased with sea level rise and it will increase more with further rises. For example, at the beginning of the 20th century **St Mark's Square** in **Venice** flooded less than **10** times per year, and in **1996** it was flooded almost **100** times.

2) **Submergence of low-lying islands**.
    Lots of low-lying islands have **disappeared** as sea level has risen, and loads more are **at risk** of disappearing. For example, if the sea level rises by just **0.5 m** from the current level then most of the **Maldives** would be submerged.

3) **Changes in the coastline**.
    As sea levels rise the coastline changes — **islands** are **created** and the **area** of **land** is **decreased**. E.g. over the last 10 000 years sea level rise has separated Britain from mainland Europe. If the sea level rises **0.3 m** from the current level **8000 km²** of land in **Bangladesh** will be lost.

Barry and Ami wish they hadn't delayed their holiday to the Maldives.

Don't forget that all these impacts have **further impacts**, e.g. damage to coastal **infrastructure**, decrease in **tourism**, decrease in **agriculture**, loss of **homes** etc.

Sea Level Changes

Sea Level Rise Results in Coastlines of Submergence

When sea level rises relative to the coast, the sea **submerges** (drowns) the existing coastline.
This creates different **landforms**:

① **RIAS** are formed where **river valleys** are partially **submerged**, e.g. Milford Haven in South Wales is a ria. Rias have a **gentle** long- and cross-profile. They're **wide** and **deep** at their **mouth**, becoming **narrower** and **shallower** the further **inland** they reach.

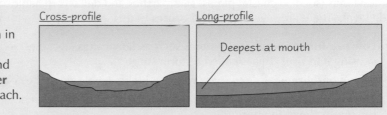

② **FJORDS** are a lot like rias, but they're **drowned glacial valleys** rather than drowned river valleys. They're relatively **straight** and narrow, with very **steep sides**. They have a **shallow mouth** caused by a raised bit of ground (called the **threshold**) formed by deposition of material by the glacier. They're very **deep** further **inland**, e.g. Sognefjorden in Norway is over 1000 m deep in places.

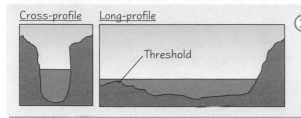

③ In areas where **valleys** lie **parallel** to the coast, an increase in sea level can form a **DALMATIAN COASTLINE**. Valleys are flooded, leaving **islands** parallel to the coastline. It's named after the Dalmatian coast in Croatia.

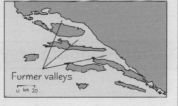

Sea Level Fall Results in Coastlines of Emergence

When sea level falls relative to the coast, new coastline **emerges** (appears) from the sea. This creates different **landforms**:

1) **Raised beaches** are formed when the fall in sea level **exposes wave-cut platforms** and their **beaches**. Over time, beach sediment becomes **vegetated** and develops into **soil**.

2) The **cliffs** above raised beaches are no longer eroded by the sea, and slowly get covered by **vegetation**. They're called **relict cliffs**. It's not uncommon to see **wave-cut notches**, **caves**, **arches** and **stacks** within relict cliffs. These **raised features** are gradually **degraded** (weathered) over time.

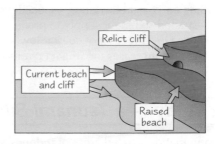

Practice Questions

Q1 State two causes of eustatic sea level change and two causes of isostatic sea level change.

Q2 Give two examples of landforms that show there must have been a drop in sea levels.

Q3 Sketch a diagram showing the cross-profile of a fjord.

Exam Questions

Q1 Describe the possible impacts of sea level rise. [8 marks]

Q2 Describe and explain how coastal submergence can result in a range of landforms. [8 marks]

I'd start moving up onto high ground now...

You need to know that sea levels are rising, and the impacts of sea level rise. Examiners love asking questions about current issues and rising sea levels are a hot topic in the news at the moment — so make sure you're hot on all the details too.

Coastal Flooding

As well as a slow rise in sea level, coastal areas are at risk of flooding because of a number of physical and human causes...

Coastal Flooding Occurs Naturally Due to Physical Causes

Coastal lowlands (such as coastal plains, salt marshes and deltas) are liable to flooding when the sea rises above normal high-tide level. There are several **physical causes** of this:

1) **Low pressure atmospheric systems** such as **hurricanes** (cyclones) reduce atmospheric pressure on the sea surface, causing it to **rise**. This is called a **storm surge**.

2) **Strong onshore winds** can force water to higher levels along the coast, allowing waves further inland.

3) **Tidal currents** and **surges** may be funnelled into a coastal bottleneck such as the Bay of Bengal, or English Channel, forcing sea levels higher.

4) **High rainfall** may cause **high river discharge**. If sea level at the river mouth is high, e.g. due to high spring tides or storm surges, the large volume of river water may be **unable to drain** into the sea and can cause flooding.

5) When a **combination of the above factors** coincide. E.g. a hurricane making landfall in Florida may cause a storm surge and high rainfall (which may be unable to drain to the sea). The storm surge and wave energy may both be intensified by strong onshore winds.

6) **Tsunamis** are huge ocean waves caused when water is displaced by **landslides**, **volcanic eruptions** or **submarine earthquakes** that shift the ocean floor. When travelling in open water (i.e. out at sea) they have a very small wave height (less than a metre) and travel at hundreds of kilometres an hour. As the waves approach the coast, the bottom of the waves slow considerably due to friction with the sea bed, causing the wave height to increase enormously.

Coastal Flooding May Also be Caused or Intensified by Human Activity

1) **Management of river systems** — some management strategies (e.g. dams) trap sediment and so reduce the amount being deposited at the river's mouth. This causes deltas and salt marshes to shrink, providing less protection against high tides and storm surges.

2) **Management of coastal systems** — some management strategies alter sediment movement, reducing the amount of protective beach material further along the coast. E.g. coastal defences at Barton in Hampshire have reduced sediment transport to the east, allowing Hurst Spit to be breached more often, flooding lowlands behind.

3) **Building on coastal lowlands**, especially sand dunes, has restricted sediment supply to protective beaches and marshes. Development of coastal lowlands, such as Florida, also **increases** the **impact** of any coastal floods.

4) **Reclamation of coastal lowlands**, such as the Dutch polders, and reclaimed marshes along the east coast of England. Draining this land to reclaim it causes the land to shrink to become lower than sea level.

Case Study — a Tsunami Struck Southern Asia on 26th December 2004

The **tsunami** that devastated areas of **Indonesia**, **Sri Lanka**, **Thailand** and **India** in December 2004 was caused by a submarine **earthquake** in the Indian Ocean. The earthquake is estimated to have measured **9.0** on the Richter scale, making it one of the **strongest earthquakes** ever recorded. The map below shows some of the countries **most affected** by the tsunami.

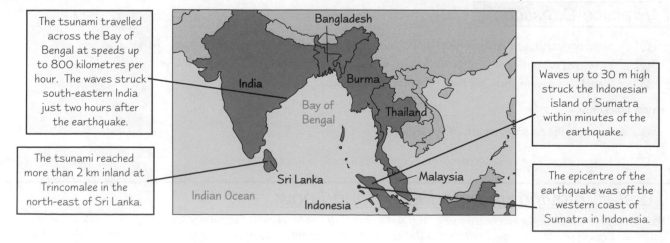

The tsunami travelled across the Bay of Bengal at speeds up to 800 kilometres per hour. The waves struck south-eastern India just two hours after the earthquake.

The tsunami reached more than 2 km inland at Trincomalee in the north-east of Sri Lanka.

Waves up to 30 m high struck the Indonesian island of Sumatra within minutes of the earthquake.

The epicentre of the earthquake was off the western coast of Sumatra in Indonesia.

Coastal Flooding

The Tsunami Had Severe *Social, Economic* and *Environmental Impacts*

Social

1) It was the **deadliest** tsunami **ever recorded**, with an estimated **230 000** people **killed** or **missing**.
2) It's estimated that **1.7 million people** were made **homeless**.
3) Many sources of fresh **drinking water** were **polluted**, either by **sewage** or by **saltwater**.
4) An estimated **400 000 lost their jobs** in **Sri Lanka** alone.

The remains of a house in a destroyed village in Indonesia.

A destroyed fishing boat on a beach in Phuket, Thailand.

Economic

1) Estimates of the **cost** of the initial **damage** caused by the tsunami are between **$8 billion** and **$15 billion**.
2) **Fishing** is a large part of the economy for many of the areas hit by the tsunami. **Boats**, **nets** and other **equipment** were **destroyed** or **lost**, severely affecting the livelihood of fishermen.
3) **Salinisation** (increase in salt content) of land has severely **reduced soil fertility**. **Crop production** will be **lower** for several years to come.
4) **Tourism** is important to the economy of many of the countries affected. **25%** of hotels in southern **Thailand** were **closed** for at least **6 months** because of damage and the number of **foreign visitors** to the island of **Phuket** dropped **80%** in **2005** as the area was perceived to be less safe.

Environmental

1) **8 million litres of oil** were released into the environment after **two oil plants** in Indonesia were **destroyed**. The oil caused widespread **pollution** at sea and **contamination** of the soil, posing **health risks** to humans in the area.
2) **Mangrove forests** as far away as the **East African coast** were **damaged** by the force of the waves, or **covered in layers of silt**.
3) The **high salt content** of the floodwater **destroyed** the natural balance of many **ecosystems**, e.g. the **Karagan Lagoon** in southern **Sri Lanka**.

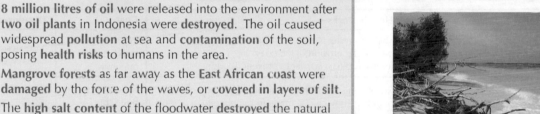
Mangrove trees uprooted by the waves.

Human Activity Increased the Impact of the Flooding

1) **Mangrove forests** protected parts of the **Sri Lankan coast** by **absorbing wave energy**. Pressure for **tourist development** and the creation of intensive **prawn fisheries** has led to the **destruction** of mangrove forests in other areas around the Indian Ocean. It's estimated that **Thailand** has lost up to **half** of its mangrove forests since **1975**. The lack of protection meant that waves could reach **further inland** and the **flooding** was **much worse** than in areas protected by mangroves.

2) It's thought that healthy **coral reefs** surrounding the **Maldives** acted as a **breakwater** (reducing the power of the tsunami waves) and prevented the complete destruction of the low-lying islands. Illegal **coral mining** and the use of dynamite in explosive **'blast fishing'** has **destroyed** many offshore coral reefs in the Indian Ocean. This reduced the level of natural protection from the waves.

Practice Questions

Q1 What is a storm surge?
Q2 Describe how the characteristics of a tsunami change as it approaches the coast.
Q3 Describe three physical and three human causes of coastal flooding.

Exam Question

Q1 Describe and explain the causes and effects of coastal flooding in a named coastal area. [10 marks]

Coastal flooding — it really is no joke...

You can see from these pages the huge impact of coastal flooding on humans and the environment. Make sure you know a case study of the causes and effects of coastal flooding in a specific area — it's one the examiners love to ask you about.

Coastal Management

Coastal management is a complex thing. Fixing up one coastal area can have the unintended effect of messing up another area nearby.

See pages 25 and 29 for some examples of the impacts of coastal erosion and flooding.

Only **Some Parts** of the **Coast** are **Managed**

The aim of coastal management is to **protect homes**, **businesses** and the **environment** from **erosion** and **flooding**.

This is because flooding and erosion of the coastline can have severe **social**, **economic** and **environmental impacts**.

All coastal settlements want to be defended, but the amount of **money available** is **limited** so not everywhere can be defended. Choosing which places are defended (and how) is based on a **cost-benefit analysis**. The money available is usually used to protect **large settlements** and important **industrial sites**, rather than isolated or small settlements.

There are **Four Options** for **Coastal Management**

1) **Hold the line** — maintain the **existing** coastal defences.

2) **Advance the line** — build **new** coastal defences **further out to sea** than the existing line of defence.

3) **Do nothing** — build **no** coastal defences at all, and deal with erosion and flooding **as it happens**.

4) **Retreat the line** — build no coastal defences, but **move people away** from the coast.

Coastal Defences Include *Hard Engineering* and *Soft Engineering*

Hard Engineering Defences Involve *Built Structures*

Defence		How it works	Cost	Disadvantage
Sea wall		The wall reflects waves back out to sea, preventing erosion of the coast. It also acts as a barrier to prevent flooding.	Expensive to build and maintain	It creates a strong backwash, which erodes under the wall.
Revetment		Revetments are slanted structures built at the foot of cliffs. They can be made from concrete, wood or rocks. Waves break against the revetments, which absorb the wave energy and so prevent cliff erosion.	Expensive to build, but relatively cheap to maintain	They create a strong backwash, as above.
Gabions		Gabions are rock-filled cages. A wall of gabions is usually built at the foot of cliffs. The gabions absorb wave energy and so reduce erosion.	Cheap	Ugly
Riprap	boulders	Boulders piled up along the coast are called riprap. The boulders absorb wave energy and so reduce erosion.	Fairly cheap	Can shift in storms.
Groynes	longshore drift	Groynes are fences built at right angles to the coast. They trap beach material transported by longshore drift. This creates wider beaches, which slow the waves (reducing their energy) and so gives greater protection from flooding and erosion.	Quite cheap	They starve down-drift beaches of sand. Thinner beaches don't protect the coast as well, leading to greater erosion and flooding.
Breakwaters	waves	Breakwaters are usually concrete blocks or boulders deposited off the coast. They force waves to break offshore. The waves' energy and erosive power are reduced before they reach the shore.	Expensive	Can be damaged in storms.
Earth bank		Mounds of earth act as a barrier to prevent flooding.	Quite expensive	Can be eroded.
Tidal barrier		Tidal barriers are built across river estuaries. They contain retractable floodgates that can be raised to prevent flooding from storm surges.	VERY expensive	Really, VERY expensive.
Tidal barrage		Tidal barrages are dams built across river estuaries. Their main purpose is to generate electricity. Water is trapped behind the dam at high tide. Controlled release of water through turbines in the dam at low tide generates electricity. They also prevent flooding from storm surges.	VERY expensive	They disrupt sediment flow, which may cause increased erosion elsewhere in the estuary.

Coastal Management

Soft Engineering Defences Involve Coaxing Natural Processes Along

1) **Beach nourishment** is where **sand** and **shingle** are added to beaches from elsewhere (e.g. **dredged** from offshore). This creates **wide** beaches, which **reduce erosion** of cliffs more than thin beaches.

2) **Beach stabilisation** can be done by **reducing the slope angle** and planting **vegetation**, or by sticking **stakes** and **old tree trunks** in the beach to stabilise the sand. It also creates **wide** beaches, which **reduce erosion** of cliffs.

3) **Dune regeneration** is where sand dunes are **created** or **restored** by either nourishment or stabilisation of the sand. Sand dunes provide a **barrier** between land and sea, **absorbing wave energy** and preventing flooding and erosion.

4) **Land use management** is important for dune regeneration. The vegetation needed to stabilise the dune can easily be **trampled** and destroyed, leaving the dune **vulnerable** to **erosion**. Wooden **walkways** across dunes, and **fenced-off areas** that prevent walkers, cyclists or 4×4 drivers from gaining access to the dunes, all **reduce vegetation loss**.

5) **Creating marshland** from mudflats can be encouraged by **planting** appropriate vegetation (e.g. glassworts). The vegetation **stabilises** the sediment, and the stems and leaves help **reduce the speed** of the waves. This **reduces** their **erosive power** and **how far** the waves reach **inland**, leading to **less flooding** of the area around the marsh.

6) **Coastal realignment** (also known as **managed retreat**) involves breaching an existing defence and allowing the sea to flood the land behind. Over time, vegetation will colonise the land and it'll become **marshland**.

Soft Engineering is More Sustainable than Hard Engineering

Hard engineering is often expensive, and disrupts natural processes. Soft engineering schemes tend to be cheaper and require much less time and money to maintain than hard engineering schemes. Soft engineering is designed to integrate with the natural environment and it creates areas like marshland and sand dunes, which are important habitats for coastal plants and animals. So soft engineering is a more sustainable management strategy than hard engineering because it has a lower environmental impact and economic cost.

Management Strategies for the Future Must be Sustainable

1) **Rising sea level** means **more** coastal management will be **needed** to protect coastal settlements and developments. **Storms** also seem to be getting **more frequent** and **more severe**, increasing the need further.

2) There's growing emphasis on the need for **more sustainable management strategies**, i.e. soft engineering.

3) Deciding how to manage a coastline is now done in a more **integrated** way to **improve sustainability**. For example, a **Shoreline Management Plan** (SMP) is a plan for how the coastline in one **sediment cell** (see p. 20) should be managed. SMPs are developed by **local authorities**. All the local authorities in one sediment cell **co-operate** when planning their coastal management strategy, so that defences in one area don't increase erosion in an adjacent area in the same cell.

4) The **process** of trying to come up with an integrated, sustainable management plan is called **Integrated Coastal Zone Management** (ICZM).

Practice Questions

Q1   What is the aim of coastal management?

Q2   What are: a) gabions,
　　　　　　　　b) groynes,
　　　　　　　　c) revetments?

Q3   What other options are there for coastal management, apart from hard and soft engineering?

Exam Question

Q1   Explain why soft engineering schemes are more sustainable than hard engineering schemes.　　　　[6 marks]

Do nothing? Retreat? Sounds like a lousy revision strategy to me...

Coastal management sounds like a difficult and unending job. Even after spending hundreds of thousands of pounds on a nice big concrete wall to keep the waves out, and some wooden groynes to hold the beach in place, it can still all go horrendously wrong. When it goes wrong, it costs even more money. These days they try to use sustainable methods instead, but it's still hard.

Coastal Management — Case Studies

You need to know case studies of coastal management. Wait a minute, what's this I see...

Hard Engineering Has Been Used Along Holderness

The Holderness coast is the fastest eroding coastline in Europe. Page 25 outlines the main reasons for the rapid erosion and the social, economic and environmental impacts of the erosion. A total of **11.4 km** of the 61 km coastline is currently protected by **hard** engineering:

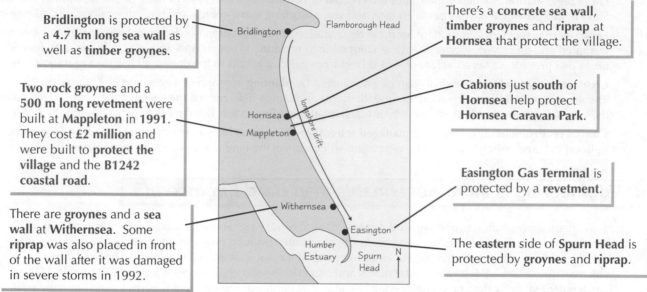

Bridlington is protected by a **4.7 km long sea wall** as well as **timber groynes**.

Two rock groynes and a **500 m long revetment** were built at **Mappleton** in **1991**. They cost **£2 million** and were built to **protect the village** and the **B1242 coastal road**.

There are **groynes** and a **sea wall** at **Withernsea**. Some **riprap** was also placed in front of the wall after it was damaged in severe storms in 1992.

There's a **concrete sea wall**, **timber groynes** and **riprap** at **Hornsea** that protect the village.

Gabions just **south** of **Hornsea** help protect **Hornsea Caravan Park**.

Easington Gas Terminal is protected by a **revetment**.

The **eastern** side of **Spurn Head** is protected by **groynes** and **riprap**.

The Schemes are Locally Successful but Cause Problems Down-drift

1) The groynes **trap sediment**, increasing the **width** of the **beaches**. This **protects** the **local area** but **increases erosion** of the cliffs **down-drift** (as the material eroded from the beaches there isn't replenished). E.g. the Mappleton scheme has caused **increased erosion** of the cliffs **south** of Mappleton. **Cowden Farm**, just south of Mappleton, is now at risk of falling into the sea.

2) The **sediment** produced from the erosion of the Holderness coastline is normally washed into the **Humber Estuary** (where it helps to form **tidal mudflats**) and down the **Lincolnshire coast**. Reduction in this sediment **increases the risk of flooding** along the Humber Estuary, and **increases erosion** along the Lincolnshire coast.

3) The protection of local areas is leading to the **formation of bays** between the areas. As bays develop the wave pressure on headlands will increase and eventually the **cost** of maintaining the sea defences may become **too high**.

4) All these problems make the existing schemes **unsustainable**.

See p. 31 for more on SMPs.

Possible Schemes All Have Problems

1) The **SMP** for Holderness for the next 50 years recommends '**holding the line**' at **some settlements** (e.g. at Bridlington, Withernsea, Hornsea, Mappleton and Easington Gas Terminal) and '**doing nothing**' along more **unpopulated stretches**. However, this is **unpopular** with owners of land or property along the stretches where nothing is being done.

2) **Coastal realignment** of businesses has been suggested, e.g. relocating **caravan parks** further inland. This would be a **more sustainable** scheme as it would allow the coast to be eroded as normal without endangering businesses. However, there are issues surrounding how much businesses will be **compensated** by for relocating. Also, relocation isn't always possible, e.g. farmland can't be 'relocated', and there may be no land for sale to relocate buildings to.

3) A **sea wall** has been proposed to better protect **Easington Gas Terminal**. This would cost **£4.5 million**. The problem is that it would reduce sediment flow to the south, **increasing erosion** at the **village of Easington** (with a population of **700 people**). A **longer sea wall** could be built that would protect the village as well as the gas terminal, but that would cost **£7 million**.

4) **Offshore reefs** made from **concrete-filled tyres** have been proposed to protect the coastline. They act like **breakwaters**. Similar reefs have been built in the USA and have reduced erosion. Some people think that the reefs will **harm the environment** though (although there's currently no evidence of this).

Coastal Management — Case Studies

Soft Engineering Has Been Used Along Blackwater Estuary

Blackwater Estuary is part of the **Essex** coastline. Land in the estuary is being eroded at a rate of **0.3-1 m/year**. In some exposed areas (e.g. **Cobmarsh Island**) the erosion rate is **2 m/year**. The area is also **at risk from flooding** as sea level is rising and the **South** of England is **sinking** relative to the sea. There are some hard engineering schemes in the estuary, but these are becoming too expensive to maintain, so **soft** engineering approaches are now being implemented:

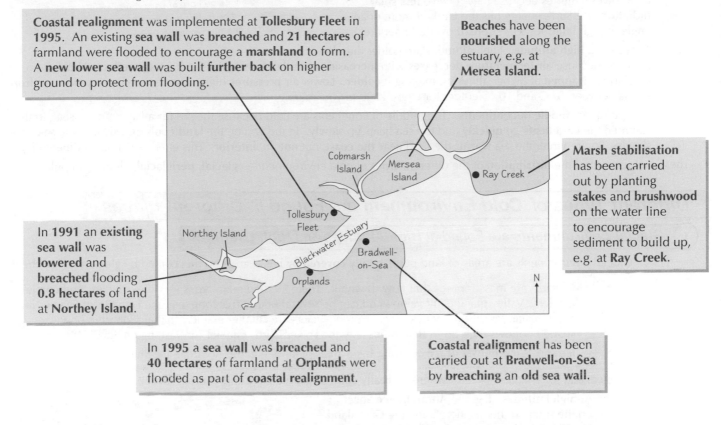

Coastal realignment was implemented at **Tollesbury Fleet** in 1995. An existing **sea wall** was **breached** and **21 hectares** of farmland were flooded to encourage a **marshland** to form. A **new lower sea wall** was built **further back** on higher ground to protect from flooding.

Beaches have been **nourished** along the estuary, e.g. at **Mersea Island**.

Marsh stabilisation has been carried out by planting **stakes** and **brushwood** on the water line to encourage sediment to build up, e.g. at **Ray Creek**.

In **1991** an **existing sea wall** was **lowered** and **breached** flooding **0.8 hectares** of land at **Northey Island**.

In **1995** a **sea wall** was **breached** and **40 hectares** of farmland at **Orplands** were flooded as part of **coastal realignment**.

Coastal realignment has been carried out at **Bradwell-on-Sea** by breaching an old sea wall.

The Schemes are More Sustainable than Hard Engineering Schemes

1) The schemes are **more sustainable** in the **long term**. E.g. to repair the sea wall at Orplands would have cost more than £600 000 (and it would only last for 20 years). The 40 hectares of farmland flooded was valued at around £600 000, but the marshland created would defend the coast for **longer** as it's **self-repairing**.

2) The schemes have created **more marshland**, which provides a larger **habitat** for **wildlife**.

3) However, some areas **haven't changed** to marshland (e.g. parts of the Orpland site are still bare mud, which is easily eroded). Also, **grazing land** has been **lost**.

Practice Questions

Q1   List the types of hard engineering used along the Holderness coast.

Q2   List the types of soft engineering used along the Blackwater Estuary in Essex.

Exam Question

Q1   Evaluate the success of a named coastal management scheme.   [15 marks]

More case studies — what a pain in the groyne...

The best thing to do here is learn the annotated map for each case study. Draw them out over and over again until they're practically tattooed on the inside of your eyelids (it'll hurt a lot less than missing a load of easy marks in the exam, I promise).

Distribution of Cold Environments

You're probably thinking that all cold environments are the same — they're all just, well, cold. Well it turns out that there are different types of cold environment, and it's not quite as simple as chilly, cold and blimmin' freezing.

There are **Three** Main **Reasons** Why Environments Might be **Cold**

1)   They're at a **high latitude**. High latitudes are **colder** than lower latitudes because they receive **less solar radiation** (the Sun's energy hits the Earth at more of an **angle** at high latitudes so it's spread over a larger area).

Latitude lines go horizontally round the Earth, like the equator — the higher you go in latitude (either north or south) the further away you get from the equator.

2)   They're at a **high altitude**. High altitudes are colder than lower altitudes because **air temperature decreases** with **increasing altitude**. **Less** of the Sun's energy **reflected** back from the Earth is **trapped** at higher altitudes, making it **colder**. Lower **air pressures** higher up also mean temperatures **drop**. It gets between 6 °C and 10 °C colder for every 1000 m you go up.

3)   They're in the **middle** of **continents**. The middle of continents are cold because they're **far away** from the **sea**. In the summer, the **land heats** up **quickly** and the **sea** heats up **slowly**. In the winter, the **land cools quickly** and the **sea** cools **slowly**. So, in winter the sea **warms** the land **near the coast**, but **not** the **interior**. This effect is called **continentality**.

These factors control the **distribution** of the different **types** of cold environment — **glacial**, **periglacial**, **alpine** and **polar**.

Different Types of **Cold Environment** are **Found** in **Different Places**

1   **Glacial Environments** are Found at **High Altitudes** and **High Latitudes**

1)   Glacial environments are areas of land permanently **covered by ice**. Land can be covered by **glaciers** or **ice sheets**:

-   Glaciers are masses of **ice** that flow **downhill**. There are two main types — **valley** glaciers and **corrie** glaciers. Valley glaciers **fill valleys** and can be **several kilometres long** (e.g. the Franz Josef Glacier in New Zealand is 12 kilometres long). Corrie glaciers are **smaller** glaciers that are found in bowl-shaped hollows high up in **mountains** (e.g. the Lower Curtis Glacier in Washington State, USA).
-   Ice sheets are **domes of ice** covering **huge areas** of land, e.g. the Antarctic Ice Sheet.

2)   Glaciers and ice sheets only form where it's **really cold**, so glacial environments are found:

-   At **high latitudes**. E.g. the **Antarctic Ice Sheet** (in the southern hemisphere), and the **Greenland Ice Sheet** (in the northern hemisphere) are both entirely **above 60°** latitude.
-   At **high altitudes** (regardless of the latitude). E.g. glaciers are found in the **Himalayan mountains** even though they're at a **low latitude** (around **30°**). This is because it's the **highest** mountain range in the world. Glaciers even form at latitudes **close to** the **equator** (e.g. the Antizana glacier in Ecuador).

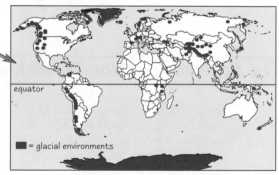

equator

■ = glacial environments

3)   Even though it can be really cold on low altitude land in the middle of continents, glaciers don't form as there's not enough snow.

2   **Periglacial Environments** are Found at **High Altitudes** and **Latitudes** and in **Continental Interiors**

1)   **Periglacial** environments are places where the temperature is frequently or constantly **below freezing**, but **not covered by ice**. They contain a layer of **permafrost** (permanently frozen ground) **on** or **below** the surface.

2)   They form where it's persistently **below 0 °C**, so they're found:

-   At **high latitudes**. E.g. the northern parts of Asia, North America and Europe are all periglacial environments with large areas of permafrost.
-   At **high altitudes**. Periglacial conditions exist **around ice masses** in **mountain ranges**. They're also found on high altitude **plateau** areas, e.g. the Tibetan plateau in Asia, and the Bolivian plateau in South America.
-   In the **interior** of land masses. Periglacial conditions exist at lower latitudes and lower altitudes because of the effect of **continentality**, e.g. Siberia, central Asia.

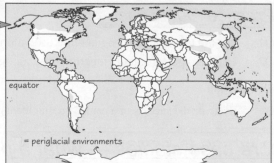

equator

= periglacial environments

Distribution of Cold Environments

3) Alpine Environments are Found at High Altitudes

1) Alpine environments are cold areas of land at an altitude **above** the **treeline**. The treeline is the **limit** of the area that trees can grow in — above the treeline it's **too cold** for trees to grow.

2) Alpine environments are **always** found at **high altitudes**. Alpine conditions can be found above the treeline on **mountain ranges**, e.g. the Himalayas (Asia), the Andes (South America) and the Alps (Europe). They can exist at **any latitude**, e.g. alpine conditions exist along much of the Rocky mountains in North America, which run north to south from above 50° to around 30° latitude.

3) Alpine environments may **include periglacial** and **glacial** conditions. **Temperature decreases** as altitude increases — permafrost (periglacial conditions) may exist above (and below) the treeline, permanent snow and ice (glacial conditions) may exist even higher up.

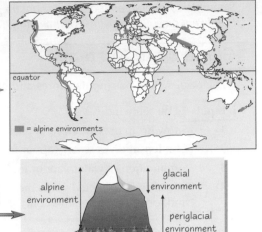

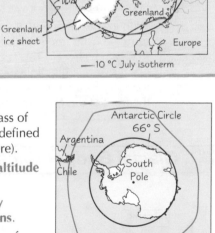

4) Polar Environments are Found around the Poles

There are **two** polar environments — one around the **North Pole** (the **Arctic**) and one around the **South Pole** (the **Antarctic**).

1) The Arctic polar environment is **cold** because it exists at a **high latitude**.

2) The Arctic polar environment can be defined either by the **Arctic circle** (**66° N**) or by the **10 °C July isotherm** (areas north of this line have an average temperature **below** 10 °C in **July**, the **hottest** month).

3) The area around the north pole is made up of **sea ice** (frozen sea water). The area of sea ice **shrinks** in the **summer**, leaving **open sea**, and **refreezes** in the **winter**.

4) Much of the Arctic polar environment is made up of the **northern land areas** of Asia, **North America** and **Europe**. The land-based polar environment can include **glacial** environments, e.g. the Greenland Ice Sheet, and **periglacial** environments, e.g. northern Russia.

1) The Antarctic polar environment is **cold** because of its **high latitude** — the Antarctic circle (**66° S** latitude) doesn't go all the way round the land mass of Antarctica though, so the polar environment around the south pole can be defined by the **10 °C January isotherm** (the hottest month in the southern hemisphere).

2) Some of the Antarctic polar environment is also cold because it's at a **high altitude** — the ice in some places is so thick it reaches an altitude of over **4000 m**.

3) The **interior** of Antarctica is also **cold** because of the effect of **continentality** — the centre is hundreds of kilometres from the **warming** effect of the **oceans**.

4) A large area around the Antarctic land mass is made up of **sea ice**. The area of sea ice changes throughout the year, **shrinking** in summer and **refreezing** in winter.

5) Most of the Antarctic polar region is on the huge **land mass** of **Antarctica**. The land-based polar environment includes **glacial** environments, e.g. the Antarctic ice sheet.

Practice Questions

Q1 Where are alpine environments found?
Q2 What's the latitude of the Arctic circle?
Q3 Give three reasons why Antarctica is cold.

Exam Question

Q1 Describe and explain the global distribution of glacial and periglacial environments. [15 marks]

So which is better — north or south? Let's take a poll...

It might not seem like it yet, but cold environments are actually pretty interesting. To really get yourself in the mood for these next few pages, try turning the heating off and opening all the windows, and read them with your scarf and gloves on.

Glaciers

Since plenty of cold environments contain glaciers, you need to know a fair bit about them.
I do like a nice glacier. Pity you have to go to the Alps or Norway to see the nearest ones.

Glaciers are **Systems**

The glacial system has **inputs**, **stores** and **outputs**.

Inputs These include:

1) **Snow** (from **precipitation** or **avalanches**).
2) **Condensation** of water vapour from the air (which then freezes).
3) **Sublimation** of water vapour from the air directly to ice crystals.
4) Bits of **rock** collected when the glacier carves away at the landscape, and rocks that have fallen onto the glacier from above.

Sublimation involves a direct change of state from a gas to a solid without passing through the liquid stage.

Stores

1) The main store is obviously **ice**.
2) **Meltwater** is a small part of the glacier. It can be found **on the ice**, **in the ice** or **below the ice**.
3) Glaciers also carry **debris** (rocks, gravel and sand).

Meltwater is considered a store when it's actually in the glacier. When it's flowing down the valley well away from the glacier, it isn't a store in the system any more.

Outputs Outputs are the **losses** from a glacier.

1) Ice can **melt** and **flow out** of the glacier as **meltwater**.
2) Surface snow can **melt** and **evaporate**.
3) Ice and snow can **sublimate** to water vapour.
4) Snow can be **blown away** by strong winds.
5) With glaciers that end at the **sea**, blocks of ice fall from the **front** (the snout) of the ice mass into water to create **icebergs**. This is called "**calving**" — as if the glacier were a big old ice cow giving birth to a little ice calf. It can also happen where there's a **lake** at the front of the glacier.

INPUTS
snow
condensation
sublimation
rock material

STORES
ice
meltwater
debris

OUTPUTS
meltwater
sublimation

meltwater

A **Glacial Budget** is the **Balance** between a Glacier's **Inputs** and **Outputs**

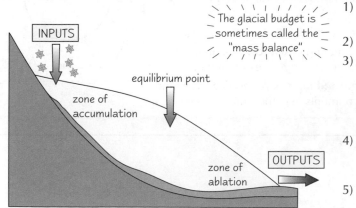

INPUTS

The glacial budget is sometimes called the "mass balance".

equilibrium point

zone of accumulation

zone of ablation

OUTPUTS

1) **Accumulation** is the **input** of snow and ice into the glacial system. Most accumulation is snow.
2) **Ablation** is the **output** of water from a glacier.
3) The **glacial budget** is the balance between accumulation and ablation over a year — it shows whether the volume of water in the glacial system has **increased** or **decreased**. This determines whether the **front** of the glacier **advances** forwards or **retreats** back.
4) You get **more accumulation** than ablation in the **upper** part of a glacier — so it's called the **zone of accumulation**.
5) You get **more ablation** than accumulation in the **lower** part of a glacier — so it's called the **zone of ablation**.

6) The place where accumulation and ablation are **equal** is called the glacier's **equilibrium point**.
7) If there's **more accumulation** than ablation over a year, the glacier has a **positive regime** (or a positive mass balance). The glacier grows and **advances** (moves forward).
8) If there's **less accumulation** than ablation over a year, this is a **negative regime** (or a negative mass balance). The glacier shrinks and **retreats** (moves back).
9) If there's the **same amount** of accumulation and ablation over a year, the glacier stays the same size and the position of the snout **doesn't change**.

Glaciers

The Glacial Budget **Changes** Throughout the **Year**...

1) You get **more ablation** during **warmer** times of the year — which makes sense, as more ice melts when it's warm.

2) During the **colder** months, there's **more accumulation** than ablation.

3) Over the year, this might **balance out** — the glacier **advances** in winter but **retreats** in summer, so overall the volume of water in the glacier **stays the same**.

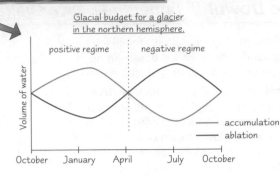

Glacial budget for a glacier in the northern hemisphere.

Hannah and Betty had a very positive regime.

...and Over **Several Years**

Changes in **global temperature** over long periods of time affect the glacial budget.

1) Temperatures in the **19th century** were **colder** than in the 18th century, so in general there was more accumulation than ablation. This meant that many glaciers **advanced** because they had a positive regime.

2) In the **20th century**, global temperature **increased** so glaciers tended to have a negative regime and **retreated**.

Glaciers Form when Snow **Accumulates** and **Turns Into Ice**

1) First, **snow settles**. It has a loose, fluffy, snowflakey consistency at this point.

2) The **weight** of **more snow** falling on top turns the snow into a denser, more granular kind of snow called **firn**.

3) **Air** is squeezed **out**, and particles of ice are **compressed together** by the continuing accumulation of snow and ice.

4) Water also **melts** and **refreezes** in the **air spaces**, making the ice **more dense**. Et voilà — a glacier is formed.

Glaciers can be **Cold-Based** or **Warm-Based**

Glaciers can be classified according to the **temperature** of their **base** (the bit where the ice touches the valley floor).

The melting temperature of ice at the base of a glacier is slightly lower than the normal melting point of ice (0 °C), because of the pressure of all the ice on top of it.

1) In **warm-based glaciers**, the base is **warmer** than the melting point of ice. It's warmer because of heat from **friction** caused by the glacier moving, or because of **geothermal heat** from the Earth. The ice at the bottom of the glacier melts, and the **meltwater** acts as a **lubricant**, making it easier for the glacier to move downhill. Ice at the **surface** also melts if the temperature reaches 0 °C, and meltwater moves down through the glacier, lubricating it even more. Lots of movement means **lots of erosion**.

2) In **cold-based glaciers**, the base is cold (the temperature is usually well **below** the ice's **melting point**) so there's very **little melting**. The ice is frozen to the base of the valley, so there's **very little movement**. There's hardly any melting at the surface either, even in summer. This means that cold-based glaciers **don't** cause very much **erosion** at all.

Practice Questions

Q1 What are the main inputs, stores and outputs in a glacial system?

Q2 What are accumulation and ablation?

Q3 How does the glacial budget change throughout the year in the northern hemisphere?

Exam Questions

Q1 What is a glacial budget? Explain how a glacial budget shows whether a glacier is advancing or retreating. [3 marks]

Q2 Describe the main differences between warm-based and cold-based glaciers. [5 marks]

Brrr. Might need an extra jumper on...

Nope, you're not reading an accountancy revision guide by mistake — glaciers have budgets too. Glacial budgets are all about the ins and outs of the glacier. Stuff comes in mainly in the form of snow, and goes out mainly as meltwater. If more comes in than goes out then the glacier advances, and if more goes out than in it retreats — not so hard after all.

Glacial Processes

Glaciers are moving all the time — they don't stop to think about the erosion they might be causing...

Glaciers Move Downhill under their Own Weight

1) **Meltwater** underneath a glacier allows the glacier to **slide** over the ground. This is called **basal sliding**, and it's the main way that warm-based glaciers move.

2) There's **more melting** around bits of **rock protruding** from the valley floor, because there's **more pressure** on the ice (so the ice melts at temperatures lower than 0 °C). Meltwater can **refreeze** downstream of the obstruction where there's less pressure, so the flow tends to be faster around the obstruction, and slower downstream.

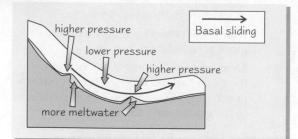

3) Glaciers move in an **arc shape** when they're in a **hollow** (by basal sliding). This is called **rotational flow** (which is a bit weird as it isn't really rotation as in "going round and round").

4) **Internal deformation** is where the ice **bends** and **warps** to flow downhill like a liquid. It's caused by ice crystals shifting past each other. It's the main way **cold-based** glaciers move.

5) At the **head** of a glacier the valley is steep, so there's a strong **gravitational force** pulling the ice downwards. This makes the ice **move quickly**. When ice moves quickly there's more **tension** (pulling apart forces), which causes the ice to **fracture** into thick layers. The **layers** then **slip downwards** — this is called **extensional flow**.

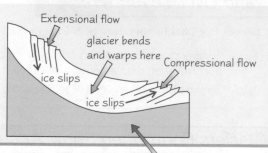

6) **Lower down** the glacier the ice is moving more **slowly** because the valley is less steep. The faster ice from the head of the glacier **pushes down** on the slower ice and **compresses it**. The **high pressure** causes the ice to **fracture** into layers, and the layers **slip forwards** — this is called **compressional flow**.

- The main things that determine the **speed** at which a glacier flows are the **gradient** of the valley floor, the **thickness** of the ice and the **temperature** at the base of the glacier.

- The **steeper** the valley, the **faster** the glacier will flow. The **thicker** the **ice** the **faster** it will flow — in a **warm-based** glacier thicker ice exerts **more pressure** on the valley floor, causing **more melting**, which makes it flow faster. In a **cold-based** glacier thicker ice means there's **more internal deformation**, which makes it flow faster. The **warmer** the **base** of the glacier the **faster** it will flow (see p. 37).

- Ice **moves faster** near the glacier's **surface** than at the **base** — **friction** at the base slows the glacier down.

- Ice also moves faster near the **middle** than at the **edges**.

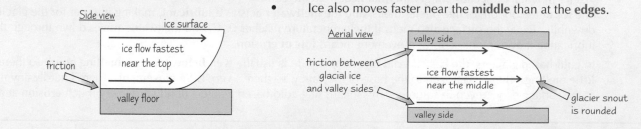

Glaciers Crack as they Move Down the Valley

1) Stresses and strains cause cracks called **crevasses** to form in the glacier.

2) Stress can be caused by **extensional** and **compressional flow**, **calving**, or **tension** between the ice attached to the **valley sides** and **back wall** and the rest of the glacier.

3) The tension caused by the glacier pulling away from the ice attached to the **back wall** produces a big **semicircular crevasse** at the back of the glacier called the **bergschrund**.

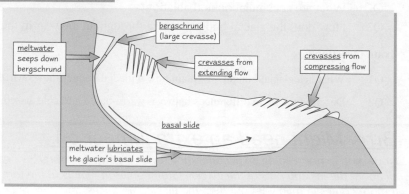

Glacial Processes

Glaciers **Erode** the **Surrounding Rock**

Glaciers erode the valley floor and sides by plucking and abrasion

1) **Plucking** — ice in contact with rock surfaces can thaw slightly then **refreeze around rocks** protruding from the valley sides and floor. When the glacier **moves forward**, it **plucks** the rocks away from the valley sides and floor.

2) **Abrasion** — **debris** carried along by the glacier can **scrape** material off the valley walls and floor.

frost shattering breaks bits of rock off the mountain face

plucking breaks bits of rock off the mountain face and makes the back wall steeper

abrasion grinds and gouges the valley floor

Meltwater erosion shapes the valley floor

Glaciers can produce huge quantities of **meltwater**, making streams that are powerful enough to erode the valley floor and sides by normal **fluvial (river) processes** (see p. 6).

The **amount** and **rate** of erosion is increased in areas of **less resistant rock**, and if the glacier is **thick** or if it's **moving quickly**. It's also increased if there's **lots** of **debris** or if the debris is made of **resistant rock**.

Weathering also contributes to the shaping of the glacial valley

Frost shattering breaks rocks off the **back** and **side walls** of the valley. **Meltwater** from snow gets into **cracks** in the valley walls and then **freezes** — when it freezes it **expands**, so it exerts **pressure** on the rock and bits of the rock get broken off. These bits of rock often **fall onto**, or **into**, the glacier (adding to the debris that **abrades** the valley).

Glaciers **Transport Debris**

1) Glaciers carry large loads of **debris** — this is material that the glacier has gathered by plucking, or bits of rock that have been broken off the back wall or valley sides and fallen onto (or into) the glacier. Debris ranges from **fine sediment** to **huge boulders**.

2) There are **three** main ways debris is transported. **Supraglacial** material is carried **on top** of the glacier's surface. **Englacial** material is carried **within** the body of the glacier. **Subglacial** material is moved along **at the base** of the glacier.

Glaciers **Deposit** their Load as they **Move** and as they **Melt**

1) The **unsorted** mixture of material **deposited** by the glacier is called **till** (it's sometimes called "boulder clay" too). It includes everything from massive boulders down to pebbles and clay. Glaciers drop any size of till anywhere.

2) **Lodgement till** is spread onto the valley floor beneath the ice by **moving** glaciers.

3) **Ablation till** is dropped by a glacier as it **melts**. The till is mainly deposited close to the glacier snout because this is where most ablation happens — the glacier drops debris as the ice around the debris melts.

4) Till **points** in the **direction** that the glacier is flowing.

5) Till is often **deposited** as landforms called **moraines** (see p. 41).

Practice Questions

Q1 What is rotational flow?
Q2 How is a bergschrund formed?
Q3 What are the main ways that debris is transported by a glacier?

Exam Questions

Q1 Explain what is meant by extensional flow. [4 marks]

Q2 Name and explain the two methods of glacial erosion. [4 marks]

Glaciers move r e a l l y s l o w l y — bit like you on a Sunday morning...

Alright, I'll admit that these two pages are slightly harder than the last two. It can be tricky at first to get your head around the different ways that glaciers move. Try reading over the first page a couple of times, then at least you'll know that rotational flow isn't a dance move. Don't forget that glaciers erode valleys in two different ways — by plucking and by abrasion.

Glacial Landforms

These pages are about the landscapes that glaciers leave behind them. Mountain climbers and geography teachers get very excited about the beauty of glacial landscapes. Whether or not they move you, you still need to learn about them.

Glaciers Create Basins called Corries (also called Cirques or Cwms)

1) Glaciers normally form on one side of a mountain peak — the side that gets **least sun** and the **coldest winds**. That's where there's **most accumulation** and **least ablation**.

2) Snow collects in hollows and turns to **ice**. **Basal sliding** (rotational flow) with **abrasion** and **plucking** deepen the hollow into a **corrie** (a bowl-shaped hollow).

3) When the ice in the hollow is thick enough, it **flows** over the lip and downhill as a glacier. Frost shattering and plucking **steepen** the back wall of the corrie.

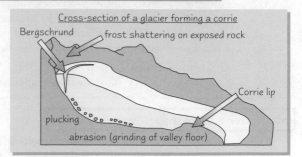

Cross-section of a glacier forming a corrie
Bergschrund — frost shattering on exposed rock
Corrie lip
plucking
abrasion (grinding of valley floor)

Glacial Erosion Changes the Landscape of Valleys

Glaciers moving through valleys produce **erosional landforms**, which change the way valleys **look** after the ice has **gone**.

1) An **arête** is a steep-sided **ridge** — it's formed when two glaciers flow in parallel valleys. The glaciers erode the sides of the valley, which **sharpens** the mountain ridge **in between** them.

2) A **pyramidal peak** is a pointed mountain peak with at least **three sides**. It forms where **three** or more **corries** form **back to back** (their back walls make the mountain peak).

3) **Glacial troughs** (also called U-shaped valleys) are **steep-sided valleys** with **flat bottoms**. They're formed by the erosion of **V-shaped river valleys** by glaciers. As the glacier erodes through the V-shaped valley it makes them **deeper** and **wider**.

4) **Hanging valleys** are valleys formed by **tributary glaciers** — they erode the valley floor much less **deeply** because they're **smaller** than the main glacier. So, when the glaciers melt, the valleys get left at a **higher level** than the glacial trough formed by the main glacier. You get **waterfalls** from hanging valleys into the main glacial trough.

> A tributary glacier is a smaller glacier that flows into the main glacier.

5) **Truncated spurs** are formed when **ridges of land** (spurs) that **stick out** into the main valley are **chopped off** (truncated) as the main valley glacier moves past.

6) **Valley steps** are (funnily enough) steps in the glacial trough. They're formed when the glacier erodes the valley floor **more deeply**. This happens when **another glacier joins** it or where there's **less resistant** (softer) rock.

7) **Tarns** are **lakes** that form in **corries** after a glacier has retreated.

8) **Ribbon lakes** are long, thin lakes that form after a glacier retreats. They form in **dips** caused by erosion of bands of **less resistant** rocks, or **behind dams** of **debris** left by the glacier.

9) **Fjords** are long, deep inlets that form when a valley that's been eroded by a glacier is **flooded** by sea level rise after the ice has **melted**.

10) A **roche moutonnée** is a **resistant** (hard) mass of rock on the valley floor. The **upstream** (stoss) side is **smooth**, because it was smoothed by **abrasion** as the glacier went over it. The **downstream** (lee) side is steep and **rough** where the glacier **plucked** at it.

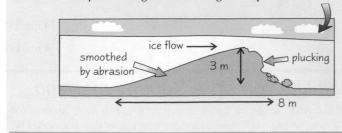

smoothed by abrasion
ice flow
plucking
3 m
8 m

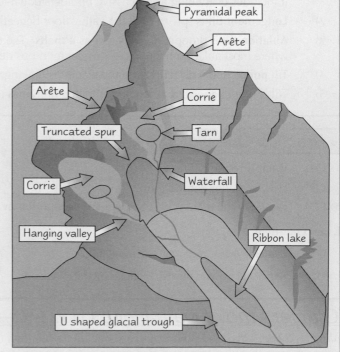

Pyramidal peak
Arête
Arête
Corrie
Truncated spur
Tarn
Corrie
Waterfall
Hanging valley
Ribbon lake
U shaped glacial trough

Glacial Landforms

Glaciers Form **Moraines** by **Depositing Till**

Moraine is the name for different formations of **till** deposited by a glacier as it melts. There are **three** different types of moraine:

1) **Lateral moraine** is deposited where the **sides** of the glacier were.

2) **Medial moraine** is deposited in the **centre** of the valley where two glaciers **converge** (the two lateral moraines join together).

3) **Terminal moraine** builds up at the **end** of the glacier, and is deposited as semicircular hillocks of till.

<u>Till</u> is all the stuff that a glacier leaves behind — unsorted boulders, stones and clay (see p. 39). <u>Moraine</u> is the name given to particular formations of till.

lateral moraine

medial moraine

lateral moraine

terminal moraine

till

Till can also be Deposited as **Hills** called **Drumlins**

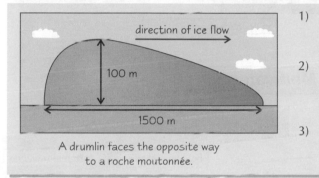

direction of ice flow

100 m

1500 m

A drumlin faces the opposite way to a roche moutonnée.

1) **Drumlins** are **half-egg shaped hills** of till, up to 1500 m long and 100 m high. The **upstream** (stoss) end is **wide and tall**, and the **downstream** (lee) end is **narrow and low**.

2) Nobody's really sure **why** drumlins are egg-shaped — it may be that till got stuck around a rock or a little hill sticking out into the glacier. It may be that an original mound of dropped till got streamlined when the ice **readvanced** over it.

3) Drumlins often form in **groups**. There are drumlins in the **Ribble Valley** in Lancashire. There are also a whole bunch of drumlins under the water level in Clew Bay, Ireland.

Erratics are **Boulders** that have been **Carried** a **Long Way** by Glaciers

1) Erratics are rocks that have been **picked up** by a glacier or an ice sheet, **carried along** and **dropped** in an area of **completely different geology** (rock type).

2) For example, in the Yorkshire dales at Norber, loose black **Silurian** rocks sit on top of white **Carboniferous** limestone.

3) There are erratics in **Eastern England** that were originally picked up by an ice sheet in **Norway** and carried all the way to England during the Ice Ages.

Les was good at long-distance boulder carrying, but not quite as good as a glacier.

Practice Questions

Q1 What is the name of the ridge formed by two glaciers in parallel valleys?

Q2 Name three erosional features of glaciated valleys.

Q3 What is the name for rocks that are transported by a glacier or an ice sheet and dropped into an area with a different rock type?

Exam Questions

Q1 Describe and explain the landforms shown in the photo on the right. [8 marks]

Q2 Describe the three different types of moraine. [3 marks]

Corries? I'm more of an Emmerdale fan myself...

There are a fair few features to learn here, but don't let that get you down. You just need to learn the names of the features, what they look like and how they're formed. Even the names of the features are a bit tricky though — cirque, arête, roche moutonnée... anyone would think this was a French exam. At least you don't need to know how to pronounce them.

Fluvioglacial Processes and Landforms

The sad news for all you glacier fans is that glaciers don't always stay around forever. But don't worry, they don't go down without a fight — even when they're melting, they still manage to change the landscape.

Meltwater Streams Erode the Landscape

1) When glacial ice melts, water runs out and forms streams of **meltwater**. **Warm-based** glaciers and **retreating** glaciers produce **lots** of meltwater.

2) **Surface** meltwater **filters** through the glacier (e.g. through crevasses) and flows through **tunnels** underneath the glacier, before running out of the snout of the glacier.

3) Meltwater streams cause **erosion** in the same way as normal rivers — but they cause **more** erosion than rivers of the same size. This is because the pressure of the ice means that meltwater streams flow very **quickly** — so they can carry **lots** of material that **erodes** the landscape.

4) Meltwater streams form deep **troughs** in the landscape called **meltwater channels**. Because meltwater streams have a lot of **erosive power**, the meltwater channels they produce are very **wide** and **deep**. After the glacier has **retreated**, the deep meltwater channels are left with very **shallow streams** running through them.

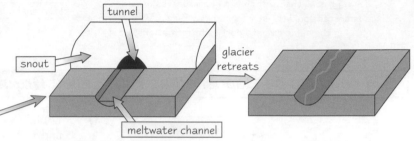

Fluvioglacial Deposits come from Glacial Meltwater

1) Glacial meltwater carries a **large load** of **sediment** of various sizes (from inside, on top of and underneath the glacier).

2) Meltwater streams **deposit** their load on the **valley floor** as they flow away from the glacier.

3) Meltwater streams are often **braided** — they split into lots of mini streams that cross over each other. This is because when the meltwater is flowing more **slowly** (e.g. in winter, when the amount of meltwater is lower) it can't carry its load — so it **deposits** the sediment on the ground, and **splits** into two streams to get round it.

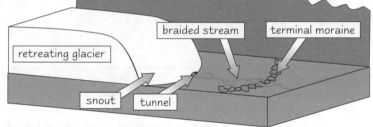

4) There's a difference between **glacial deposition features** formed by **glaciers** dropping debris as they melt (see p. 41) and **fluvioglacial deposition features** formed by **meltwater** carrying debris, then depositing it away from the glacier.

5) **Fluvioglacial** deposits are **sorted** — the fine sediment is **separated** from the larger sand, which is separated from the gravel, and so on. **Glacial** deposits are **unsorted**.

Melting Glaciers leave Outwash Plains and Kettle Holes

1) An **outwash plain** is a layer of gravel, sand and clay that forms in **front** of where the snout of the melting glacier used to be. Meltwater flows out of the glacier, and carries the sediment with it.

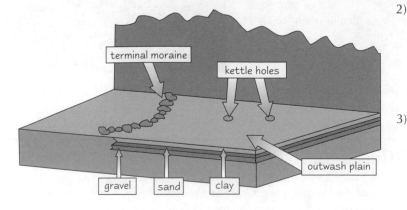

2) Sediments on outwash plains are **sorted** into layers. **Gravel** gets dropped **first** because it's **heavier** than sand and clay, so it forms the **bottom layer** of the outwash plain. **Clay** is dropped **last** and gets carried furthest away from the snout because it's the lightest sediment — it forms the **top layer** of the outwash plain.

3) **Blocks of ice** that have broken off from the front of the glacier can get surrounded and partly buried by the **fluvioglacial deposits**. When the blocks of ice **melt**, they leave **holes** in the outwash plain, called **kettle holes**.

Fluvioglacial Processes and Landforms

Meltwater Streams Deposit *Kames* and *Eskers*

1) **Eskers** are long, winding **ridges** of sand and gravel that run in the **same direction** as the glacier. They're deposited by meltwater streams flowing in **tunnels** underneath the glacier — when the glacier retreats and the stream dries up, the load remains as an esker. Eskers show you where the glacial tunnel used to be.

2) **Kames** are **mounds** of sand and gravel found on the valley floor. Meltwater streams **on top of** glaciers collect in depressions and **deposit** layers of debris. When the ice **melts** the debris is dumped onto the valley floor.

3) **Kame terraces** are piles of deposits left against the **valley wall** by meltwater streams that run between the glacier and the valley sides. They look like lateral moraine, but they're **sorted** into layers — meltwater streams deposit their **heaviest** loads first, so kame terraces have **gravel** at the **bottom** and **sand** on **top**.

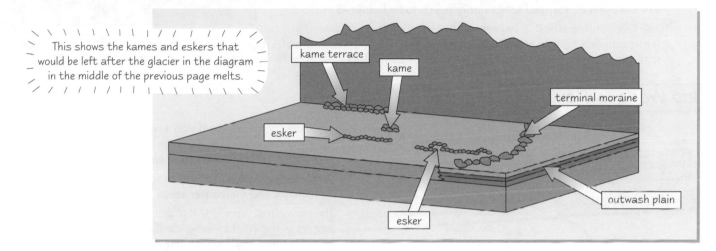

This shows the kames and eskers that would be left after the glacier in the diagram in the middle of the previous page melts.

kame terrace · kame · terminal moraine · esker · esker · outwash plain

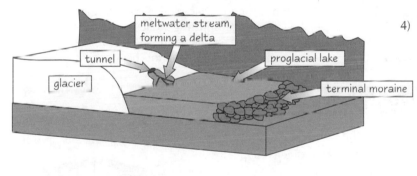

meltwater stream, forming a delta · tunnel · glacier · proglacial lake · terminal moraine

4) Lakes (called **proglacial lakes**) can form in front of glaciers, e.g. when the flow from meltwater streams gets dammed by the terminal moraine. As meltwater streams flow into a proglacial lake, they **slow down** and **deposit** their sediment on the ice — these deposits are known as **deltas**. When the ice melts, these deltas are dumped on the valley floor, forming **delta kames**.

Practice Questions

Q1 What are meltwater channels?

Q2 What's the main difference between glacial deposits and fluvioglacial deposits?

Q3 What is an outwash plain?

Q4 How are kettle holes formed?

Q5 What are eskers?

Exam Questions

Q1 Describe how kame terraces are formed. [2 marks]

Q2 Explain how delta kames are formed. [4 marks]

I'm melting! Meeeeeelting!

Well, this is just typical of glaciers if you ask me. Not content with ripping bits of rock out of mountains and scattering them all over landscapes, glaciers then have to go and melt, and wash all kinds of bits of rock all over the place. If only they didn't have to be so, well, <u>messy</u> about it — then you wouldn't need to know what a kame or an esker was. Oh well, tough luck, eh.

Periglacial Processes and Landforms

Periglacial areas are cold areas that aren't covered in ice.
There's usually ice in the soil though — I knew it'd be there somewhere.

Permafrost is Permanently Frozen Ground

1) **Periglacial** areas contain **permafrost** — **permanently frozen ground** with a top layer that can **melt** in the **summer** (called the **active layer**). **20-25%** of Earth's land surface is **permafrost**.

2) Areas of permafrost can be **continuous** (**all** the ground is frozen), or **discontinuous** (only **patches** of the ground are frozen).

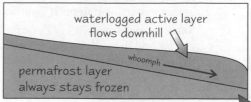

waterlogged active layer flows downhill

whoomph

permafrost layer always stays frozen

3) For **discontinuous** permafrost to form the **mean annual temperature** needs to be **below 0 °C** for at least **2 years**. For **continuous** permafrost to form the mean annual temperature needs to be **below –5 °C**.

4) The layer of permafrost is **impermeable** (water **can't** flow through it). If the temperature gets **above 0 °C** in the summer, the active layer **melts**, but the water can't go anywhere. This means that the active layer gets **waterlogged** and will **easily flow** wherever there's a **gradient**. This flow is called **solifluction**.

Ice Wedges Develop in Permafrost Soil

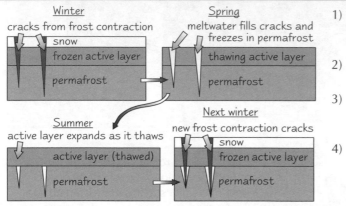

Winter
cracks from frost contraction
snow
frozen active layer
permafrost

Spring
meltwater fills cracks and freezes in permafrost
thawing active layer
permafrost

Summer
active layer expands as it thaws
active layer (thawed)
permafrost

Next winter
new frost contraction cracks
snow
frozen active layer
permafrost

1) When temperatures **drop very low** in winter, the ground **contracts** and **cracks** form in the permafrost. This is called **frost contraction**.

2) When temperatures **increase** in spring, the active layer **thaws** and **meltwater seeps** into the **cracks**.

3) The permafrost layer is still frozen, so the water **freezes** in the cracks — the ice-filled cracks formed in this way are called **ice wedges**.

4) Frost contraction in following years can **re-open** cracks in the same place, **splitting** the ice wedge. More water seeps in and freezes, **widening** the ice wedge. The ice wedge gets **bigger** each time this happens.

Ground Water Freezes causing Frost Heave

1) Water freezing in the ground can make humps on the surface.

2) When the active layer freezes in winter, the ice forms a kind of lens shape.

3) In fine-grained soil (like silt or clay) the ice lifts (heaves) up the surface layers of soil. This is called frost heave.

ice heaves soil upwards

ice forms lens shape

4) Ice lenses also form underneath stones because stones lose heat faster than the soil around them, so when temperatures drop it's colder beneath the stones.

5) As the ice lenses expand, they push the stones upwards towards the surface of the ground. The ice lenses underneath the stones stop the stones from slipping back down. If the ice thaws, fine material fills in the space where the ice was, so the stones don't fall down. Eventually the stones rise above the surface of the ground.

stone   ice lens

ice pushes stones upwards

Patterned Ground is Formed by Frost Activity

Sometimes **stones** on the surface of the ground are arranged in **circles**, **polygons** or **stripes** — this is called **patterned ground**. Patterned ground can be formed in two ways — by **frost heave** and by **frost contraction**:

1) Stones can get pushed to the surface by **frost heave**. Once they reach the surface, they **roll down** to the **edges** of the **mounds** that have formed, so they form **circles** around them (**polygons** form when the mounds are **close together**). If the mounds are on a **slope**, the stones roll downhill and form **lines**.

2) **Frost contraction** causes the ground to **crack** in **polygon shapes**. The cracks get **filled in** with **stones**, forming polygon patterns on the surface.

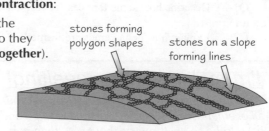

stones forming polygon shapes

stones on a slope forming lines

Periglacial Processes and Landforms

Nivation makes Hollows Deeper by Freezing and Thawing

Freezing   Thawing

1) When snow gets into a **hollow** in the ground, it can **increase** the size of the hollow.

2) The temperature in periglacial environments often **fluctuates** around **0 °C**, so a lot of **freezing** and **thawing** happens — when the temperature's **above** 0 °C, the snow **melts**, and when it's **below** 0 °C, the water refreezes as **ice**.

3) Every time the ice **freezes**, it **expands**, so **frost shattering** eventually breaks bits off the rock at the base of the hollow. When the snow **melts**, the meltwater carries the broken bits of rock (debris) **away**.

4) Slopes **collapse** because they're **waterlogged** and they've been **eroded** — the material is **washed away** by meltwater.

5) Eventually the hollow becomes **deeper** and **wider**. The processes that cause this are collectively called **nivation**, and the hollows formed by nivation are called **nivation hollows**. Nivation hollows can be the beginning of a **corrie**.

Solifluction Produces Lobe Formations

1) The **waterlogged active layer** of soil **flows** easily over the frozen impermeable layer beneath.

2) Solifluction produces **lobe** formations where one section of the soil is **moving faster** than the soil around it, e.g. because it's on **steeper** ground, so it flows down **further** to create a **tongue** shape.

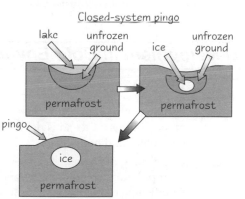

Pingos are Ice-Filled Periglacial Hills

1) A pingo is a **conical hill** with a **core** of ice. Pingos can be as large as 80 m high and about 500 m wide.

2) There are **two types** of pingo — **open-system** and **closed-system**.

3) **Open-system pingos** form where there's **discontinuous** permafrost. **Groundwater** is forced up through the **gaps between** areas of permafrost (from unfrozen layers lower down). The water **collects** together and **freezes**, forming a **core** of ice that **pushes** the ground above it **upwards**.

4) **Closed-system pingos** form in areas of **continuous** permafrost where there's a **lake** at the surface. The lake **insulates** the ground, so the area beneath it remains **unfrozen**. When the lake **dries up**, the ground is no longer insulated and the permafrost **advances** around the area of unfrozen ground. This causes water to **collect** in the centre of the unfrozen ground. The water eventually **freezes** and creates a **core** of ice that **pushes** the ground above it **upwards**.

5) If the ice core **thaws**, the pingo **collapses**, leaving behind a **pond** of meltwater surrounded by **ramparts** (walls of soil).

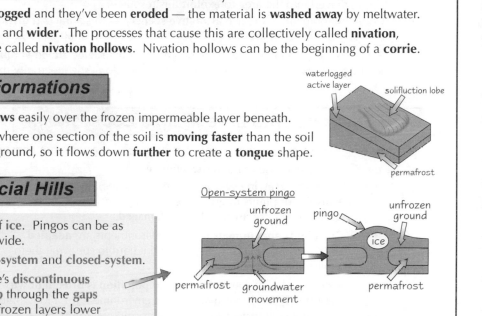

Practice Questions

Q1 What is permafrost?

Q2 How do ice wedges develop?

Q3 What's the difference between open-system pingos and closed-system pingos?

Exam Question

Q1 Describe the processes that lead to the formation of patterned ground in periglacial environments.   [6 marks]

I always thought Pingo was one of the Beatles...

The trouble with this lot is that there are so many different processes going on, and all of them are to do with water freezing and then thawing. But at least you can sleep soundly now you know that patterned ground is caused by frost activity and not aliens.

Issues in Cold Environments

Cold environments might not be great for beach holidays, but they've still got some great resources. There'll always be people who want to exploit those resources, even if it means damaging the environment in the process.

Cold Environments Contain Valuable Resources, which Attract Development

1) Many cold environments (and the **seas** around them) **contain resources** that **attract development**. These include:

- **Whales**, **seals** and **fish** — e.g. in **northern Russia** whales and seals are hunted for their skins, meat and blubber, while its **fishing industry** is one of the **largest** in the world.

- **Minerals** — e.g. the discovery of **gold** in **Canada** and **Alaska** triggered gold rushes and led to the establishment of towns based around mining that still exist today.

- **Oil** — e.g. **Alaska** has a lot of **oil**, and over the last few decades **oil companies** have moved into the area to **exploit** this resource.

Barry didn't like the sound of 'development'.

2) Cold environments also have **attractive scenery** — this attracts **tourism**. E.g. the number of tourists visiting **Antarctica** each year has risen from **6700** in **1992** to **46 000** in the **2007/2008** season.

3) Some cold environments have the potential for **hydroelectric power production** as they have natural lakes at high altitudes. **Norway** currently supplies **99%** of its domestic electricity through HEP plants.

Cold Environments have Fragile Ecosystems

1) Fragile ecosystems are ecosystems that struggle to **recover** from **damage**.

2) They're fragile because of the **harsh climate**:

- The **short growing season** (when there's enough **light** and **warmth** for plants to grow) means that plants **don't have much time** to **recover** if they're **damaged**.

- The **plants** and **animals** in cold environments are **adapted** to the cold conditions, so they find it hard to survive if their **environment changes**.

- **Decay** is **slow** because it's cold, so **pollution** is **broken down** very **slowly** (and so remains in the environment for a long time).

3) **Tundra** is a fragile ecosystem found in some cold environments, e.g. in periglacial environments.

> **Tundra** is found where it's **too cold** for **trees** to grow, either because of **high altitude** or **high latitude**. **Arctic tundra** is found in Greenland, northern Russia and Canada. **Antarctic tundra** is found in islands around Antarctica, e.g. South Georgia. **Alpine tundra** occurs in alpine environments. Vegetation includes **shrubs**, **grasses**, **mosses** and **lichen**. Animals found there include **seals**, **penguins**, **seabirds**, **hares**, **foxes**, **caribou** (reindeer) and **bears**.

Development in Cold Environments can Damage the Ecosystem

Fishing

1) Fishing can **disrupt food chains**, e.g. **krill** fishing in the **Southern Ocean** is depleting food supplies for whales and penguins.

2) **Overfishing** of a species can severely **deplete** its **population**, sometimes beyond recovery. Overfishing of the **Patagonian Toothfish** in the **Antarctic** is currently a concern.

3) **Bottom trawling** catches fish by dragging nets along the sea-bed. This **disrupts** the **ecosystem** (by **reducing light levels** through increasing turbidity) and **catches other species** as well as the target one. It's carried out in the **Gulf of Alaska**, the **Greenland Sea** and the **Barents Sea**.

Oil extraction

1) **Oil spills** can occur **during transport** of oil from the area. For example, in **1989** there was a huge **oil spill** off the coast of **Alaska** when the **Exxon Valdez oil tanker** crashed. Over **40 million** litres of oil spilled into the ocean, and over **250 000 birds** and **fish** were **killed**.

2) **Oil spills** can occur if **pipelines leak**. Between **1977** and **1994** there were, on average, **30 to 40** spills a year from the **Trans-Alaska pipeline**. Some of these were caused by **intentional attacks** and **forest fires**.

Hydroelectric power production

1) **Hydroelectric dams** can **block** the normal **migratory path** of fish. This can prevent them reaching **spawning grounds**, and so cause the fish **population** to **decrease**.

2) Hydroelectric dams also **heat up** the water, which can endanger **fish** that are used to **colder** temperatures.

Tourism

1) Large **cruise ships** increase **pollution** in the areas (from the ships and from the tourists).

2) Tourists and tourism developments (e.g. roads, hotels) disrupt **wildlife** and **damage habitats**, leading to **reduced biodiversity**.

Issues in Cold Environments

Mining

1) Mining can lead to **ground and surface water contamination**, either by **chemicals** used **during mining** or by the materials **being mined**. E.g. the lead-zinc mine in **Maarmorilik** (Greenland) was closed in 1990 but **lead** and **zinc** are still released, **polluting** nearby fjords.

2) Mining produces both **solid waste** and **wastewater** that has to be disposed of. In some cases, e.g. in the **Red Dog Mine** in **Alaska** and the **Kubaka** mine in **Russia**, the facilities are not built to deal with the quantities produced and the **waste** is **released** into the **environment**.

Development in Cold Environments has Affected the Locals

1) Even though the **climate** in **tundra** areas is very **harsh**, native **tribes** have lived there for **thousands** of years.

2) For example, the **Inuit** people are a group of tribes who live in the tundra in the northern parts of **Canada**, **Greenland** and **Russia**. Their traditional way of life involves **hunting** and **fishing** — they **eat** the **meat** and make **clothes** and **shoes** from the animal **fur** and **skin**.

3) **Newcomers** from Europe and the US started to take an **interest** in tundra areas during the **17th century** because of the opportunities for hunting **whales** and **seals**. **Seals** were hunted for their warm **fur** and their **oil** — the oil was used as **lamp fuel** and to make **leather**. **Whales** were mainly hunted for their **oil**, which was used to fuel **lamps**, make **candles** and also an ingredient in **margarine**.

4) The arrival of the **newcomers** had a very **negative** effect on the people living in the tundra, because they brought new **diseases** with them — many of the Inuit were infected and **died**. E.g. In the late 19th and early 20th century **90%** of the Inuvialuit (a Canadian Inuit tribe) were **killed** by diseases like tuberculosis, measles, smallpox and flu.

5) Also, an increase in **whaling**, **sealing** and **fishing** in the tundra areas **reduced** the **number** of whales, seals and fish available for the Inuit people to catch.

6) So development in tundra areas has had a big impact on the **lifestyles** of the indigenous people. E.g. in Canada:
   * There **aren't enough resources** for Inuit tribes to **support themselves** by hunting and fishing (and many young Inuits no longer learn the skills needed for this) so they have to find **paid employment**. This is difficult as the few job opportunities that exist are usually taken by the generally more educated white population.
   * With **unemployment** at nearly **50%** amongst some Inuit communities, they have to rely on government help.
   * The change of employment has also led to Inuits living in **permanent settlements** rather than being nomadic.

Development in Cold Environments can be Made More Sustainable

For development to be sustainable it has to **not deplete resources** and not cause **long-term environmental damage**. It's pretty **difficult** for development to be totally sustainable, but there are things that make it **more sustainable**. For example:

1) **National parks** have been set up to allow **tourism** whilst **protecting** the environment — e.g. **Denali National Park** in Alaska was set up in 1917, and then expanded in 1980 to include a greater area of land. Cars and private vehicles are **banned** from the park, so visitors have to travel in park buses on approved routes. The most vulnerable parts of the park don't have any **roads** at all, so the ground is **protected** from the damaging effects of vehicles.

2) **Fishing quotas** have been introduced (e.g. in the **Barents Sea**), to **limit** the number of fish caught and **prevent overexploitation** of the resource.

3) **Oil pipes** have automatic **shut-off valves** in order to minimise **oil spills** if the pipelines are damaged.

Practice Questions

Q1 Name three resources that can be found in cold environments.

Q2 What kind of wildlife is found in tundra areas?

Exam Questions

Q1 Describe the impact of development on cold environments. [6 marks]

Q2 Explain how the traditional way of life of native tribes in tundra areas has been affected by development. [6 marks]

Personally, my main issue with cold environments is chilblains...

Exploitation of cold environments is kind of a sad story, but at least it's not too hard to get your head around. Just make sure you learn what kind of resources are found in cold environments, and how exploiting them can damage the environment and affect the lifestyles of the native people. And always check the label on margarine to make sure there's no whale oil in it — urgh.

Issues in Cold Environments — Case Study

You've probably noticed by now that geography teachers love a good case study. Well it turns out that the examiners are just the same — case studies are their absolute favourite thing in the world. So they'd probably love these pages...

The **Antarctic** is a **Unique Wilderness Area**

Antarctica is the land mass, 'the Antarctic' is the area within the Antarctic Circle (it includes Antarctica).

1) A wilderness area is an area that has been **unaffected** by large-scale **human activity**.

2) Antarctica is the **largest** wilderness area on Earth — it covers an area about **14 million km²**, so it's **larger** than **Europe**.

3) It contains **90%** of all the **ice** on Earth — around **70%** of all the Earth's **fresh water** supplies.

4) The **Antarctic ice sheet** covers most of the land mass of Antarctica all year round. The **ice sheet** extends into the **sea** — the ice masses that extend out over the sea are called **ice shelves**. The two largest ice shelves are the **Ross Shelf** and the **Ronne Shelf**. Chunks of ice can become detached from the ice shelves and fall into the sea as **icebergs**.

5) There are several **islands** off the coast of Antarctica, e.g. **Elephant Island**.

The **Antarctic** has a **Fragile Ecosystem**

1) There's **very little available water** in Antarctica for plants to grow. Inland areas receive **less than 166 mm** of precipitation per year (which is low enough to classify it as a **desert**) and most precipitation that falls is **frozen**.

2) It's **very cold** — the average temperature is **–49 °C**.

3) There's also **very little sunshine** in winter (the sun doesn't rise for several months because of the Earth's tilt).

4) This means that **very few** plants and animals **can survive** there, and the ones that do have to be specially **adapted**. Antarctica's plant life is mainly made up of **mosses** and **lichens**, and only **two** species of **flowering plants** grow. There's abundant **bird life**, e.g. **albatross** and **penguins**.

5) The lack of water, warmth and sunlight in Antarctica means that the land environment is very **fragile** — it takes a long time for it to **recover** from **damage**.

6) There's abundant **sea life**, e.g. **fish**, **seals** and **whales**.

7) The **sea ecosystem** is also **fragile** — if the population of one species **decreases** it affects other species in the **food chain**, e.g. if the population of krill decreases it would affect the whale population as some whales feed on them.

The **Antarctic** has Lots of **Valuable Resources**

1) Although the Antarctic appears to be **barren** it has a lot of **natural resources**:

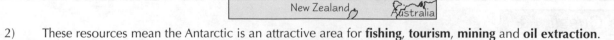

There are around **300** species of **fish** and **eight** species of **whale** in the waters around Antarctica. The **Weddell** and **Ross** Seas are both rich in fish.

Antarctica has very **attractive scenery**.

There are large underground deposits of **coal** and **iron ore** in the **Transantarctic Mountains**.

There are large reserves of **oil** underneath the **Southern Ocean** around Antarctica.

Argentina
Weddell Sea
Chile
South Pole
Transantarctic Mountains
Ross Sea
New Zealand
Australia

2) These resources mean the Antarctic is an attractive area for **fishing**, **tourism**, **mining** and **oil extraction**.

3) The Antarctic is also very attractive to **scientific researchers** because it's unique.

The **Antarctic** is **Protected** by the **Antarctic Treaty**

1) Antarctica has **no native people**, so no one can claim the land as their own. This has caused **conflict** over the **ownership** of the region since it was discovered in the 18th century — lots of different countries have **tried** to **claim ownership** of bits of the continent and the right to **exploit** its **resources**.

2) Since the Antarctic has a **fragile** ecosystem the **impact** of any development on the **environment** could be **devastating**.

3) To try and **protect** the Antarctic from environmental damage, the **Antarctic Treaty** was set up **1961**. 12 countries agreed to set aside disputes over who owns Antarctica and came up with **laws** to **protect it**.

4) The treaty includes many **protocols** and **conventions** that **control** or **prohibit** certain activities (see next page for more).

Issues in Cold Environments — Case Study

Oil Extraction, Mining and Whaling are Currently Banned in the Antarctic

OIL EXTRACTION and MINING

1) Due to the **possible** huge **environmental impact** of oil extraction and mining in the area they're currently banned.

2) The **Madrid Protocol** (part of the Antarctic Treaty) came into force in **1998**, banning all mining activity and oil extraction. The ban is in force for **50 years** — it's due to be **reviewed in 2048**.

3) Some people think the ban may be **lifted** in 2048 due to the **need for minerals** and **oil** (caused by depletion of reserves in the rest of the world).

WHALING

1) Whaling **was allowed** in the Antarctic, but caused a **decrease** in **whale populations**, e.g. it's estimated that there were **250 000 blue whales** in the Antarctic a century ago, now there are fewer than **1000**.

2) In **1994** the whole Antarctic area was declared a **whale sanctuary** and **commercial hunting** was **prohibited** (some whaling is still allowed for scientific research).

Efforts have been Made to Make Other Activities More Sustainable

1) Currently **tourism**, **scientific research** and **fishing** are allowed in and around Antarctica.

2) In the **2007 2008** season **46 000 tourists** visited the area.

3) There are around **5000 scientific researchers** in the Antarctic in **summer**, and about **1000** in **winter**.

4) **Fishing** is huge in the **Southern Ocean**, e.g. over **16 000 tonnes** of **Patagonian toothfish** were caught in **2000**.

5) These activities are controlled to **reduce** their **environmental impact** and to make them **more sustainable**:

Activity	Control
Tourism	• The <u>Antarctic Treaty</u> prohibits discharging of <u>oil</u> or <u>plastics</u> from cruise ships. • Tour operators have to stick to Antarctic Treaty rules, but they're mostly self-regulated by the <u>IAATO</u> (International Association of Antarctica Tour Operators). The IAATO imposes restrictions on tourist activity to reduce the environmental impact, for example no more than 100 passengers are allowed on shore in one place at a time and only one ship is allowed at a landing site at a time.
Scientific research	The <u>Protocol on Environmental Protection</u> came into force in <u>1998</u> as part of the Antarctic Treaty. It includes rules that protect Antarctica from damage caused by scientific research, e.g. scientists have to <u>remove</u> most of their <u>waste</u> from the Antarctic, and <u>treat sewage</u> before they dispose of it into the sea.
Fishing	The <u>Convention for the Conservation of Antarctic Marine Living Resources</u> came into force in <u>1982</u> as part of the Antarctic Treaty. It includes <u>quotas</u> (limits) on fish catches such as the Patagonian toothfish, krill and icefish.

6) **Not everyone** thinks that **tourism should be allowed**. The number of visitors is expected to increase to **80 000** per year by **2010**, which would **increase** the **environmental impact** of tourism.

7) It's very difficult to police the seas in the Antarctic so a lot of **illegal fishing** occurs despite the quotas, e.g. in the **2003-2004** season it was estimated that **2622 tonnes** of **Patagonian toothfish** were caught illegally.

Practice Questions

Q1 Name three of the resources that are found in Antarctica.

Q2 What is the Antarctic Treaty?

Exam Question

Q1 How is the Antarctic being protected from the impact of development? [15 marks]

Insert your own Aunt Arctica joke here...

Antarctica seems like quite a lively place considering nobody actually lives there. There's lots to learn on these pages, but at least it's all pretty interesting. Anyway, that's the end of cold environments — I hope you've enjoyed it as much as I have.

Desert and Desert Margin Characteristics

In my mind, deserts are full of towering sand dunes and camels, but in reality they're a bit different to that...

Rainfall is Low in Deserts and Desert Margins

1) **Deserts** are **arid** (dry) environments. Environments are classed as arid if they get **less than 250 mm** of **rainfall** a **year**.

2) **Desert margins** (land at the **edges** of a desert) are **semi-arid** environments. Environments are classed as semi-arid if they receive between **250** and **500 mm** of **rainfall** a **year**.

3) The **aridity** (dryness) of an environment depends on **rainfall** and the **rate of evapotranspiration**.

4) **Not all** deserts are **hot**, e.g. the **Gobi desert** in Asia is a **cold desert**. You **only** need to know about **hot** deserts for the **exam**.

Evapotranspiration is evaporation and transpiration (evaporation through plants).

Most Deserts and Desert Margins are Found...

① Around 30° North and South of the Equator

1) Air moves in **circular patterns** between the **equator** and about **30° north** and **south** of it. These **circular air patterns** are called **Hadley cells**.

2) In a Hadley cell **air rises** at the **equator**. The air cools as it rises, moisture **condenses** and falls as **rain**, leaving the air **dry**.

3) The **dry air descends** around **30° north** and **south** of the equator.

4) In areas where the **air descends** a zone of **high pressure** is created.

5) **Winds** blow **outwards** from high pressure areas — so **no moisture** can be **brought in** by the wind.

6) This means that the area has **very low precipitation**, which means desert margins and deserts are found there, e.g. the **Sahara**.

30° north
equator
30° south

② In the Middle of Continents

1) The **central** parts of **continents** are usually **more arid** than coastal areas.

2) **Moist wind** from the sea **moves inland** and the **moisture** held is **dropped** as precipitation.

3) So when the **wind reaches** the **centre** of a large **continent** it's carrying **very little moisture**, so very **little rain** falls.

4) For example, the **Turkestan** desert exists because it's in the **central** part of **Asia**.

Tropic of Cancer

Equator

Tropic of Capricorn

30°

30°

☐ Desert (arid)

■ Desert margin (semi-arid)

③ Next to Mountain Ranges

1) Tall mountain ranges **force winds upwards**.

2) As the air rises it **cools** and its ability to **hold moisture** is **reduced**.

3) Any moisture held is dropped as **precipitation** over the mountains, so the wind that moves inland has **very little moisture**, which means that **very little rain falls** there.

4) This is called the **rain shadow effect**.

5) For example, the **Atacama** desert in South America exists because of the rain shadow effect of the **Andes** mountains.

④ Near Cold Ocean Currents

1) In some places **cold ocean currents** run along the coastline.

2) Wind is cooled as it travels over the cold water and its **ability to hold moisture** is **reduced**.

3) **Moisture** that's stored in the atmosphere is **released** as precipitation over the ocean **before** reaching **land**.

4) So when the wind **reaches** the **land** there's **very little moisture left**, so **very little rain falls**.

5) For example, the **Namib** desert in **Africa** exists because of the **Benguela Current** (a cold ocean current) that runs up the **west coast** of Africa.

Desert and Desert Margin Characteristics

Hot Deserts are Hot and Have Large Variations in Temperature

1) The **mean annual temperature** of most hot deserts is **high** — usually between **20 and 30 °C**.
2) There are large **seasonal variations** in **temperature** — up to **50 °C** in summer and **below 0 °C** in winter.
3) There are also large **daily variations** in **temperature** — up to **50 °C** in the day and **below 0 °C** at night. Large variations are due to the dry desert air, which can't **block sunlight** during the day or **trap heat** at night.

The temperature in **desert margins** is a bit lower:

1) The **mean annual temperature** of most **desert margins** is **lower** than in deserts — between **10 and 20 °C**.
2) The **temperature variations** in **desert margins** are usually **less extreme** (between **10 and 35 °C**).

There's Little Vegetation in Hot Deserts

1) The **biomass** (total amount of living matter) in a desert is **low** because the **lack of water** makes it **difficult** for things **to grow**.
2) The amount of vegetation within a desert **varies** — there can be **none** where there are sand dunes, and a **variety** of small **shrubs**, **grasses** and **cacti species** in other areas.
3) Plants are **specialised** to **survive** in the hot and arid conditions, e.g. cacti have special ways to **collect**, **store** and **conserve** water.

The vegetation in **desert margins** is a little different:

1) There's **more** vegetation in desert margins than in deserts.
2) Vegetation includes **shrubs**, **grasses** and **trees**.
3) The **amount** of vegetation generally **increases** the **further away** from the **desert** you go, because there's **more water**.

Adaptations of Cacti

The enlarged stem stores water.

The thick waxy coating reduces transpiration and protects from strong winds.

Small spiny leaves reduce transpiration, and protect them from being eaten by herbivores.

Long, shallow roots absorb water from a large area, whilst longer taproots reach deeper water.

The Soil in Hot Deserts is Very Dry and Not Very Fertile

1) You usually think of deserts as just being made from **sand**, but there are areas of **bare soil** and also **soil underneath** the sand.
2) Desert soils **aren't very fertile** because they don't contain very much organic matter. This is because **few plants grow** there.
3) The soils are often **sandy** (in areas with sand dunes) or **stony** (in rocky areas).
4) The soils are **very dry** due to the **low rainfall** and **high temperatures**.

The soil in **desert margins** is a bit better:

1) The soil in desert margins is **more fertile** than the soil in deserts, because there's more vegetation.
2) The soil contains **more water** than desert soil.
3) The soil is **less sandy** and **stony** than in deserts because there's **more weathering**.

Practice Questions

Q1 How much rainfall do desert margins receive per year?
Q2 Explain how the rain shadow effect causes aridity.
Q3 Why do deserts have large daily temperature variations?

Exam Question

Q1 The graph on the right shows the climate in Riyadh, Saudi Arabia.

a) Describe the climate in Riyadh. [6 marks]

b) Riyadh is 25° north of the equator. Explain how its location leads to low levels of precipitation. [5 marks]

c) Suggest what the vegetation in Riyadh is like, and explain your answer with reference to the climate in Riyadh. [4 marks]

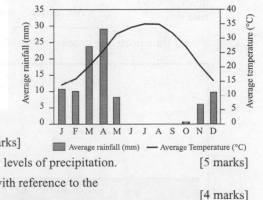

WLTM hot desert — must have a dry sense of humour...

You need to know all about where deserts are, why they formed there and what they're like. So get learnin'. Now, with all this talk of deserts I can't stop thinking about chocolate chip cheesecake. Which reminds me — don't forget it's spelt with one 's'.

SECTION 4 — HOT DESERT ENVIRONMENTS

Processes in Hot Desert Environments

It's a hard life being a rock in the desert — wind and water erode you and weathering makes bits fall off willy-nilly...

Rocks are Broken Down by Weathering

There are several **different types** of **mechanical weathering** that **break down rocks** in hot deserts. They include:

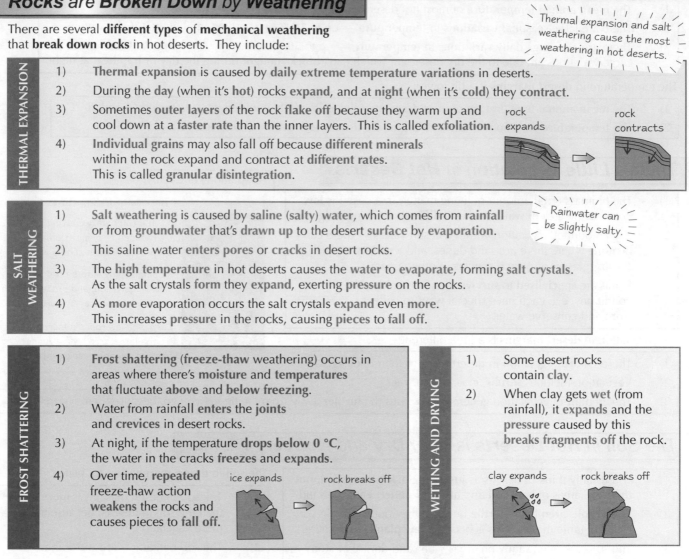

THERMAL EXPANSION

1) **Thermal expansion** is caused by **daily extreme temperature variations** in deserts.
2) During the **day** (when it's **hot**) rocks **expand**, and at **night** (when it's **cold**) they **contract**.
3) Sometimes **outer layers** of the rock **flake off** because they warm up and cool down at a **faster rate** than the inner layers. This is called **exfoliation**.
4) **Individual grains** may also fall off because **different minerals** within the rock expand and contract at **different rates**. This is called **granular disintegration**.

> *Thermal expansion and salt weathering cause the most weathering in hot deserts.*

rock expands   rock contracts

SALT WEATHERING

1) **Salt weathering** is caused by **saline (salty) water**, which comes from **rainfall** or from **groundwater** that's **drawn up** to the desert **surface** by **evaporation**.
2) This saline water **enters pores** or **cracks** in desert rocks.
3) The **high temperature** in hot deserts causes the **water** to **evaporate**, forming **salt crystals**. As the salt crystals **form** they **expand**, exerting **pressure** on the rocks.
4) As **more** evaporation occurs the salt crystals **expand** even **more**. This increases **pressure** in the rocks, causing **pieces** to **fall off**.

> *Rainwater can be slightly salty.*

FROST SHATTERING

1) **Frost shattering** (**freeze-thaw** weathering) occurs in areas where there's **moisture** and **temperatures** that fluctuate **above** and **below freezing**.
2) Water from rainfall **enters the joints** and **crevices** in desert rocks.
3) At night, if the temperature **drops below 0 °C**, the water in the cracks **freezes** and **expands**.
4) Over time, **repeated** freeze-thaw action **weakens** the rocks and causes **pieces to fall off**.

ice expands   rock breaks off

WETTING AND DRYING

1) Some desert rocks contain **clay**.
2) When clay gets **wet** (from rainfall), it **expands** and the **pressure** caused by this **breaks fragments off** the rock.

clay expands   rock breaks off

Wind Erodes Desert Rocks and Transports Particles

1) Wind can **erode** desert rocks in **two** ways:
   ① **Deflation** — the **removal** of **fine, loose particles** from the surface of rocks.
   ② **Abrasion** — **small particles** being **carried** by the wind **scrape off** particles from the rock surface.

2) It then **transports** the eroded material by **three** processes:

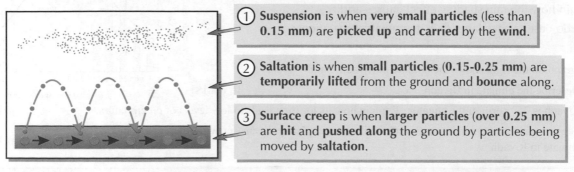

   ① **Suspension** is when **very small particles** (less than **0.15 mm**) are **picked up** and **carried** by the **wind**.

   ② **Saltation** is when **small particles** (**0.15-0.25 mm**) are **temporarily lifted** from the ground and **bounce** along.

   ③ **Surface creep** is when **larger particles** (over **0.25 mm**) are **hit** and **pushed along** the ground by particles being moved by **saltation**.

3) **More particles** are **transported** when the wind is **strong** and comes from a **constant direction**.
4) When there's a **reduction** in **wind speed**, the wind **drops** some of its **load** — this is **deposition**.

Processes in Hot Desert Environments

There are Three Types of River in Hot Deserts

1) **Exogenous** rivers have a **source outside** the **desert margin**. They flow **throughout the year** despite **evaporation** reducing their volume. For example, the source of the **Colorado river** in the **USA** is in the **Rocky Mountains**. It flows through the **Sonoran Desert** and the **Grand Canyon** to the sea.

2) **Endoreic** rivers **terminate inland** in the form of an **inland sea** or **delta**. For example, the **River Jordan** terminates in the **Dead Sea** — an inland sea in the **Middle East**.

3) **Ephemeral** rivers flow **intermittently** or **seasonally** after **rainstorms**. For example, the **Todd River** in the **Simpson Desert** (**Australia**) only flows a few days a year and remains a **dry river bed** for the rest of the year.

Derek promised them an ephemeral river was coming soon...

Flooding Erodes the Desert

Most **rainfall** in hot deserts is **light** and **infrequent**. However, **sometimes** there may be a **sudden**, **high intensity rainstorm** that lasts for a **short period** of time. This can cause **two types** of **flood** in a desert — **flash floods** and **sheet floods**.

Flash Floods

1) A **flash flood** is a **sudden**, **strong** and **rapid** flow of water through a **channel**.

2) They occur because **heavy** rainfall **can't** be **absorbed** by the **dry**, **hard desert soil** — so the **runoff** collects in **channels** and **flows rapidly downhill**.

3) Flash floods have **enough energy** to transport **large pieces** of desert rock by **traction**. They also transport **pebbles**, **gravel** and **sand** by **suspension** and **saltation**. The rocks in the water are **eroded** into **smaller fragments** by **attrition** (rocks smashing into each other).

4) The material carried by flash floods **erodes** the channels by **abrasion**, making them **deeper**.

5) At the **mouth** of a **channel**, the flash flood waters **spread out**, **slow down** and **soak into** the **ground** (unless they meet another body of water).

See page 6 for more on how water erodes and transports material.

Sheet Floods

1) A **sheet flood** is a **slow-moving**, **even flow** of water **over land** (i.e. it **isn't** confined to a **channel**).

2) Like flash floods, they occur **after** a period of **intense rainfall**, where water **collects** across the **dry**, **impermeable desert floor** and flows down **gentle slopes** as a **sheet** of water.

3) Sheet floods have **less energy** than flash floods, but can still **transport pebbles**, **gravel** and **sand** by **suspension** or **saltation**.

4) The **material** carried by sheet floods **erodes** the **desert surface** by **abrasion**.

Practice Questions

Q1 Name four types of mechanical weathering that occur in hot deserts.

Q2 Describe two ways in which wind can erode desert landscapes.

Q3 What is suspension?

Q4 What is surface creep?

Exam Questions

Q1 Describe the mechanical weathering processes that can occur in hot desert environments. [8 marks]

Q2 a) Describe the three types of river that can be found in hot desert environments. [3 marks]

    b) Outline how flash floods and sheet floods can erode hot desert landscapes. [6 marks]

Surface Creep — Grandad's new disco dance move...

There are tons of technical terms to get to know on these two pages — saltation, exogenous, ephemeral... It's tricky enough to get the spelling right, let alone what they mean. But if you shut the book and test yourself a few times you'll soon have 'em sussed.

Landforms in Hot Desert Environments

Wind and water in the desert do really neat things, like sculpting crazy landforms. Ooooooh, aaaaaaaahh.

Wind Erosion Forms Yardangs and Zeugen

Yardangs

Yardangs are **narrow, streamlined ridges** that are usually **three to four** times **longer** than they are **wide**. **Strong winds** (blowing in **one direction**) carry sand in **suspension**, which **erodes rocks** by **abrasion**. **Softer** rock is **eroded faster** than **harder** rock, so **ridges** of hard rock are created (yardangs). The ridges **aren't** always **continuous**.

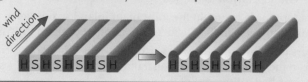

Zeugen! — That wind is capable of some nifty sculpting.

Zeugen

Zeugen are **long, block-shaped ridges** of rock (a **single** ridge is called a **zeuge**). They're formed in areas where a layer of hard rock sits **above** a layer of softer rock. If **cracks** form in the **hard rock** due to **weathering** processes such as **frost shattering** (see page 52), the **wind** can **erode** through the **cracks** and into the softer rock beneath by **abrasion**. Again, the **softer rock** is eroded **more** than the **hard rock**, and ridges (zeugen) are formed.

Sand Dunes Form When the Wind Deposits Sand

1) **Sand dunes** form when **sand grains** carried by **suspension** are **deposited** as the wind **slows down**.

2) **Vegetation**, **rocks** and **other dunes** slow wind down, causing it to **drop** its load.

3) The **shape** and **layout** of dunes is affected by several factors:

   See page 52 for more on how wind transports sand.

   - The **speed**, **direction** and **consistency** of the **wind**.
   - The **amount of sand** being transported — the **more** sand, the **larger** the dune.
   - The nature of the **ground surface** — e.g. **rocky outcrops** or **uneven ground** slow wind down.
   - The **amount** and **type of vegetation** — **deposition** occurs **downwind** from vegetation and **around its base**, **deforming** the shape of dunes. Also, **plant root networks** help to **stabilise sand** and **hold** dunes in place.

4) There are lots of **different types** of sand dune:

Barchan dunes (crescent-shaped)

1) These are **isolated** dunes that develop from mounds of sand. They form in the **direction** of the **prevailing wind** as sand is **deposited**.

2) When the slope of the dune becomes **too steep, sand avalanches** occur, depositing sand at the **base** (downwind).

3) **Swirling wind currents (eddies)** help to keep the slope **steep**.

4) The dune **slowly moves forward** in the direction of the wind.

5) If there's a **lot of sand** being deposited, many barchan dunes **connect** with each other to form a **barchanoid ridge**.

Seif dunes (long wiggly lines)

1) **Seif dunes** are **long, wiggly ridges** of sand.

2) They form **from barchan dunes** if a **change** of **wind direction** occurs.

3) When wind blows from **alternate sides** the **'arms'** of barchan dunes are **elongated** and form a wiggly line.

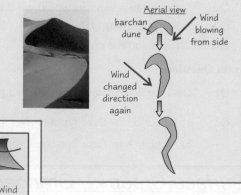

Star dunes (urm... star-shaped)

1) Star dunes have **multiple steep faces** caused by winds from **many directions**.

2) As more sand is added they grow in **height**.

Landforms in Hot Desert Environments

Water Erosion Creates Many Different Desert Landforms

The **fast-moving water currents** that follow **torrential rainfall** in the **desert** can create many different **landforms**:

1 Pediments

Pediments are **desert plains** — **gently sloping** areas of **rock** (usually covered in a thin **layer** of **debris**). They're formed by the **erosion** of rock by **sediment** carried in **sheet floods** or **small streams**.

2 Inselbergs

Inselbergs (e.g. **Ayers Rock**) are **steep-sided hills** that rise up from pediments. They're made of **hard rock** that's more **resistant** to **erosion** than the **surrounding rock**. The surrounding rock is **eroded** by **water**, leaving the harder rock **standing out**. Inselbergs can also be formed by **wind erosion**.

3 Mesas and buttes

A **mesa** is an **isolated, flat-topped, steep-sided** landform found only in **arid** places. They're a **type** of **inselberg** composed of a **hard horizontal rock layer**. They form in the **same way** as inselbergs. **Buttes** are **smaller** and **narrower** versions of mesas.

4 Salt lakes

Salt lakes form when **desert rivers**, which contain salt, are **endoreic** (**terminate** in an **inland sea**). The water can't **leave** the lake and **evaporation** is **high**, resulting in a lake with a **high salt content** (sometimes higher than **sea water**). Some salt lakes are **ephemeral** — evaporation is **so high** that they **dry up** at certain times of the year, leaving the salt behind to form **salt pans** (**ground** covered with **salt**).

5 Wadis and alluvial fans

A **wadi** is a **gully** or **ravine** that's been eroded by **seasonal rivers**. Depending on the **strength** of the river, a wadi can have **shallow** or **very steep** valley sides. If there's a flat desert plain at the **mouth** of a **wadis** the water **spreads out** on to the plain. This leads to **sediment** being **deposited** as **energy** is **dissipated**, forming an **alluvial fan**.

6 Badlands

Badlands are so called because they're **difficult** and **dangerous** to travel through. Badlands are **vast areas** of **uneven terrain** with **deep, interlocking canyons**, **steep ridges, loose sediment** and **deep sands**. **Wadis** and **buttes** can be found there. **Erosion** occurs from **flood waters** and **wind**. **Softer rock** layers and **clay soils erode** to form **canyons**, while **hard rock** layers are **eroded less** to form **ridges**.

Practice Questions

Q1 Give three factors that affect the shape and layout of sand dunes.

Q2 What are pediments?

Q3 Name two features of badlands.

Exam Questions

Q1 Describe and explain the formation of yardangs and zeugen. [7 marks]

Q2 The diagram above shows a desert landscape.

a) Identify the landforms A, B and C. [3 marks]

b) Landform D is a mesa. Describe what it is and how it formed. [4 marks]

c) Suggest what E is and how it formed. [4 marks]

So, the yardangs fight the zeugen and the inselbergs save the world...

...what's that... we're not talking about Star Trek... Oh. Sounded like we were. Best make sure then that you really do know your yardangs from your zeugen, your pediments from your inselbergs — I suggest you get that butte into gear and sha-wadi-wadi.

Desertification

Desertification isn't the cheeriest topic around but it's definitely important.

Desertification is a Form of Land Degradation

Desertification is the **degradation** of **semi-arid** land by **human activities** and **changes in climate**. It leaves land **unproductive**. **Africa** and **Asia** are the **worst affected areas** but desertification is a problem across the globe.

1) A **third** of land worldwide is **at risk** of **desertification**. 110 countries have regions that are threatened, with those likely to be worst affected in **Africa**, **Asia** and **Latin America**.

2) **250 million people** across the globe are already affected by desertification, the **largest proportion** of which are in **Asia**.

3) **46%** of **Africa** is **at risk** of desertification (**25%** is at **high** or **very high risk**).

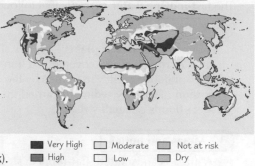

World map of desertification risk

| ■ Very High | □ Moderate | ▨ Not at risk |
| ▨ High | □ Low | ▨ Dry |

Climate Change is a Physical Cause of Desertification

Climate change is causing desertification by **reducing rainfall** and **increasing** the **temperature** in some areas:

Lower rainfall

1) Climate change will probably **reduce rainfall** in **sub-tropical regions** (where most semi-arid environments are).

2) If there's **less rain** then **surface water** and **groundwater** will be **reduced** (as it's used up or evaporates but isn't replenished).

3) This means that the volume of **water** available for **vegetation growth** is **reduced**, which leads to the **death** of vegetation.

4) The **roots** of **plants** and **trees bind the soil together**. **Fewer plants** and **trees** mean **fewer roots**, leading to **soil erosion**.

Higher temperatures

1) **Global surface temperature** has **risen** by **0.6 °C** over the last century and is predicted to **continue rising**.

2) As **temperatures increase** the **rate of evapotranspiration** also **increases**.

3) This **dries out soils** and **lowers surface water levels**, leading to soil erosion in the same way as lower rainfall does (vegetation dies).

Human Activity is the Main Cause of Desertification

1) **Overgrazing** — **reduces vegetation**, so leads to **soil erosion** (due to lack of **plant roots**). Trampling by large numbers of animals **compresses** and **breaks down** the **structure of soil**, which also makes **erosion more likely**.

2) **Overcultivation** — **reduces soil productivity** as the over-exploitation of the soil leaves it **without** enough **nutrients** to support plants. Without plants (and plant roots) the soil is **easily eroded**.

3) **Deforestation** — removing **trees** and therefore **tree roots** means that (once again) soil is more **vulnerable to erosion**. Forests are cleared to provide **land** for **farming** as well as **wood** for **fuel** and **building materials**.

4) **Irrigation** — can cause desertification in a number of ways:

- Irrigation **depletes surface water** and may involve **unsustainable pumping** of **aquifers**. As **water levels** are **lowered**, **water availability** for plants **decreases**, leading to **soil erosion**.

- Some **irrigation techniques** can **erode soil directly**, e.g. surface irrigation, where large amounts of water are added to the soil in a short amount of time, **washing topsoil away**.

- If **too much water** is used to irrigate crops the excess can **sink** into the soil and **raise groundwater levels**. If the aquifer is **saline** this may bring **high concentrations** of **salt** too close to the surface, **increasing** the **salinity** of the **soil** too much for plants to survive.

Aquifers are underground rocks containing water that can be extracted.

5) **Population growth** — **increases pressure** on the **land** as more and more **food** is needed to meet the **growing demand**. This leads to **further overgrazing**, **overcultivation**, **deforestation** and **irrigation**, therefore increasing desertification.

Desertification Impacts on Land, Ecosystems and Populations

As **fertile topsoil** is **eroded** the land becomes **less productive** (i.e. less can be grown). **Less plant life** means that **less animal life** can be supported and **biodiversity decreases**. If agricultural productivity decreases to the point where farmers **can't feed** their **families** or **earn a living** from the land then they have to **migrate** from the area. This **increases pressure** on the **land** in the **areas** that they **migrate to**. If people are **unable** to move then desertification can lead to **famine**, as families or whole communities are unable to produce the food they need from the degraded land.

Desertification

There are Strategies to Manage Arid Environments

Desertification can be prevented by using strategies that...

...make agriculture more sustainable by reducing overgrazing, overcultivation, and improving the fertility of the soil

1) Leaving areas of land fallow (not cultivated) — this allows the soil to recover from grazing.

2) Adopting nomadic farming — nomadic herders constantly move animals on, which stops areas being overgrazed.

3) Rotating crops — different crops need different nutrients, so rotating crops stops the same nutrients being depleted year after year. This improves soil fertility. Adding compost can also improve soil fertility.

4) Planting legumes (e.g. clover) — these improve soil fertility by increasing the amount of nitrogen present.

...make water use more sustainable by reducing use

1) Growing crops that need little water (e.g. millet, sorghum and olives) — this can reduce water use.

2) Using drip irrigation — this technique adds small volumes of water to the soil at a time. It reduces wastage of water and also prevents soil being eroded by large volumes of water being added in one go.

...increase or maintain the level of vegetation to reduce erosion

1) Planting trees — these act as windbreaks, protecting soil from wind erosion.

2) Using alternative energy sources — technology such as solar cookers can help reduce deforestation to provide wood for fuel. These cookers use the sun's energy to heat food and are cheap and easy to make.

External Aid May be Needed to Implement These Strategies

Implementing strategies to combat desertification costs money, either for equipment (e.g. drip irrigation systems) or for programmes to educate and train local people. In developing countries this money often comes from external aid. For example, in 1988 the International Fund for Agricultural Development funded a programme costing US $1.5 million to combat desertification in Northern Sudan.

Sustainable Strategies Address the Causes of Desertification

1) Most of the strategies above are sustainable because they prevent desertification and once implemented they can be carried on by the local community without external help or money. E.g. once people have been trained how to make a solar cooker, further external aid isn't needed as that knowledge is now within the community.

2) Some strategies just address the problems caused by desertification and so aren't sustainable (as they won't prevent desertification happening again in the future).

3) Examples of unsustainable strategies are transporting water to areas at risk of desertification, and using external aid to provide relief from famine.

4) To address the threat of desertification many countries are drawing up National Action Plans, which aim to prevent desertification using sustainable solutions and involving local communities.

Practice Questions

Q1 What is desertification?

Q2 Describe three strategies that reduce desertification.

Q3 What makes an anti-desertification strategy sustainable?

Exam Question

Q1 Outline the causes of desertification. [10 marks]

Dessertification — now that sounds like a topic I could get on board with...

If a third of land was at risk of being turned into sticky toffee pudding, the world would be a much better place. Sadly, that's not the case and desertification is causing problems across the globe. The good news is that if you take the time to learn these two pages really well it shouldn't cause you a smidge of a problem in your exam. Every cloud and all that...

Desertification Case Study — The Sahel

Down to specifics... The Sahel — it's a real place, with real problems.

Desertification is *Already Happening* in the *Sahel*

1) The **Sahel region** is a roughly **3900 km long belt** that runs east to west across **Africa**. It separates the hyper-arid Sahara from the wetter and more fertile savanna further south.

2) The Sahel runs through **10 countries** (see map), which are some of the poorest countries in the world.

3) It receives **200-600 mm** of rain per year, mostly between **May** and **September**, but **rainfall** can **vary** massively from year to year.

4) Some areas are **already suffering** from **desertification**, and others are at **very high risk**.

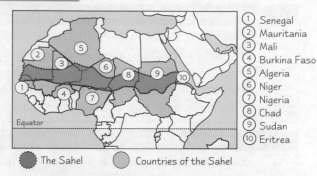

1. Senegal
2. Mauritania
3. Mali
4. Burkina Faso
5. Algeria
6. Niger
7. Nigeria
8. Chad
9. Sudan
10. Eritrea

⬤ The Sahel ⬤ Countries of the Sahel

Desertification is *Caused* by *Climate Change*, *Agriculture* and *Deforestation*

Climate change

1) Between **1968** and **1997 rainfall** in the Sahel **decreased** between **29%** and **49%**.

2) Low rainfall led to a **five year drought** from **1968** to **1973** and **droughts** were **common** across the Sahel from then right through to the early 1990s. While drought alone **doesn't cause** desertification (well managed land will recover when the drought ends) it can **contribute** to desertification when the **land** is **badly managed**, as the land will become degraded to a degree that it **can't recover from**.

3) The **average temperature** of the region has **increased** over the last century. This **increases** desertification by **increasing evapotranspiration**, which **reduces ground** and **surface water supplies**.

Agriculture

1) Between **1968** and **1998** the **population** of the Sahel **increased** from **274 million** to **628 million**. As the population increases **more food** has to be produced from the land to feed everyone.

2) At the same time, the **area of good agricultural land** has **reduced**, as more and more land is used as **game parks** for **tourists**.

3) With **less land available** and **more people** to feed the **pressure** on remaining agricultural land has **increased**. This has led to **overcultivation** and **overgrazing**, which has **increased desertification**.

4) The **total** area of land that's used for agriculture has **increased** from **8 million hectares** in **1960** to over **16 million hectares** in **2000**, as land that's **less suitable** for agriculture is used.

5) **Restriction** of **nomadic farmers** (those who move their herds depending on the weather, season or state of pasture) by **border closures** has forced farmers to stay in **one area**, causing **overgrazing**. Some nomads have also adopted a more **settled lifestyle**, which has had the same effect as restricting movement.

6) **Political instability** and **war** has led to **migration** of people to refugee camps, putting huge pressure on the surrounding environment to provide **enough food** for the **enlarged population**. E.g. between **1998** and **1999**, **30 000** people migrated to **Sudan** to escape the war between **Ethiopia** and **Eritrea**.

Deforestation

1) To create **more space** for **agriculture** large areas of **forests** have been **cleared** in the Sahel (usually by burning), leaving the ground vulnerable to **erosion**.

2) **Deforestation** to provide **wood** for **fuel** is a major problem in the Sahel, where **82%** of **total energy** used in homes and for industry comes from **wood**.

3) The demand for fuel wood has led to some people switching **from agriculture to wood collection** to earn a living. As increasing amounts of wood are collected the area of land that's deforested also increases. Wood for use in **Zinder** (a city in **Niger**) is now collected up to **200 km** away from the town.

Desertification Case Study — The Sahel

Desertification Has Environmental, Social and Economic Impacts

1) Erosion of topsoil has **reduced** the **area** of **productive agricultural land** in the Sahel. In **Mauritania** all that's left is a **200 km wide** strip running across the country, whilst in **Niger 2500 km²** of land is lost **each year** to desertification.

2) As land area decreases, so does the **amount of food produced**. E.g. some areas of **Niger** now produce **less than a 20th** of the food they could **40 years ago**. This causes **loss** of **livelihoods** and, in the worst cases, **famine**.

3) Many people have had to **migrate** from areas where the **land can't support them** any longer. E.g. over **2 million** people have migrated from **Mali** and **Burkina Faso** as a result of desertification.

4) With **fertile soil** becoming increasingly **scarce**, **tensions** have grown between **settlement farmers** and **nomadic herders** over use of the land, sometimes leading to **violence**.

5) The **changing conditions** in the Sahel have led to **animal migrations**. E.g. **rodents** from the Sahara are travelling further south, **destroying crops** and bringing **new diseases**.

Strategies to Reduce Desertification are Being Implemented

Some strategies to reduce desertification are **traditional techniques** that have been used for many years. For example:

The plant *Jatropha curcas* is grown as hedges **around food crops** by farmers in **Mali**. It's able to grow in **poor quality soil** and **isn't eaten by animals**. Its roots help **bind soil together** and it **protects** the soil from wind and water **erosion**. **Oil** produced from the plant can be **sold**, providing a valuable source of **income**. This strategy has **reduced poverty** and **erosion** in the area. The plant can also be burnt as **fuel**, **reducing** the need for **deforestation**.

Contour bunding is a **low-cost** technique where stones are placed **around agricultural lands** to keep **rainfall** there long enough for it to **soak in**. It's used to **maximise water use** and **prevent soil erosion**. It's **increased** some yields by **40%** in **Burkina Faso**, but can only be used in areas with **sufficient stones**.

Other strategies are more **recent** developments and have relied on **external aid** for implementation. For example:

In **Niger**, **Non-Governmental Organisations** (NGOs) are helping farmers to **reduce soil erosion** by providing **free seeds** of plants that are **suitable** for growing in **arid conditions**. These plants grow an **extensive root system** that **holds** the soil together. Long roots also mean that the plant can **absorb water** from **deeper** in the ground, so they're **less vulnerable to drought**. This scheme has been successful in **reducing soil erosion** but some people are concerned that it **encourages poor farmers** to continue agricultural production that's **high-risk**.

Similar schemes are also run in Sudan and Senegal.

In **Eritrea**, a **more efficient** version of the mogogo (a traditional stove) has been introduced. It needs **50% less wood** than the older version and therefore **reduces the need to cut down trees for fuel**. **Funding** for the project has come from NGOs and **international aid agencies**. A similar project has been launched in **Chad**, where new stoves run on **manure** rather than wood, therefore **reducing deforestation** and the risk of desertification. The new stoves have **reduced pressure** on **wood supplies** and the number of **respiratory diseases** has **decreased** as they produce **less smoke** than the old ones.

In **Chad**, NGOs have launched schemes to **reduce soil erosion** by **educating villagers** about the importance of maintaining plenty of **vegetation** and by helping them grow and plant **seedlings**. The schemes also **promote cooperation** between **neighbouring villages** to try to avoid over-exploitation of resources and to **share techniques** for good land management.

External aid can have **negative impacts** if the projects they fund aren't managed properly. During the 1968 to 1973 drought thousands of **wells** were built using aid money. Many farmers used the wells to **increase** the **size** of their **herds**, but the land couldn't cope with the **overgrazing** that followed. **Large areas** of land became **desertified** as a result.

Practice Questions

Q1 How is agriculture causing desertification in the Sahel?
Q2 Describe the impact of desertification on the Sahel.

Exam Question

Q1 Evaluate the strategies used to reduce desertification in the Sahel. [15 marks]

I drought you'll have too much of a problem learning this...

Like with all case studies you need to make sure that you learn lots of details and examples. Having a general idea that there are some problems with desertification in the Sahel isn't going to cut it. You need to learn the causes, impacts and the strategies.

Desertification Case Study — Southern Spain

*It's not just developing countries at risk — desertification's causing problems all over the place.
The Med may be fantastic for holidays, but all those tourists have an impact...*

Desertification is Already Happening in Southern Spain

1) **Spain** is in **Southern Europe**, close to North Africa and the Sahara desert.

2) Roughly **50%** of Spain is classified as **arid**, making it the **driest** country in Europe.

3) In 2008 it was estimated that **37%** of Spain is **at risk** of **desertification** (with **18%** of the land at **high** or **very high** risk).

4) The **most vulnerable areas** of the country are in the **south**, e.g. Andalusia and Murcia.

The map on the right shows the vulnerability of different areas to desertification.

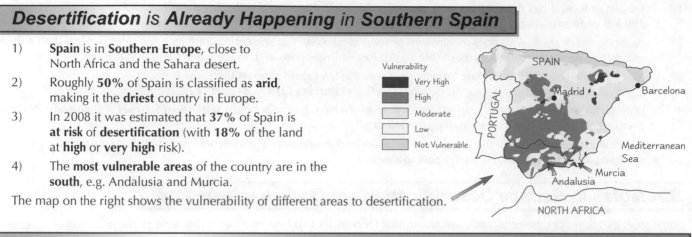

Desertification is Caused by Climate Change, Agriculture and Development

Climate Change

1) The **average temperature** in Spain has **risen** by **1.5 °C** in the last century, **increasing** the rate of **evapotranspiration**.

2) **Rainfall** has **decreased** throughout Spain. Between **1991** and **2000** rainfall in **Andalusia** fell by **9.5%**.

3) Higher temperatures and lower rainfall have **reduced surface water resources**. Less water is available to recharge groundwater supplies, leading to **falling groundwater levels**. As there's **less water fewer plants** can grow, meaning **fewer roots** to hold the soil together. This leads to **soil erosion** and desertification.

4) As the climate gets hotter and drier there's **increased risk** of **forest fires**, causing **deforestation** and desertification.

Agriculture

1) **Overcultivation** is causing desertification as the **nutrient content** of the soil is **reduced** to the point that it's no longer productive. **80 million tonnes** of **topsoil** is **lost** each year in **Andalusia** because of intensive cultivation of **olive trees**.

2) **Overgrazing** is **reducing vegetation cover**, causing desertification.

3) Groundwater resources are being pumped to **irrigate crops**. This is **lowering groundwater levels**. Increasingly more water is being used for irrigation because...

- **Agriculture** is carried out in areas that **aren't** really **suitable** for it. E.g. the region of **Almeria** (in Andalusia) is an important agricultural area as produce grown there for export contributes **$1.5 billion** to the economy each year. Almeria is the driest area in Europe though, so this is only possible with **intensive irrigation**.

- **Crops** that need **more water** than the area can **supply** are being grown for **export**. E.g. Spain is Europe's largest producer of **strawberries**, and **95%** of its exports are grown in **Andalusia**. As Andalusia is so arid **intensive irrigation** is needed to supply the strawberries with the **large amounts** of **water** they need to grow.

Although there are restrictions in place to protect aquifers, many farmers are using **illegal boreholes** to secure water supplies for their crops.

Development

1) There's been a huge **increase** in **tourism** in Southern Spain in the last 50 years. In the last few years an estimated **180 000 holiday homes** have been built along the Spanish coast every year.

2) This is increasing strain on water supplies as there's more and **more demand** for **water** for **swimming pools**, **water parks** and **irrigation** of **golf courses**.

3) Although there are regulations in place to protect water supplies for agriculture, many developments get around them by **reclassifying** grass on golf courses as "**crops**" or holiday villas as "**farms**". This ensures that, like farms, they get **allocated water**. This contributes to desertification by **depleting water levels**. It also **reduces water availability** for farms, **reducing** their **productivity**, which leads to desertification spreading.

Desertification Case Study — Southern Spain

Desertification Has Environmental, Social and Economic Impacts

1) The demand for water to fill swimming pools and irrigate crops and golf courses has led to **conflict** over water. A **black market** for water has developed, supplied by water from **illegal boreholes**. An estimated **40%** of land in some parts of the **Segura basin** (Murcia) is illegally irrigated and **10%** of wells in the **Guadalquivir river basin** (Andalusia) are illegal.

2) Exploitation of groundwaters has led to **loss of habitats**, such as wetlands, and **reduced biodiversity** in the region. E.g. nearly **150 000 ha** of **marshland** surrounding **Doñana National Park** has been **lost** since 1900 — most of which has been deliberately drained for farming.

3) As groundwater levels lower the water can become **salinised** (very salty). When this happens the water is no longer suitable for drinking or irrigation and the **resource** is **lost**. Many wells have had to be abandoned.

4) As **aquifers** become **salinised** so do the **soils** around them, which leads to **further desertification**.

5) Desertification leaves soil **unusable for farming** and deprives farmers of their **livelihood**.

Strategies to Reduce Desertification are Being Implemented

The government's **Programme of National Action Against Desertification** aims to tackle desertification in several ways:

The **National Hydrological Plan** was adopted in **2001** to ensure that water supply meets demand by:

1) **Transferring water** from areas with a **plentiful supply** to areas with **very little**.

2) Building **desalinisation plants** to produce fresh water from saline aquifers at a cost of **€1.2 billion**.

3) **Reducing** the amount of water **wasted** during irrigation by **improving irrigation infrastructure**, e.g. by investing in technology for sprinkling and drip irrigation. The aim is to **reduce** the amount of **water** used for irrigation by **10%** (from 2002 levels), whilst **increasing** the area of **land irrigated** by 7%.

4) Reducing pressure on water supplies by **introducing management strategies** for **aquifers** and funding awareness-raising activities to **promote efficient use** of resources.

> The National Hydrological Plan is **controversial** as it's very expensive and some elements **aren't sustainable**. **Raising awareness** and **improving infrastructure** can help **reduce desertification**, but transporting water from one area to another is only a **short-term** solution to the shortage of water (it doesn't tackle the overuse of water that's causing desertification). Irrigation will continue to **increase** and desertification will **spread**.

Areas at **high risk** of **forest fires** are being identified and **defence plans** drawn up for them so that fires can be dealt with quickly. Areas that are destroyed have to be **reforested** and many **new areas** are being planted with trees and bushes. Since the scheme was introduced **550 000 hectares** have been forested.

> Reforestation and forest management **reduces soil erosion** and so desertification.

An official **water trading scheme** has been set up that allows farmers to buy water. It costs them three times the normal price but is **lower than the black market price** and therefore aims to **reduce illegal exploitation** of **aquifers**.

> Water trading can help to reduce **illegal** exploitation of aquifers. If water resources are **sustainably managed** then the scheme could **reduce desertification**, but if resources continue to be **over-exploited** then water trading is unlikely to reduce desertification.

Practice Questions

Q1 Which areas of Spain are most vulnerable to desertification?
Q2 Why has the volume of water needed for irrigation increased?
Q3 Describe two impacts of desertification in Spain.

Exam Question

Q1 Compare the strategies used in Spain and the Sahel to tackle desertification. [15 marks]

Last year I went to sunny Spain — and helped spread desertification...

You know the drill by now — learn all the specifics, don't skimp on the examples, blah blah blah. The more information you know the more marks you can get. And once you've learnt these pages, you're done with deserts and arid environments. Finally.

Population Change Basics and the DTM

Populations are dynamic — they're always changing. These pages will help you understand how and why — it's all to do with birth and death rates and population migrations. And don't forget the famous DTM.

There are **Loads** of **Terms** and **Definitions** to Learn

1) **Birth rate** — the **number** of live **births** per 1000 people, per year.

2) **Death rate** — the **number of deaths** per 1000 people, per year.

3) **Fertility rate** — the **average number of children** a woman will have between the ages of **15** and **44** (**reproductive** age).

4) **Infant mortality rate** — the **number of children** (out of every 1000 born alive) who **die before their first birthday**.

5) **Life expectancy (longevity)** — the **average age** (in years) a person can **expect to live**.

6) **Migration rate** — the **difference** between the **number** of people who **migrate in** (**immigrants**), and the number of people who **migrate out** (**emigrants**) per **100 000** (or 1000) of the population, per year.

7) **Population density** — the **number** of people per **square kilometre** (km²).
It's the **total population** of an area **divided** by the **size of the area** (in km²).

Migration is the movement of people between or within countries.

8) **Changes in the population over time:**

- **Natural change** — the change in population (**increase** or **decrease**) because of the **difference** between **birth rate** and **death rate** (not including changes due to **migration**). For example, when **birth rate > death rate**, the population will **grow naturally** (if migration rate is **zero**). When **death rate > birth rate**, the population will **fall** (unless enough people **migrate in**).

< means 'less than'
> means 'more than'

- **Zero growth rate** — the population is **neither increasing** nor **decreasing** (e.g. **birth rate = death rate**).

The **Demographic Transition Model (DTM)** Shows **Population Change**

The **demographic transition model** (**DTM**) shows how the **population** of a country **changes** over time through **five stages**. The model shows changes in **birth rate**, **death rate** and **total population**.

'Demographic' means it's to do with human populations.

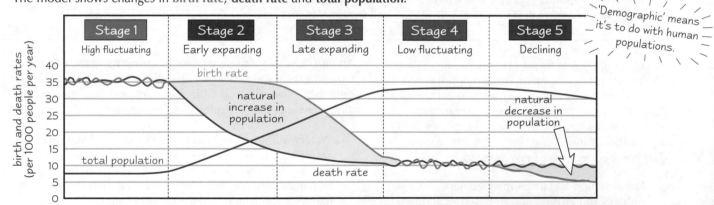

As Countries **Develop** They **Move Through** the **Stages** of the **DTM**

As countries become **more developed** their birth rate and death rate **change**, which causes the **total population to change**.

Stage 1 — high birth rate and high death rate

Birth rate and death rate **fluctuate** at a **high level** — the population remains **stable** but **low**.
There **aren't any countries** in Stage 1, but some **tribes** in the rainforests of **Brazil** are in this stage.

1) **Birth rate is high** because there's **no birth control** or **family planning**, and **education is poor**.

2) It's also high because there's **high infant mortality**, so people have **more children** to replace those who've **died**.

3) **Death rate is high** and life expectancy is **low** because there's **poor health care**, **sanitation** and **diet** — leading to **disease** and **starvation**.

Birth rate — around **35/1000**   **Death rate** — around **35/1000**

The values for the birth rate, death rate and population for each stage are just rough estimates, not exact figures.

Population Change Basics and the DTM

Stage 2 — high birth rate, death rate falls

Death rate **falls**, but birth rate remains **high** — the population **increases rapidly**.
Countries like **Nepal** and **Afghanistan** are in **Stage 2**.

1) **Birth rate** is still **high** as there's still **little birth control** or **family planning** and **education is poor**.
2) Birth rate also stays **high** for **labour reasons** — family members (including **children**) all have to **work**, e.g. on **farms**. A **larger** family can tend to a **larger** farm, helping to bring in **more food** and **money**.
3) **Death rate falls** and **life expectancy increases** due to improved **health care**, **sanitation** and **diet**.

Birth rate — around **35/1000**   **Death rate** — falls to around **15/1000**

Stage 3 — birth rate falls a lot and death rate falls slightly

Birth rate **declines rapidly**, while death rate **falls slowly** — the population **increases at a slower rate**.
Countries like **Egypt** are in **Stage 3**.

1) **Birth rate decreases** due to the **increased** use of **birth control and family planning**, and **improvements** in **education**.
2) The **birth rate** also **drops** as the **economy** moves towards **manufacturing** — **fewer children** are needed to **work** on farms, so having a **larger family** isn't as **advantageous** as it once was.
3) **Birth rate falls** further still as **more women work** rather than stay at home to have children.
4) Some countries introduce **government population policies** to try to **reduce the birth rate**.

Birth rate — falls to around **13/1000**   **Death rate** — falls to around **10/1000**

Stage 4 — low birth rate and low death rate

Birth rate and death rate **fluctuate** at a **low level** — the population remains **stable** but **high**. Most **developed countries**, e.g. most of **Europe** and the **USA**, are in **Stage 4**. Birth rate stays low because **increased access and demand** for **luxuries** like **holidays** and **material possessions** means there's **less** money available for having children (they're **expensive** to raise). Also, there are **fewer advantages** to having children, e.g. they're **not needed** to work for the family.

Birth rate — falls to around **10/1000**   **Death rate** — around **10/1000**

Stage 5 — birth rate drops below death rate

Birth rate begins to **decline** further while death rate remains **stable** — the population begins to **decrease**. Some **highly developed** countries, e.g. **Japan**, are in **Stage 5**.

1) The **birth rate decreases** because children are **expensive** to raise and many people have **dependent** elderly relatives, so lots of people choose **not** to have children.
2) **Death rate** remains **steady** as there are **more elderly people** so more people die (of **old age**) despite **advances** in health care.

Birth rate < **Death rate**

Hmm, have children or buy myself a shiny new car...

Practice Questions

Q1   Define fertility rate.
Q2   Define population density.

Exam Question

Q1   The table shows some population data for a country since 1600.
       With reference to the DTM, describe and explain the changes in the population shown by the data.   [10 marks]

Date	Birth rate (per 1000 per year)	Death rate (per 1000 per year)	Population (millions)
1600	38	37	2
1700	35	34	3
1800	35	18	7
1850	26	15	15
1900	18	12	21
1950	12	10	26
2000	8	10	28

Rabbits never seem to get much past Stage 2...

You're expected to know your way around the DTM. Make sure you understand the diagram and how all the different rates change over time. You need to be able to explain why the rates change too. Then you can apply it to any country or set of stats.

Applying the DTM

So you're now a dab hand at the ol' DTM and how the stages differ from one another.
It's a nice model but it doesn't work for every country, and you get to learn why. Joy.

Most MEDCs are in Stages 4-5 of the DTM

1) **Most countries** that are classed as MEDCs (**More Economically Developed Countries**) have **passed through** Stages 1, 2 and 3. They have **low birth and death rates, long life expectancies** and **slow population growth.**

2) During Stages 2 and 3 their **rapid population growth** was accompanied by **industrial growth, farming improvements** and **increasing wealth.** This is where they **changed** from being LEDCs (**Less Economically Developed Countries**) to MEDCs.

3) Some MEDCs are in **Stage 5**, e.g. **Italy, Japan** and **Germany.** Birth rate is **lower** than death rate, causing the population to **shrink.** The population is also **ageing,** as **more people** live for **longer** — a greying population.

4) Being in Stage 5 can cause **problems** for a country:

   • There are too **few children** to **replace** the current, ageing **workforce** — the workforce may not be large enough to carry out the work, which could cause the **economy** to **slow down** or **stop growing.**

   • A **smaller population** means a **reduction** in **spending,** which could also cause the **economy** to **slow** or **stall.**

   • There are **fewer taxpayers,** so there's **less money** for **services.** This is made worse by the **increasing cost** of **services** for the **elderly** — **more old people** means **more money** is needed for **pensions** and **health services** (carers etc.).

Most LEDCs are in Stages 2-3 of the DTM

1) Most countries classed as **LEDCs** are in **Stage 2** (e.g. **Afghanistan**) or **Stage 3** (e.g. **India**).

2) Lots of countries entered **Stage 2** in the **1950s,** e.g. **Kenya** and **Bangladesh. Improved health care** and **sanitation** led to a **reduced death rate,** while birth rate **stayed high.** Many of these countries have become **overpopulated** — they don't have the **resources** (e.g. **money** or **services**) to **cope** with the expanding population.

3) Some **former LEDCs** have moved into **Stage 3** in the last few decades, e.g. **Newly Industrialised Countries** (**NICs**) like **Malaysia** and **Taiwan.** The **death rate** is still **falling,** leading to **increasing populations.** Some **governments** have introduced **policies** to reduce **birth rate** and **prevent** overpopulation, e.g. **one-child** policies.

> *You need to be aware that although most countries used to be classified as either MEDCs or LEDCs, it's now thought that this system is too simplistic — there are too many stages of development to divide countries into only two categories.*

The UK's Demographic History Matches the DTM Model

Stage 1 (prehistoric times to about 1760)

Total population was **small** — e.g. **6 million** in **1700. Poor diet** and **hygiene,** as well as **wars** and **diseases** such as the **Black Death** and **cholera,** caused a **high death rate,** which **cancelled** out the **high birth rate.**

Stage 2 (1760-1880)

The population **grew quickly** — it was **5 times** bigger by the **1880s** (6 million in 1700 to **30 million** by 1881). Improvements in **farming** and **medicine** reduced **starvation** and **disease,** so **death rate fell. Birth rate** remained **high** and the **economy grew** quickly. **Urban populations** grew particularly **rapidly.**

Stage 3 (1880-1940)

The population was still **growing,** but at a **slower rate** — **47 million** by **1941. Birth control** improved and was used **more frequently,** so the **birth rate fell. Death rate continued to fall** (except during **World War 1**) as **food supply, medicine** and **hygiene** continued to **improve.**

Stage 4 (1940-today)

Population growth has **slowed down** — **56 million** by **1981. Death rate** was **low,** except during **World War 2,** and **birth rate** was also **low,** except for **baby booms** (**large increases** in **birth rate**) after World War 2 and in the **1960s.**

Stage 5 (today+)

Death rate today is **almost** exactly the same as birth rate and the population is **ageing** — pensioners **outnumber** children and it's been estimated that by **2030, a quarter** of the UK's population could be **over 65.** The population could begin to **decline** if birth rate **drops below** death rate because there are too few young people, or death rate becomes larger than birth rate because the large population of elderly people **die.**

> *Look back at the last two pages to refresh your memory of the DTM.*

Applying the DTM

The *DTM* is *Useful*...

1) The **DTM** gives a good **generalised** picture of how a **population** can **change** over time.

2) It's easy to **compare** a **country** with the DTM — if you know a bit about how the **population** and **birth** and **death rates** of a country have changed, you can analyse what **stage** of the DTM it's in.

3) You can then **forecast** how its population may change — which can help governments decide on **policies** such as **one-child limits** and **immigration laws**.

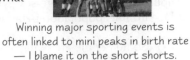

Winning major sporting events is often linked to mini peaks in birth rate — I blame it on the short shorts.

...But It Has *Limitations*

1) The **original data** used to **create** the DTM was from **more developed**, richer countries (e.g. **European** countries, **Japan** and the **USA**). This means it might **not** be a **valid model worldwide** — what happened in these countries might not be the **same** as what's happening in others, e.g. countries in **Asia** or **Africa**.

2) The original DTM **didn't** have **Stage 5** — it's been **added** since some countries have moved **out of Stage 4**.

3) The DTM doesn't take things like **education** and the role of **women** into account separately and these affect **birth rate** quite a lot, e.g. **increased higher education** means more people **delay** having a family.

4) The **population** in countries with **different customs** may change in different ways, e.g. the **Catholic** church **condemns contraception**.

5) **Extreme poverty** and **low levels of development** may cause a **lack of population growth** and **prevent** many **LEDCs** from passing through **all** the stages.

6) The DTM **can't predict** exactly **when** countries will **reach** each stage, or **how long** each stage will **last**.

7) It doesn't consider **migration** — **international migration** can have a large effect on **population change**.

8) **Other factors** can also affect the population so a country **no longer fits** the DTM:

Population control policies (e.g. France and China)

High levels of population growth or decline have forced some governments to introduce **population policies** — **discouraging** or **encouraging** larger families. For example, population growth in **France** is very **low**, so the government has introduced things like **subsidised childcare** to encourage **larger families**. In **China**, the **opposite** is occurring. The government has tried to **reduce** birth rate using a **one-child per family policy**.

Infectious disease (e.g. HIV/AIDS, Malaria)

Some countries may have particularly **high levels** of **infectious disease**, which keeps the **death rate high**, **reducing** the population or stalling population **growth**. For example, some **African countries** like **Nigeria** and **Botswana** have very **high HIV/AIDS** rates, leading to **high death rates**.

Civil War (e.g. Rwanda, Sierra Leone, ongoing in Sudan)

War leads to an **increased death rate** and **decreased birth rate**, especially if **large numbers** of men and women of **reproductive age** are **killed** or **involved** in the conflict. Also, **civil war** often leads to **emigration**, decreasing the population, as people **flee** the fighting. For example, thousands of people **died** during the civil war in **Sierra Leone (1991-2002)** and thousands more **fled** to **neighbouring countries**.

Practice Questions

Q1 Describe two problems faced by countries in Stage 5 of the DTM.

Q2 In 1800, what stage of the DTM was the UK in?

Q3 Describe one factor that can affect the population size so that a country no longer fits the DTM.

Exam Question

Q1 Discuss the uses and limitations of the DTM. [15 marks]

Baby boom — the noise babies make as they break the sound barrier...

OK, so not the greatest CGP pun ever, but at least I'm trying. You better be trying to learn all these DTM facts — my blood, sweat and tears have gone into this page. Well tears anyway — that joke really isn't great, it's a 'must try harder' for sure.

Population Structure and Migration

Population structure pyramids are very exciting — not as exciting as cheerleader pyramids, but still better than nowt.

Population Structure *is How the* Population *is* Made Up

Population structure is the **number** or **%** of **males** and **females** in different **age groups** within a population.
Population pyramids (age-sex pyramids) **show** population structure. You can **learn** a lot about the **demographics** of a place from its population pyramid. For example, the pyramid below shows the **population structure of France**:

(A) Some people are living to be **100**, which shows a **high life expectancy**.

(B) **Women** are living **longer** than **men**.

(C) There are **fewer** people aged **75-85**, because there was a **low birth rate** when they were **born** (around **World War 1** – WW1) and they've suffered from a **high death rate** (lots killed in **WW2**).

(D) There are also **fewer** people aged **50-60**, also because of a **low birth rate** when they were born (around **WW2**).

(E) There are **lots** of people aged **25-50** because of a **baby boom** after WW2.

(F) There are **fewer** people aged **0-10** because of a **low birth rate** for the last 10 years.

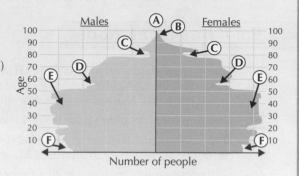

Population Structure Varies *from* Place to Place *and* Over Time

1) Population pyramids for **different countries** vary because of different **demographic factors** — **birth** and **death rates**, **fertility rates**, **wars**, **migration** etc.

2) A country's population structure **changes** through **time** as it moves through the **stages** of the **DTM** (see page 62).

3) This means a **population pyramid shape** can show **which** stage of the DTM a country is in:

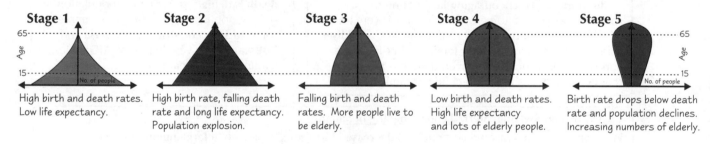

Stage 1
High birth and death rates. Low life expectancy.

Stage 2
High birth rate, falling death rate and long life expectancy. Population explosion.

Stage 3
Falling birth and death rates. More people live to be elderly.

Stage 4
Low birth and death rates. High life expectancy and lots of elderly people.

Stage 5
Birth rate drops below death rate and population declines. Increasing numbers of elderly.

Migration *Can Change* Population Structure

Migration is the (often permanent) movement of people **between** or **within** countries. **Immigration** is the movement of people **into a country** (or area) and **emigration** is the movement of people **out of a country** (or area). Migration can **alter population structure**, which can be seen in the **population pyramids** for the areas affected. Migration can affect **any part** of the population pyramid — it depends **how old** the migrants are.
Here are some examples:

1) **Internal migration (migration within a country)**
Internal migration from **rural** areas to **urban** areas often affects the number of **young adults** (people of **working** and **reproductive age**). They **move away** from the countryside **into** the cities to find **jobs**. This is called **rural-urban migration**. This can **affect birth rate** too as the migrants are of reproductive age.

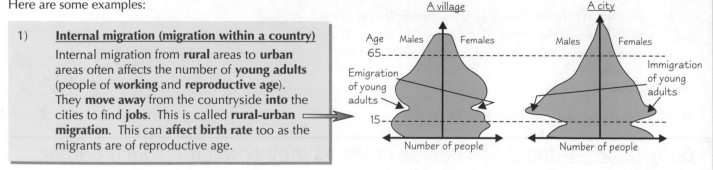

Population Structure and Migration

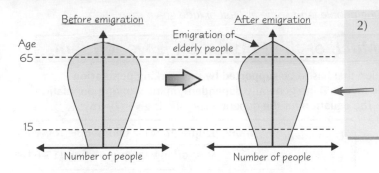

Before emigration

After emigration

Age 65

Emigration of elderly people

15

Number of people

Number of people

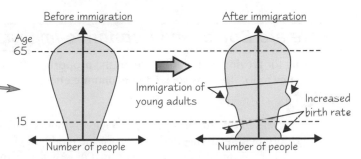

2) **Emigration away from countries at later DTM stages**

Emigration **away** from countries at **later DTM stages** into other countries **decreases the population** of the country they've left. E.g. **elderly people** in the **UK retiring and emigrating** to other countries. This **reduces** the number of elderly in the UK, but **increases** the number in the countries they **move to**.

3) **Immigration into countries at later DTM stages**

Immigration **into** countries at **later** DTM stages (e.g. MEDCs) **from** those at **earlier** DTM stages (e.g. LEDCs) **increases the population** of people of **working** and **reproductive age**. This **increases** the population of young people and **increases birth rate**. For example, immigration into the **UK** (Stage 4).

Before immigration

After immigration

Age 65

15

Number of people

Number of people

Immigration of young adults

Increased birth rate

Migration Occurs Because of Push and Pull Factors

The **reasons** for migration can be divided into **push** (**negative**) and **pull** (**positive**) factors:

Push factors — these are things that **make** people want to **move out** of the place they're in. They're **negative factors** about the place they're **leaving**, e.g. **lack of jobs** or **poor living conditions** and **services**, fear of **political persecution**.

Pull factors — these **attract** people to a **new place**. They're **positive factors** about the place they're **moving to**, e.g. **better jobs** and **more job opportunities**, **better** living conditions and **services**.

Migration is also affected by **obstacles** and **opportunities**:

Obstacles — these are things that make migration **more difficult**, e.g. the **cost** of moving.

Opportunities — these are opportunities individuals **encounter** that mean they **stop** before they reach their **intended destination**, e.g. **Polish** migrants heading for **Ireland** for **work** might stop in **London** because there are plenty of **jobs** there.

Hmm, he's got his own boat, but it's a shame about the beard. I'll give him a pull factor of 5.

Practice Questions

Q1   What is population structure?

Q2   What do population pyramids show?

Q3   What is internal migration?

Q4   How does immigration into a country at a later DTM stage affect the population of young people?

Q5   How do obstacles and opportunities affect migration?

Exam Question

Q1   Describe what is meant by push and pull factors.   [4 marks]

Large, shiny tractors — rural pull factors...

The diagrams on these pages might look horribly complicated, but they're a good visual way of showing how populations change (plus the colours look nice). I'd bet they make great revision aids and pretty handy additions to exam answers. Hint hint...

Impacts and Management of Population Change

Some countries are full of old people, some are full of young people, and some are full of little green men...

The **Dependency Ratio** Shows **How Much** of the **Population** is **Dependent**

The **dependency ratio** gives the **proportion** of the population that has to be **supported** by the **working population** (aged **15-64**). **Young people** (aged **0-14**) and **older people** (**over 65**) are generally **dependent** on the working population — they need to be **looked after** or **supported financially**. The **equation** for the dependency ratio is given below:

A **high dependency ratio** means there's a **greater proportion** of dependent people, e.g. **Uganda** has a **high dependency** ratio of **1.1** — there's **more than one** dependent person for **each** working person.

$$\text{Dependency ratio} = \frac{\text{Young people (0-14) + Old people (over 65)}}{\text{Working age population (15-64)}}$$

There are **Social** and **Economic** Impacts of an **Ageing Population**

An **ageing** (or **greying**) **population** means the **proportion** of older people is **increasing**, which causes an **increase** in the **dependency** ratio. This has **social** and **economic effects**:

Social

1) **Increased pressure on public services** — there's **greater demand** for services like **hospitals** and **hospices**. **More** people are needed to **care** for the elderly, so **more carers** and **nurses** will need **training**. Also, more people will act as **unpaid carers** to their **own** elderly family members, putting pressure on them **socially** and **financially**.

2) **Unequal distribution of older people** — e.g. **Eastbourne** in the UK is a **resort** with a high proportion of **retired**, older people. Areas like this may have **inadequate facilities** for **young people**, e.g. **bars** or **youth clubs**.

3) **Reduced population growth or population decline** — the working population may have **fewer children** because they already have older dependants, leading to a **reduction** in **birth rate**.

4) **Longer working life** — the **state pension** is **low** because there are **so many** retired people. It's often **not enough** to support people in their retirement so some may have to **work beyond** normal **retirement age** — to build up **personal pensions** or **savings**, or to **add to their income** from the state pension.

Economic

1) **Reduced work force** — a **smaller proportion** of the population is working, which may **slow economic growth**.

2) **Increased taxes** — **pensions** and **services** are paid for by **taxes**. A greater proportion of older people **claiming** pensions and support could mean **higher taxes** for the working population.

3) **Spending** — the elderly have **savings** and **pensions** to spend (the **grey pound**).

There are **Social** and **Economic** Impacts of a **Youthful Population**

A **youthful population** means there's a **large** proportion of **young people** in the population. This has **social** and **economic effects**:

Social

1) **Increased pressure on public services** — greater demand for services like **schools** and **childcare**.

2) **Rapid population growth** — the large numbers of children grow up and have **families** too, **increasing** the population. This may lead to **overpopulation** if there **aren't enough resources** to cope with the number of people.

Economic

1) **Too few jobs** — there **aren't enough jobs** for young people when they grow up. **More unemployed** means more people are dependent on **government support**.

2) **Increased poverty** — **more** young people are born into families that are **already poor**, so there are **more people in poverty**. Some children may have to **work to** help **support** their large family, so they **can't go to school**, which means they can't **break out of poverty**.

There are **Political Impacts** of **Ageing** and **Youthful Populations**

Whether a population is getting **older** or **younger**, the impact on **politics** is the same — it changes what's important in **elections** and how people **vote**, and it affects **policies** such as **immigration laws** and **taxes** and **pensions**.

1) **Ageing population** — elderly issues will be important to **voters**, e.g. changes to **national pensions** or **heating allowances**. **Immigration laws** may be **relaxed** to encourage people of **working age** to **enter** the country.

2) **Youthful population** — youth issues will be important, e.g. **student loans** and **childcare provision**. The government may need to **increase teacher salaries** to **encourage** more people into the **profession**.

Impacts and Management of Population Change

There are *Strategies* to *Manage Ageing Populations*

1) **Encouraging larger families** — e.g. the **Swedish government** makes having children more **manageable** by giving both parents **18 months' paid leave** when they have a child. Encouraging larger families should result in a **larger working population** when the children grow up, which can provide **more taxes** for **better pensions** and **services**.

2) **Raising retirement age** — the **working population** is made **larger**, so **more people contribute** to the **state pension fund** and to personal pensions for **longer**. People will also **claim** the state pension for **less time**.

3) **Encouraging the immigration of working-age people** — e.g. in recent years **Japan** has **increased** its number of **foreign workers** because there **aren't enough** working-age Japanese people to fill the jobs **available**. This **increases** the **working-age population**, which helps to support the ageing population by **paying taxes**.

4) **Increasing health care provision** — large numbers of older people puts pressure on **health care systems**. This **doesn't** manage the **population change** but it could help ease the problem of **poor health** in the **elderly**.

There are *Strategies* to *Manage Youthful Populations* Too

1) **Controlling birth rate** — some countries that are **overpopulated** try to **slow** further growth by introducing policies that **limit** the number of children couples can have. For example, **China** introduced a **one-child policy** for some couples in **1979**. It's thought this has **prevented** more than **300 million births** since it was introduced.

2) **Limiting the immigration of younger people** — **limiting** the number of immigrants of **reproductive age** (15-44) would mean birth rates aren't **made any higher** by immigrants having children.

3) **Encouraging family planning and the use of contraception** — governments can offer **sex education** and **free** contraception, allowing couples to **plan** and **limit** the number of children they have.

4) **Increasing childcare provision** — countries can **invest** in **more** and **better childcare** so parents can **work** instead of caring for children. This **doesn't** manage the population change, but helps to address some of the **problems caused** by a younger population.

Management Strategies Should Aim Towards *Sustainable Development*

Sustainable development is all about developing and **growing** to meet the **needs** of people **today**, without **hindering** the ability of people in the **future** to meet their **own** needs. It involves **getting** what we need now without **damaging** or **altering** the **environment** in an **irreversible** way.

Generally, the **strategies** to manage growing elderly or youthful **populations** don't help sustainable development **on their own** — achieving sustainable development requires **lots** of **strategies** in lots of **different** areas.

1) **Encouraging larger families** — this creates an **even larger population** that'll need **housing**, **transport**, **food** etc. This **isn't** sustainable unless the population's **needs** are met in a **sustainable way**, e.g. **carbon-neutral homes**, **low** or **no** emission transport, food that's produced in an **environmentally friendly** way with **few food miles**.

2) **Encouraging the immigration of working-age people** — on its **own** this doesn't help towards sustainable development. E.g. **more** working people require **more jobs**, which could be in **heavily polluting industries**, or in **offices** that use **electricity** etc. Unless **these** needs are met in a **sustainable way**, this strategy on its own isn't sustainable.

3) **Controlling birth rate** — this **helps towards** sustainable development as the population **won't** get much **bigger**. But if the needs of the population still **aren't** met in a sustainable way, then it **just** stops the problem getting any **worse**.

Practice Questions

Q1 What does the dependency ratio tell you about a country or area?

Q2 Describe one strategy used to manage the effects of a youthful population.

Exam Question

Q1 Describe and explain the social and economic impacts of an ageing population. [15 marks]

This book'll have a social impact on you — you'll have to stay in and revise...

I'm sorry about this geography stuff taking up your valuable time, but think of it as an early warning. The population's ageing, so there'll be a lot of people for us to look after, and believe it or not, we'll all be old one day too so these strategies better work.

Managing Populations — Case Studies

And you thought I'd forgotten about the case studies. Case studies are good for you — you should have some for your tea.

The **UK** Has an **Ageing Population**

Like most **wealthy** and **developed countries**, the population of the UK is **ageing** (it's a **greying population**) — people **over 65** make up a **large part** of the population and it's **increasing**. In **2005**, **16%** of the population of the UK were **over 65**. This is expected to rise to **25%** by **2041** — here are a few reasons **why**:

1) **Increasing life expectancy** — between **1980** and **2006** life expectancy **rose 2.8** years for **women** and **4** years for **men**. It's currently **81.3** for **women** and **76.9** for **men**. As people live **longer**, the number of older people **increases**.

2) **Baby booms** — **lots of babies** were born in the **1940s** and **60s**. These large generations are starting to **retire**, **increasing** the number of elderly people.

3) **Falling birth rate** — there are **fewer** young people, so the **proportion** of older people is **greater**.

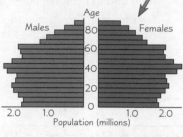

The **Ageing UK Population** Causes **Problems**

1) **Pressure on the pension system** — there aren't enough people of **working-age** to pay for an **adequate pension** for the **retired** population. **State pensions** are paid for by the **working population** through **taxes**.

  - Today, **60%** of the population (the people of **working-age**) are paying taxes that go towards the pensions of **19%** of the population (the people of **retirement age**).

  - By **2030**, only **56%** of the population will be of **working-age** but the taxes they pay will have to pay for the pensions of the **27%** of the population of **retirement age**.

2) **More elderly people living in poverty** — the state pension **isn't very large**, and many people don't have **other savings**. The working population **isn't large enough** to provide a **better pension** (see above).

3) **Pressure on the health service** — older people often need **more medical care** than younger people, e.g. the average stay in hospital in **2005** for people **over 75** was **13** nights, but only **8** nights for the UK population **as a whole**.

Different Strategies Aim to Manage Ageing Populations

1) The age of retirement has been increased — retirement age in the UK is currently 65 for men and 60 for women, but it will be raised to 68 for everyone by 2050. Increasing the retirement age means people have to work for longer, increasing the size of the working population.

2) Encouraging immigration of working-age people — the UK has allowed unlimited immigration of people from countries who joined the EU in 2004, e.g. Poland. In 2004, around 80% of immigrants that came to the UK from the new EU countries were 34 or under. This also increases the size of the working population.

3) Encouraging more women to have children — new UK pension proposals mean women won't lose out on state pensions if they take career breaks to have children. This could encourage women to have children. Working family tax credits support women (and men) who go back to work once their children are born, which might also encourage more couples to have children.

Strategies Need to Work Towards Sustainable Development

As mentioned on the **previous page**, strategies to **manage** ageing populations should support **sustainable development**. But usually they can't do this on their **own** — other actions need to be taken to help **achieve** sustainable development.

1) Increasing retirement age — this helps towards sustainable development because it doesn't increase the population. But it might mean more jobs are needed, as people work for longer. This could hinder sustainable development if the new jobs aren't provided in a way that works towards sustainability, e.g. building and working in new coal-powered power plants versus wind-turbine power plants.

2) Allowing immigration — this is only sustainable if the needs of the new people are met in a sustainable way. E.g. meeting the increased energy demand by increasing energy production from renewable sources, building new energy-efficient homes with good insulation and natural heating systems.

3) Encouraging more children — this could increase the population of a country, and so is similar to immigration.

Managing Populations — Case Studies

Uganda Has a Youthful Population

Like many **poorer** and **less developed** countries, **Uganda** has a **youthful population**. In **2007**, **50%** of the population were **under 15** and only **3%** were **over 65**. The population is becoming **more youthful** — here are a couple of reasons **why**:

1) **High birth and fertility rates** — every year there are **48** babies born for every 1000 people, and women have an average of **7 children** during their reproductive years (15-44).

2) **Low life expectancy** of around **52** years — there are **very few** older people, which means the **proportion** of the population made up of young people is **very high**.

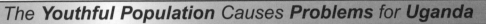

The Youthful Population Causes Problems for Uganda

The main problem caused by a **youthful population** is **overpopulation**, which is caused by a **high birth rate**. The population of Uganda is currently around **30 million**, but by **2025** it's thought it will grow to about **56 million**. When there are **too many people** for the **resources** the country has, things like the **health service** and levels of **employment** suffer:

1) **Pressure on the health service** — around **6000** women already **die** each year in **childbirth**. When the youthful population reaches **reproductive age** the pressure on the health service will be **even greater**, potentially leading to **more deaths**. The health service is also **stretched** because of **HIV/AIDS** (a deadly disease). It's passed on from **mother to child** and through **unprotected sex**, so HIV/AIDS may **spread** further when the youthful population start to have children, putting **even more strain** on the health system.

2) **Unemployment could get much worse** — in **2003** unemployment in **Uganda** was **3.2%**. However, 50% of the population are under 15 and so weren't **counted** in these figures. When the **large youth population** reaches working age there **won't be enough jobs** for them all, so unemployment will **rise further**, causing **poverty** to **increase**.

Some Strategies Have Been Introduced to Address These Problems

1) Encouraging the use of contraceptives and family planning — the use of contraceptives among married women is less than 25%. New policies encouraging the use of contraceptives allow women to plan how many children they have and when they have them, e.g. the government has brought in free contraceptives like condoms. However, family planning clinics aren't widespread, so many people don't have easy access to birth control. Since 1991, birth rate has increased, suggesting this population management method isn't working.

2) Policies to combat the spread of HIV/AIDS — in the late 1980s a programme of education called the ABC approach was used (Abstain from sex until marriage, Be faithful to one partner and use Condoms). This strategy worked — HIV infection rates fell from 15% of all adults in 1991 to 5% in 2001.

These Strategies Should Help to Achieve Sustainable Development Too

1) **Encouraging contraception** — this should **reduce birth rate** and help prevent **overpopulation** from getting any worse. This means the country can **focus** on sustainable development for the current population, without the population **increasing dramatically** and putting **pressure** on sustainable development strategies.

2) **Reducing the spread of disease** — this **relieves** pressure on the **health care system**, which **frees up** money to be used elsewhere, e.g. in **developing sustainable** irrigation techniques for **rural farming** communities.

Practice Questions

Q1 Describe one problem caused by the ageing population in the UK.

Q2 Describe one problem caused by the youthful population in Uganda.

Exam Question

Q1 With reference to a named example, evaluate the strategies used to manage population change. [10 marks]

Youthful populations — not exactly like Neverland...

You're all too old, you're all too young — hang on, nobody's the right age here. Population structures are constantly changing, causing lots of different problems. Just think, one day the youthful populations will be old, then they'll be ageing populations.

Urban and Rural Characteristics

For anyone who thinks that urban characteristics is a dance beat with a groovy bass line — read on...

Urban and Rural Areas Have Different Characteristics...

Urban areas can be divided into **zones** based on the **major land use** in each area. In **developed** countries, as you **move away** from the **town** or **city centre**, the **major urban zones** are: the **inner city**, the **suburbs** and the **rural/urban fringe**. Each of these urban zones, and the **rural area** beyond them, have their own characteristics. The table below shows the **typical characteristics** of a large urban area in the UK:

Characteristic	Inner city	Suburbs	Rural/urban fringe	Rural area
Housing	High-density terraced housing built in the 19th century and high-rise blocks of flats built in the 1960s. Some old warehouses may have been redeveloped into luxury apartments.	A mix of 20th century detached and semi-detached houses with gardens. Closer to the inner city, a high proportion of properties will be council-owned. Further out, properties will be privately owned and larger, with garages and driveways.	Low-density, high-quality private housing. May also be higher density outer-city council estates.	Larger, privately owned housing and new estates with privately owned houses.
Ethnicity	High proportion of ethnic minorities.	Proportion of ethnic minorities tends to decrease as you move out of the city.		Majority white.
Age structure	High proportion of younger people (students and young professionals).	Mostly families with children.	Mostly families with children. More elderly people.	Higher proportion of elderly people.
Wealth	The poorest sections of the urban population tend to live here. You also get more wealthy people living in redeveloped areas.	Wealth tends to increase as you move out of the city.		Wealthiest residents who've moved out of the city. Also, some less wealthy original rural residents.
Employment	High proportion of students, unemployed and unskilled or semi-skilled workers. Some young professionals living in redeveloped areas.	More employment in tertiary sector (e.g. services, clerical and professional) and skilled manual workers.	Proportion employed in tertiary sector tends to increase.	High proportion of workers in professional and managerial sectors (e.g. doctors, lawyers and bankers). Also agricultural workers.
Provision of services	Today, often an area of urban decay with derelict warehouses and industrial sites. But it's close to the city centre, which has lots of shops and services.	Some local shopping parades. Good transport routes to city centre and good availability of public transport.	The location for out-of-town shopping complexes, airports and recreational facilities such as golf courses.	Village shops may have closed as more residents shop in urban areas on their commute to work. Lack of public transport facilities.

...Which Affect the Welfare of the People Living in Each Zone

As you **move out** of the urban area **towards rural areas**, there tend to be **fewer environmental**, **social** and **economic problems**. These problems are **factors** affecting the **social welfare of people** living in each zone. In **general**, these problems and social welfare **improve** as you **move away** from the inner city:

Environmental

1) Old, **poor quality housing**, often in a state of **disrepair**, creates a **poor living environment** in the **inner city**.
2) **Graffiti** and **vandalism** levels are **highest** in the **inner city** where there may be many **empty** and **derelict buildings**. Vandalism can also be high in the **suburbs** where there's a larger population of **children** and **teenagers**.
3) **Air pollution** is highest in the **inner city** due to remaining **industrial sites** and the **high volume of traffic**.

Social

1) There can be **tension** between people of **different ethnicities** in the **inner city** because of the **higher proportion** of **ethnic minorities**. This can occur in **rural areas** too if **large numbers** of immigrants move there.
2) The **crime rate** is **high** in the inner city — possibly due to the high levels of **unemployment** and **poverty** in this area. There are often **poor relationships** between the **police** and the **community**. Crime rates tend to **fall** as you **move away** from the inner city.
3) **Rural areas** can also experience social problems, e.g. a **lack of public transport** services can **isolate** people, particularly the **elderly**, and out-migration can lead to the closure of services like **shops** and **post offices**.

Economic

1) **Industrial decline** and **lack of investment** can lead to **high levels** of **unemployment** in the inner city. Although **employment levels** are generally **higher** as you **move away** from the inner city, there is **increasing unemployment** in **rural areas** because of **agricultural decline**.
2) **Poverty** is highest in the **inner city**. This can lead to **higher death rates** and **poorer general health** due to **poor nutrition**, **poor education** and a **lack of access** to **services**.

Remember, environmental, social and economic problems all affect social welfare.

Urban and Rural Characteristics

Population Change and Migration Have Affected Urban and Rural Areas

The **character** of **urban** and **rural areas** can be affected by **population change** and **migration** (including both **rural-urban migration** and **immigration**).

Housing

1) In **developed countries**, most migrants occupy the **cheaper, run-down** areas of housing in **urban areas** such as those found in the **inner city**.

2) In **developing countries**, rural-urban migration has resulted in the growth of **shanty towns** — **unplanned** and often **illegal** settlements, usually on the **outskirts** of the urban area, where people build their **own homes** out of whatever they can **find**. Theses areas have **limited services** such as clean **water** and **power**.

Ethnicity

1) High numbers of **immigrants** can change the character of areas by bringing their **existing culture** and **customs** with them. If they **fail to integrate** into the existing community, then 'ghettos' may form — areas of cities where members of an **ethnic minority** group live, **segregated** from the rest of the city.

2) Although most immigrants move to **urban areas**, some move to **rural** areas seeking **work** in **agriculture**. This can have a **greater impact** on the **character** of small rural **villages** than it does on a large city, especially if all the migrants are from one country. E.g. Polish workers moving to the UK countryside might open Polish **shops** and **cafes** in small **villages**, which may have **few shops** for the **original residents** already.

Age Structure

1) In **developed countries**, rural areas have increasingly ageing populations due to the **out-migration** of **younger people** and the **inward migration** of **retired people**.

2) The **provision of services** will be affected by this **changing age structure**, e.g. in **rural areas schools may close** due to reduced demand, whilst there may be **increased** demand for **services for the elderly**, e.g. nursing homes.

There's more about the effects of changing age structure on p. 68

Wealth

1) In **developed countries**, increasing numbers of **second-home owners** and **commuters** increases the **wealth of rural areas**. This leads to **rising house prices**, which can force **younger residents** to leave as they **can't afford housing**.

2) As young, wealthy professionals move to **redeveloped urban areas**, they **increase the wealth** there. This can **improve inner city areas**, but can also mean **younger original residents can't afford** to buy houses there.

Employment

1) **Unemployment** will **increase** if **many people** move to urban areas without there being **enough jobs** available.

2) This is a big problem in **developing countries** as there's often a very **high rate** of **rural-urban migration** for work.

3) In rural areas, the large number of people **moving away** for work could eventually lead to a **lack of available workers**.

A lot of these effects are linked, e.g. a lack of available workers in rural areas can lead to more immigrants moving to rural areas, which can affect age structure and social welfare too.

Services

1) **Shops and services** in rural areas suffer because **residents who commute** may use shops **closer** to their **work**. Services like **bus routes** can also close as the **newer residents** tend to use **cars** instead. This could be a problem for the **original residents** of the rural areas if they rely on **public transport** to get about.

2) As people of **reproductive age** move to an area, there'll be increased need for **childcare services** and **schools**. When **elderly residents** move to an area, it **increases** the need for **carers, home help** and **health care**.

Practice Questions

Q1 How does the proportion of ethnic minorities in each zone change with distance from the city centre?

Q2 In which zone would you expect to find 19th century terraced housing?

Exam Question

Q1 Explain how population change and migration can affect the character of urban areas. [6 marks]

My barber gave me a rural/urban fringe — that affected MY social welfare...

Wow, there's quite a lot on these two pages — make sure you know the different characteristics of urban and rural areas and how they affect the welfare of the people who live there. As if all that wasn't enough, you also need to know how these characteristics can be affected by population change and migration. Look on the bright side though — it could be worse... probably...

Urban and Rural Characteristics — Case Study

Now it's time to take all that lovely theory and apply it to the real world — that's what geography's all about.

Different Areas in Preston Have Different Characteristics

The map below shows **four areas** in and around **Preston**, a city in the **North-west** of **England**. The areas correspond to **wards** (areas of roughly **equal-sized population** defined by the **city council**). There's **one area** from **each of the zones** discussed in the table on page 72. The characteristics of **housing** and the **provision of services** are **different** in **each of the areas**:

LEA — an area on the **rural/urban fringe**. It has large **semi-detached** and **detached** houses with **gardens** and **driveways**. Many of the houses are built on **modern estates**. There are **no out-of-town shopping centres**, but there are small shopping **parades** and a **supermarket**. There's a regular **bus service** to the city centre and there's also a **golf course** in this ward.

FISHWICK — an **inner city** area. Here there's mainly **high-density**, 19th century **terraced housing** built during the **industrial revolution** when Preston's **cotton industry** was at its peak. It has a few **corner shops** that sell convenience goods (e.g. **bread and milk**), but it **doesn't have** any **parades of shops** or **shopping centres**. Residents travel to the **city centre** for these services.

ASHTON — a **suburban** area. It has **terraced housing** to the east of the ward. To the west, there are **larger detached** and **semi-detached** houses with **gardens** that border **Ashton park**. The **Lane Ends** shopping area has over 40 shops and there are many **bus stops** with **frequent services** to the city centre.

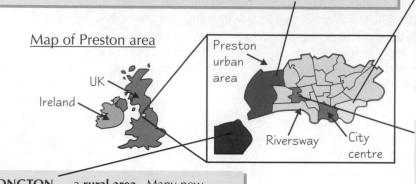

Map of Preston area

UK
Ireland
Preston urban area
Riversway
City centre

LONGTON — a **rural area**. Many new **housing estates** have been built here since the **1960s**. Housing consists of **large detached** and **semi-detached** properties with **gardens** and **garages**. The **A59 Longton By-Pass** provides easy **access** to Preston city centre for **commuters**. Longton village has a **supermarket** and many **shops** and **services**.

These Areas Fit the Expected Pattern for Urban and Rural Zones...

The table below shows **data** from the **2001 census** about the **characteristics** of the **population** in each ward. The **four areas** of Preston fit the **generalised** characteristics for **different zones** (as described on p. 72) quite well:

The % of privately owned houses **increases** as you **move away** from Fishwick (inner city).

Characteristic	Statistic	Fishwick	Ashton	Lea	Longton
Housing	% of houses privately owned	60.5	81.5	81.7	92.7
	% of houses without central heating	17.5	17.5	5.6	3.7
	% of houses with 1+ occupant per room	4.8	0.5	0.6	0.3
Ethnicity	% of population in ethnic group 'white'	66.5	93.2	95.7	99.2
Age structure	Average age (years)	32.9	38.4	35.6	43.4
	% of population aged 60 years or over	15.0	20.4	15.8	28.4
Wealth	% of households owning at least 1 car	57.4	75.7	86.2	88.5
Employment	% of 16-74 year olds unemployed	5.9	2.1	2.0	1.1
	% of working population employed in management or professional sector	15.7	28.3	30.8	30.7

The % of **elderly** residents roughly **increases** as you **move towards** Longton (rural area).

The proportion of **ethnic minorities decreases** as you **move away** from Fishwick.

The proportion of people **employed generally increases** as you move **away from** Fishwick. Also, more people are employed in **tertiary sector jobs** as you move away from Fishwick.

There's **no direct** data on **wealth**, but **car ownership** can be used as a rough **indicator** of the wealth of an area — the **greater the %** of car ownership, the **greater the wealth**. The number of people owning cars **increases** as you move **towards** Longton.

Urban and Rural Characteristics — Case Study

... But There are Some Exceptions

There are a **couple** of ways in which these areas **don't** fit the generalised characteristics:

1) There are **no** out-of-town **shopping** centres in **Lea** (**rural/urban fringe**). This could be because of the **huge redevelopment** of **Preston Docks** in the neighbouring ward of **Riversway**. This has provided shopping and **leisure** facilities (such as a **cinema**, **bars** and **restaurants**). The residents of Lea can **travel** here easily, resulting in **less demand** for these services **within** Lea itself.

2) There are **more services** in **Longton** than might be expected for a **rural area**. Many commuters use the regular **bus service** from Longton to **Preston**, rather than **driving** into the city centre. This could be because of the **difficulty** of parking in the **centre**. Because the bus services are used **more frequently**, they're less likely to get **cancelled**. It also means that commuters are more likely to do their **shopping** in **Longton**, rather than **carry** it home on the bus. This might explain why there are **lots of shops** and a **supermarket** in Longton.

The Different Characteristics Have Implications for Social Welfare

The **social welfare** of people living in and around Preston is **affected** by the **characteristics** of the different areas. **Social welfare** tends to be **worse** in the **inner city**, and improve as you move **further towards** rural areas:

1) **74%** of people in **Lea** described their **general health** in the 12 months leading up to the 2001 census as '**good**'. In **Fishwick**, only **65%** described their general health as '**good**'. This may be because a **higher percentage** of people in Fishwick live in houses that are likely to be **cold and damp** due to the **lack** of **central heating** (see table). Also, the **higher occupancy rate** in Fishwick means that **germs** spread more easily from person to person, **aiding** the spread of **disease**.

2) The **Preston Crime Audit** found that there were **161 crimes** per 1000 people in **Fishwick** between 2003 and 2004, compared to **52** in **Lea**. The high levels of **unemployment** and **low levels of wealth** in inner city areas like Fishwick can lead to **higher crime rates**. **Theft of vehicles** and theft **from** vehicles are also **higher** in Fishwick. This could be because most of the houses **don't** have **driveways** or **garages**, so vehicles are **less secure**.

3) The level of **education** is **lower** in **Fishwick** than it is in other areas — in **Ashton**, **21.4%** of the population have **no qualifications**, but in Fishwick it's **44.7%**. **Fewer** people are in **higher education** in Fishwick too — **10.3%** of the **18-74** year old population in **Ashton** are classed as **students** in **full-time education**, but this is only **6.2%** in Fishwick. Lower levels of education mean residents can't apply for **more highly skilled** or **professional work** (see data table).

4) **Less skilled workers** are usually paid **lower wages** than highly skilled professionals — this affects the **wealth** of the area. In the table, **car ownership** (i.e. wealth) **increases** towards Longton, **as the proportion** of **managers** and **professional** sector workers **increases**. A **lack of wealth** in an area can lead to other social welfare **problems** such as **increased debt**, and less money for **entertainment** and **sporting activities**, which can add to **health issues** such as **depression** and **obesity**.

Practice Questions

Q1 Name four wards found in the Preston area.

Q2 Which ward in Preston consists of mainly 19th century terraced housing?

Q3 Describe the general pattern of ethnicity for wards in the Preston area.

Exam Question

Q1 For a named region, choose **two** of the following areas:
- inner city
- suburb
- rural/urban fringe
- rural area

For these two areas, compare their characteristics and explain how they affect the social welfare of the resident population. [15 marks]

It's been a long-ton coming but you prest-on and got to the end...

Hurrah — that's the end of Population. Well, not the end of population as in the end of the world — that wouldn't be anything to cheer about. But that's the Section finished. It might have been tough at times, but you 'pressed on' and got there in the end.

Global Food Distribution

This section is all about one of my favourite topics of conversation — grub. So tuck in.

Global **Food Production** is **Unevenly Distributed**

Some countries produce **large amounts** of food and some countries produce **very little**. The map below shows the production of barley by country from 2000 to 2002. The production of other food follows a similar pattern.

East Asia, **North America** and **Europe** produce a lot of food due to:

1) **Climates** that are **good** for farming.

2) Lots of **investment** in farming.

South America and **Africa** only produce small amounts of food due to:

1) A **lack of resources** and **funding** for farming equipment.

2) Large areas of **land** that are **unsuitable** for farming as they are either **mountainous**, have **poor quality** or **little soil**, e.g. the Sahara desert.

3) **Unsuitable climates** — **low rainfall**, **too hot** or **too cold**.

Metric tonnes (1000s)
- ■ 9001 — 17200   ■ 1501 — 4000   ☐ 0 — 500
- ■ 4001 — 9000   ▨ 501 — 1500   ☐ No data

There are **Several** Different **Food Production Systems**

1) **Commercial** farming — the production of crops or livestock to make a **profit**.

2) **Subsistence** farming — when just enough food is grown to **feed the family**. It's common in Africa and Asia.

3) **Intensive** farming — **produces as much as possible** from the land. There are **two types** of intensive farming:

   - **Capital-intensive** farming has a high input of capital (money), and a low input of labour for the area of land. It often involves using fertilisers, pesticides and labour-saving machinery.
   - **Labour-intensive** farming doesn't involve much capital but uses a lot of labour.

4) **Extensive** farming — the **opposite** to intensive farming. It has a **low capital** and **labour input** for the area of land so produces **less food** than intensive farming. Small numbers of livestock grazing large areas of land is an example. Extensive farming has **less impact on the environment** and provides **better animal welfare** than intensive farming.

5) **Arable** farming — **plants** are grown for food, fuel, animal feed or materials (e.g. wood).

6) **Livestock** farming — **animals** like sheep, pigs or cows are raised for food or for materials (e.g. leather).

7) **Mixed** farming — farming of **plants and livestock**.

Global **Food Consumption** is Also **Unevenly Distributed**

Food consumption, like production, **varies** between countries. The map on the right shows the **daily calorie intake** of people in different countries.

Large populations consume more than small populations but this map shows consumption per person.

1) **More developed** areas like **North America** and **Europe** **consume a lot**. They can afford to import a large variety of foods, have a **culture** of **consumerism**, and many people have **high disposable incomes** so can **afford more food**.

2) **Less developed** areas like **Africa**, **South America** and parts of **Asia consume less food** per person as they **can't afford** as much.

3) **China** and other **newly industrialised countries** are **consuming more** as their **wealth increases**.

Daily calorie intake per person (2001-2003)
- ■ Over 3600   ▨ 2600 to 3100   ☐ 1520 to 2100
- ■ 3100 to 3600 ☐ 2100 to 2600   ☐ Not estimated

Food is **Traded Between Countries**

1) Countries that are able to **produce lots** of food often **export** it to those that can't.

2) North America, Europe, Australia, Argentina and Brazil all **export large amounts** of food.

3) Africa, Japan and Middle Eastern countries such as Saudi Arabia all have to **import large amounts** of food.

Global Food Distribution

Trans-National Corporations Play an Important Role in the Food Industry

Trans-National corporations (TNCs) are companies that operate in **more than one country**.
Many TNCs play a **major role** in the **production**, **processing** and **distribution** of food.

E.g. **Cargill**™ is a TNC based in the USA. It's the largest privately owned company in the world and operates in **66 countries**.

1) **Production**: Cargill™ **sells products** like fertilisers, equipment and seeds to farmers to help them grow crops. It then **buys** the crops from them. It also **produces its own** food, e.g. palm oil in Papua New Guinea.

2) **Processing**: It **owns processing plants** across the globe, e.g. soya bean processing plants in Paraguay, corn processing plants in China and cocoa processing plants in Ivory Coast.

3) **Distribution**: The worldwide distribution of many Cargill™ products is run from an office in Switzerland. It has its **own distribution network** in some countries, e.g. Venezuela, and **employs local people** to trade products in others, e.g. Pakistan.

ADVANTAGES OF TNCs

1) Lots of foods can be produced **cheaply**.
2) The **range of foods available** is increased.
3) TNCs **provide jobs** and **improve economic security** in countries where they operate.
4) They **invest in research** and **development** of new products and technologies that can increase farming yields.

DISADVANTAGES OF TNCs

1) They **control** the **price** of products such as seeds, fertilisers and machinery, the cost of processing and distribution, and the price of foods produced. If these prices are too high **some countries can't afford them**.
2) **Smaller companies can't compete and go bankrupt**. This causes supplies of food to become **delocalised** (countries have to buy from TNCs instead of local companies), leading to **less self-sufficiency**.
3) The **intensive farming methods** of TNCs can cause **environmental problems** (see page 80).
4) It can take a long time to process and transport the food — **reducing its nutritional value**.

The Geopolitics of Food Involves Different Issues

1) Food production and trade are **very important** to all governments for many reasons.
2) All countries want '**food security**' — they want to make sure that **their supply** of food (either from their own country or from another) **isn't disrupted** by things like poor yields, wars, or other political issues.
3) If their food supply **is** disrupted it can result in **food shortages**. These can cause serious **health issues** as well as **social** and **political instability** in that country. Not good.
4) Also, food production can account for a **huge proportion** of a country's **economy**.
5) So, countries make **agricultural policies** that **protect** their **home production** and **control** the **import** of food (see pages 82-83 for more).

Practice Questions

Q1 Why is food production in Africa low?
Q2 What is subsistence farming?
Q3 Describe the global pattern of food consumption.

Exam Questions

Q1 Compare the main characteristics of intensive farming and extensive farming. [5 marks]

Q2 Discuss the advantages and disadvantages of the involvement of TNCs in the global food industry. [8 marks]

Food fights — a serious threat to the even distribution of food...

OK, I'm fully aware that your main interest in food is probably the part where you shovel it into your mouth — but you do need to learn all the bits that lead up to that. So take the time to learn these pages properly — you could get asked about any of it.

Changes in Demand

Back in yesteryear, olden times and days of yore people had to eat whatever they could grow, which I imagine made mealtimes a trifle dull. Luckily for you and me, all that has changed...

In the Last 50 Years the Food Industry Has Become Globalised...

Before the 1960s the food we ate was usually grown in our **own country**, and was often from the local area. Since then there has been an **increase** in the **global trade** of food to satisfy **rising levels of consumption** and the increasing demand for a **wide range** of foods **all year round**. This increase in global trade is called **globalisation**.

...Which Has Had a Negative Impact on the Environment

Countries can make a lot of **money** by **exporting food** so it's in their interests to **produce large amounts**. Unfortunately, producing and transporting all this extra food can be damaging to the environment:

1) Countries that **export food** want to **produce as much as possible**. This means that they want **more land** for **farming**, which often leads to **deforestation** to provide the land.

2) The **greater** the **area** of land that's farmed, the **bigger** the **environmental impact** of farming. Growing food for export can also mean a change to more environmentally damaging **intensive farming methods**.

3) As **food exports increase**, so does the amount of **transportation** needed and the amount of **carbon dioxide** released by vehicles. Carbon dioxide is a greenhouse gas, so the more that's released the bigger the contribution to the **greenhouse effect** and **climate change**. '**Food miles**' is the distance food travels from **producer** to **consumer** and gives an indication of **how much** carbon dioxide is **released** as the food is transported.

See page 80 for the damaging effects of intensive farming methods.

The Type of Food That's in Demand Has Changed

1 Demand for SEASONAL PRODUCTS ALL YEAR ROUND has INCREASED...

1) In the 1960s most of the fruit and vegetables on sale in the UK were **locally produced** and **seasonal**. Seasonal food isn't available all year round — you can only buy it during the months that it grows.

2) Today, you can buy seasonal products at **any time** of year.

3) This is because fruit and vegetables are **imported** from **abroad**. E.g. peaches grow in the UK from August to September, but are imported all year round from Spain, Italy, France and Greece.

2 ...and so has demand for HIGH VALUE FOOD EXPORTS from POORER COUNTRIES.

1) **High value foods** are, unsurprisingly, foods that have a **high value**. They include things like exotic fruits and vegetables, coffee and chocolate.

2) Between 1980/1 and 2003/4 **high value food** exported from **poorer** countries to **richer** countries **quadrupled** — from $26 billion to $106 billion.

Crops that are grown for export are called cash crops.

Both these changes in demand were caused by...
1) A rising culture of **high consumption**.
2) **Rising incomes** in developed countries, which means more people can afford to buy the imports.
3) The **increasing popularity** of **exotic** products.

Dave was thrilled to discover his favourite vegetables were now available all year long.

There are **negative** effects of importing seasonal and high value food:
1) There are **food safety** and **agricultural health concerns** because standards vary between countries.
2) Importing food **increases food miles**, which increases the **negative impact** of transporting food on the **environment**.
3) There's **less food produced** in developed countries because it becomes cheaper to import food than produce it. This leads to **lower food security** as countries rely more and more on imported foods.
4) Many people are concerned about the fairness of **workers' pay** in developing countries, and that these countries are selling their best produce abroad at cheap prices.
5) The **best land** is often used to grow **high value foods** for exportation. This may leave **little** or **poor quality land** to grow **food** to feed the local population, which can lead to **food shortages**.

Changes in Demand

3 Demand for **ORGANIC** food has **INCREASED**...

Between 1993/4 and 2003/4 **organic food sales** in the UK **increased** over **10 times** — from £105 million to £1119 million.

This trend is caused by people's concern that...

1) **Intensive farming damages** the **environment**.
2) Eating food that may contain **pesticide residues** is **harmful**.

There are negative effects of organic produce:

1) It's more vulnerable to **pests** and **disease**.
2) It's more **expensive** to produce and buy.
3) There's **not enough** organic produce grown in the UK to **meet demand** so some has to be **imported**, which **increases food miles**.

4 ...and so has demand for **LOCAL PRODUCE**.

From 2005 to 2006 the number of UK shoppers buying **local produce increased** by 6%.

Reasons for this change in demand include more awareness of...

1) **Environmental issues**, i.e. food miles.
2) **Social issues** — the possible exploitation of workers in the developing world.

The negative effects are:

1) Local foods can be **more expensive** to produce and buy.
2) If we **import less** from the **developing world**, the **producers** there may **suffer**.

Foods Can be Produced in a *More Sustainable Way*...

For food production to be **sustainable** it has to **not damage** the **environment** and **not deplete resources**. Hardly any food production systems are totally sustainable, but there are ways to make them **more sustainable**:

1) **Relocalising food supplies** (buying food produced locally). This would **reduce food miles**.
2) Replacing intensive farming with **organic farming**. This would reduce the impact on the environment.
3) Using **less food packaging**. This would **reduce energy use** and **waste**.
4) Using **fair trade systems**. This would give growers in developing countries **fair pay** and improved **social** and **environmental** standards.

... But There are *Challenges* to Doing This

1) Food **can't** always be **grown locally** — the land might not be suitable for farming.
2) **Organic** farming methods are usually **less productive** than intensive farming methods — so **more land** is required to produce the same amount of food.
3) **Climate change**, **soil degradation** and demand for **biofuels** is **reducing** the area of **land** available for farming.
4) Also, in many areas where the **land** available for **farming** is **reducing**, the **population** is **increasing** and therefore **more food** is needed.
5) So, with **less land** available and **more people** to feed, it would be very **difficult** to **produce enough food** using **only** organic farming methods as they're **less productive** than **intensive farming methods**.

Practice Questions

Q1 What are high value food exports?
Q2 List the negative effects of the growth of high value food exports from developing countries.
Q3 List some of the ways that food could be produced in a more sustainable way.

Exam Questions

Q1 Describe and explain the changes in demand that have driven globalisation of the food industry. [4 marks]

Q2 Describe the environmental impacts of the globalisation of the food industry. [8 marks]

'Newsflash: Jet-setting vegetables to destroy planet.' Just as I suspected...

The key thing here is to be able to explain yourself. It's all very well knowing how our food supply has changed but if you can't explain why, you're going to come unstuck, which is never good. So read these pages through, scribble the details down, and you'll be able to explain to all and sundry why you can buy peaches in December. Whether they want to know is a different issue.

Increasing Food Production

So, there's no shortage of demand for good food, which leads us seamlessly on to the fact that...

Global **Food Production** Needs to **Increase**

Food production needs to increase to cope with **population growth** and **increasing consumption** in countries with increasing wealth, e.g. China, India and Brazil.

There are a Range of **Strategies** That **Increase Food Production**

① The **Green Revolution** Increased the Use of **Technology** in Agriculture

The green revolution began in the 1940s and spread the use of technology and intensive farming methods across the world.

Food production increased through the use of:

1) **Higher yielding crops** and **animals** (developed by selective breeding).

2) **Monocultures** — growing just one crop over a large area.

3) **Irrigation technologies**, e.g. groundwater pumping, electric sprinklers.

4) **Agrochemicals**, e.g. fertilisers, pesticides and herbicides.

5) **Mechanisation**, e.g. use of machines for sowing, harvesting, weeding and spraying.

The **negative impacts** of the green revolution are:

1) Bankruptcy of **small farms** that **can't afford** the **technology**, leading to **rural unemployment** and **food shortages**.

2) **Lower food security** — monoculture crops can be wiped out by a single pest, drought or disease, and there's no alternative crop to rely on.

3) The **intensive farming methods** of the green revolution can **damage** the **environment**:

- Monoculture **reduces biodiversity**.
- Over-irrigation can lead to **lower ground water levels**, **waterlogging** and **salinisation** (increase in saltiness) of soil and water.
- Agrochemicals can cause **pollution**.
- Mechanisation and over exploiting the land leads to **reduced soil fertility** and **increased soil erosion**.
- Using pesticides could lead to the evolution of "**superpests**" that are resistant to pesticides, which could result in **more damaging pesticides** being used.

Example: **India** began a green revolution programme in **1961**. It **financed agrochemicals**, **developed irrigation systems** and **imported high yielding** varieties of **wheat** and **rice**. Productivity increased rapidly as a result, e.g. **rice yields tripled** by the **1990s**.

② Genetic Modification is a **High Technology** Approach

Genetically modified (GM) crops are crops that have been altered by the addition of genes that give them **beneficial characteristics**. They were introduced in the 1990s.

Crops can be modified to make them:

1) **Produce pesticides** — making them **resistant** to some **pests**.

2) **Herbicide** and **pesticide tolerant** — this means farmers can use these chemicals without harming the plant.

3) **Resistant to disease**.

4) **Higher yielding** — either by increasing their size, or their rate of growth.

5) **Longer lasting**, i.e. with an increased shelf-life.

6) **Resistant to harsh** environmental **conditions**, e.g. drought or frost.

All of these modifications **increase food production**.

A small number of **GM animals** are also being developed, e.g. quick to mature salmon, cows that produce enriched milk, and pigs that produce lower fat bacon.

Because GM is a new technology it's still unclear what all of its **disadvantages** are. Some concerns include:

1) If crops are grown that are resistant to agrochemicals farmers might be tempted to use **more agrochemicals**, which can **damage** the **environment**.

2) Some GM crops are able to **cross-pollinate** and **transfer** their **genes** to other plants. This could lead to a gene for herbicide tolerance being transferred to a weed, which would then be difficult to kill.

3) The pesticides produced by some GM crops could **harm non-pest species**, e.g. butterflies.

Example: '**Bt maize**' and '**Bt cotton**' contain a **gene** from bacteria that enables them to produce a **toxin** poisonous to insect pests (called Bt toxin). **20% less insecticide** is needed on these crops.

Increasing Food Production

③ Land Colonisation and Land Reform Provide Agricultural Land

Land colonisation and **reform** can **increase food production** by giving people **access to land** to grow food.

Land colonisation is when humans move to an area of land that **hasn't been used before**, e.g. rainforests.

The disadvantages include **environmental damage** (such as **deforestation**) and possible **conflicts** with indigenous populations.

Example

2 million hectares of the **Amazon rainforest** are **cleared** each year to make way for subsistence and commercial **farms**.

Land reform is when land is **redistributed**, e.g. land owned by the government is given to local people.

Disadvantages include **conflicts** over who is entitled to the land (or over compensation for previous landowners). **Human rights violations** are also a concern if the previous landowners were forcibly removed.

Example

In **Albania** in the 1990s **216 large state farms** were **redistributed** to create **380 000 small farms** owned by former state **farm workers**.

④ Commercialisation is the Change from Subsistence Farming to Commercial Farming

Commercialisation **increases production** through the use of capital-intensive **green revolution technologies**. Commercial farms produce **high value food** for export and produce **cash crops**.

Example

Commercialisation of small farms in **Kenya** since the 1960s has led to it becoming the world's **4th largest exporter** of tea. Tea is now Kenya's **main source** of foreign **income**.

There are disadvantages to **commercialisation**:

1) The **best land** is usually used to produce food. This can lead to **food shortages** as there's less high quality land left to produce food for the **local population**.

2) Also, the move from subsistence to commercial farming involves the use of **green revolution technologies** and the **problems** that they cause (see previous page).

⑤ Appropriate Technology Solutions are Low Cost

Appropriate technologies are **simple, low cost** technologies that **increase food production**. They're **made** and **maintained** using **local knowledge** and **resources** only, so aren't dependent on any outside support, expensive equipment or fuel.

Appropriate technology is also known as intermediate technology.

Example

The **treadle pump** is a **human powered** pump **developed in Bangladesh** in the 1980s. It **pumps water** from below the ground to **irrigate small areas** of **land**. This is important in Bangladesh as the main crop (**rice**) needs **lots** of **water** to grow. It costs US $7 to buy. It has **increased** Bangladeshi farmers' average annual **incomes** by roughly $100, through increased irrigation and therefore increased crop yield.
Local workshops, village dealers, well drillers and pump installers have all benefited from the business that the local production and distribution of the pump has brought.

The main **disadvantage** of appropriate technology solutions is that they tend to be **labour intensive**.

Practice Questions

Q1 How have green revolution technologies increased agricultural production?
Q2 What is the difference between land colonisation and land reform?
Q3 What is commercialisation of agriculture?

Exam Question

Q1 Explain the disadvantages of using green revolution technologies to increase food supplies. [6 marks]

Food glorious food — turns out everybody wants some more...

So there you have it — five ways to increase food production. It isn't edge-of-your-seat stuff, but you could be asked to explain or compare any of these strategies, so you need to know each strategy and its disadvantages really well. Sorry about that.

Controlling Food Production and Supply

Just when you thought you had food production sussed, it turns out there's a lot more to it...

Food Production and Supply Needs to be Controlled

Production and supply of food have to be controlled in order to:

1) Ensure **food availability** and **security**, but **prevent overproduction**.

2) Ensure **fair living standards** for farmers and the **survival** of **rural communities**.

3) Encourage farmers to act as '**stewards of the landscape**' and **preserve** the natural **environment**.

In **Europe** food production and supply is controlled by the **Common Agricultural Policy** (**CAP**). CAP is a set of policies laid out by the European Commission — it controls production and supply through a range of **market** and **non-market policies**.

Market Policies Control How Profitable Products Are

Market policies control food production by controlling **how profitable** it is to farm certain produce.
There are several different **types** of **market policies**:

1 Subsidies — Paying Farmers to Produce Certain Products

Subsidies are **payments** made to **farmers** to **grow certain products**. This maintains home grown supplies and **food security**. It also ensures **fair living standards** for farmers.

> **Example**
>
> The EU is the second largest **dairy** exporter in the world due to the **subsidies** that support the industry. **€1 billion** was paid out in dairy subsidies in **2006**.

> **Negative effects** of subsidies:
>
> 1) The **cost** of paying farmers.
>
> 2) It can cause **overproduction**. This can lead to **export dumping** (when food is sold abroad for less than the cost of production).
>
> 3) Export dumping causes **disruption** of **international markets** and **problems** in **developing countries** (because farmers are unable to compete with the artificially low price of the dumped food).

2 Quotas Limit Production and How Much is Imported

Quotas limit the production of some food to **prevent overproduction**.
Import quotas protect the market by **limiting** the amount of **imported produce**.

> **Example**
>
> **Milk quotas** were introduced in the **1980s** following overproduction that created '**milk lakes**' and '**butter mountains**' (huge amounts of produce that couldn't be consumed or exported). Milk quotas have gradually been **increased** as **demand** has **increased**.

> **Negative effects** of import quotas:
>
> 1) They **prevent consumers** obtaining **cheap imports**.
>
> 2) They can **influence** international **production** and **trade**.

3 Intervention Ensures Farmers Can Sell Their Produce

1) **Intervention** is when the EU **buys produce** from farmers. It improves food security by ensuring farmers can **sell** their **produce** even when demand is low. Intervention stock is either **stored** for later **resale**, **exported** or **disposed** of.

> **Example**
>
> Currently, the EU will buy up excess stocks of **grain**, **butter** and **sugar**. The EU had over **1.5 million tonnes** of sugar **stored** in warehouses in January 2006.

> **Negative effects** of intervention:
>
> 1) The **cost** of **transport**, **storage** and **disposal**.
>
> 2) It can cause **overproduction**.
>
> 3) The risk of **export dumping** and **disruption** of **markets**.

2) **Intervention** involves **guaranteeing** a **minimum price** for certain products (pricing). It **controls production** by encouraging farmers to **produce** or **stop producing** particular products.

> **Example**
>
> The EU aims to **cut sugar production** by 6 million tonnes by 2010 to allow developing countries to export lower cost sugar. In 2006 the **guaranteed price** for sugar was **cut** by 36% to encourage farmers to **stop producing** sugar.

> **Negative effects** of pricing:
>
> 1) **Cost** of paying farmers.
>
> 2) **Increased cost** to **consumers**.

Controlling Food Production and Supply

4) Tariffs *Protect the Market for Domestic Farmers*

Tariffs are **taxes** applied to **imported goods** — they stop imports from **undercutting** domestic produce.

> **Example**
>
> The EU can produce **94%** of the beef that it needs, but if it was **cheaper** for consumers to buy **imported beef** then it would **not be profitable** for EU farmers to produce it and **production** (and so **food security**) would **decrease**. To prevent this, a **tariff** of 18 to 28% is applied to **imported** beef products, making them **more expensive** than locally produced products.

> **Negative side effects** of tariffs:
>
> 1) They **prevent consumers** buying **cheap imported products**.
>
> 2) They can **affect international production** (by reducing trade of products with high tariffs and increasing trade of products with low tariffs).

Non-market Policies *Control Production* Without Affecting Markets

Non-market policies also **control food production**, but **don't affect** how **profitable** certain products are to farmers. There are several different **types** of **non-market policies**:

1) Diversification Schemes Promote Enterprise

Diversification schemes encourage farmers to develop **new enterprises**, reducing dependence on subsidies for agricultural products.

> **Example**
>
> **Rainton Farm** in Scotland has **diversified** by producing and selling **ice cream**, and providing **tourist facilities** such as a farm shop, tea room, adventure playground, 3D maze and nature trails.

2) Environmental Stewardship *Protects* Nature

Environmental stewardship involves paying **subsidies** to farmers to use **conservation methods** when farming.

Payments are made for schemes that:

1) Protect **wildlife**.
2) Maintain or enhance **landscape quality**.
3) Protect the **environment** and **natural resources**.
4) Promote **public access** to the **countryside**.

> **Example**
>
> In the **Lake District** farmers receive subsidies to **restrict cultivation and grazing, reduce fertiliser** and **pesticide use, manage hedges, maintain ditches** and **repair** stone walls.

> **Benefits** of non-market policies:
>
> 1) They prevent **overproduction**.
> 2) They prevent **land degradation**.
> 3) They promote **sustainable farming**.
> 4) They promote a **sustainable rural economy**.
>
> **Negative effects** of **non-market policies**:
>
> 1) **Cost** of paying farmers.
> 2) **Reduced productivity** (this can be a benefit if overproduction is an issue though).

Practice Questions

Q1 What are agricultural subsidies?
Q2 Describe the negative effects of intervention.
Q3 What are the benefits of environmental stewardship schemes?

Exam Question

Q1 Describe how EU market policies control the level and nature of agricultural production. [15 marks]

More food, less food, environmentally friendly food, grrrr — enough already

Managing food supplies for a whole continent is tricky stuff — the balance needs to be just right. Luckily for you, you only need to be able to explain these policies — pity the people who actually have to come up with them. Or laugh at them. Whichever.

Managing Food Supply — Case Studies

Two highly interesting, hugely important and crucially contrasting case studies for you.

Case Study 1: Bangladesh — Production Doesn't Meet Demand

1) Bangladesh is a **developing country** with a high poverty rate.

2) Rates of **malnutrition** are **high**.

3) **Food production doesn't meet demand** due to **fast population growth** and **climatic events** that **damage production**. E.g. the annual monsoon and cyclones cause flooding as the country is situated on low-lying river deltas.

Food Supplies are Managed Through a Range of Strategies

Various organisations are working to increase productivity and ensure food supplies are sufficient. These include the government, foreign aid agencies, international research institutions and non-governmental organisations (NGOs). These groups have put a range of strategies in place to increase food supplies:

1 **Investment** in **Technology**

The government provides **subsidies** and **loans** for farmers to invest in **green revolution technologies**. The use of **high yielding rice seeds, agrochemicals** and **increased irrigation** increased rice production from 11.7 to 23.1 million tonnes between 1974 and 2000. There has also recently been more investment into **appropriate technology solutions**, due to the negative effects of green revolution technologies (see page 80).

2 **Free Market Policies Encourage** Food **Imports**

The government has **removed** many **subsidies, eliminated quotas**, and **reduced import tariffs** to **encourage imports**, which are essential to feed the population. **Disadvantages** of this strategy include **susceptibility to rising food prices** — in 2008 the rising price of grain pushed 4 million people below the poverty line.

3 **Diversification** is **Encouraged**

Bangladesh relies heavily on **rice**, which needs four times more water than most crops to grow — a problem in a country with falling water levels. **Food security, nutrition** and **health** would all improve if a **greater range of foods** was produced.

Diversification is encouraged in several ways:

1) **Small and medium businesses** are **supported** by projects that provide expertise and training.

2) **Financial incentives** are given to livestock farmers, e.g. tax holidays and duty exemptions.

3) **EU trade preferences** allow goods to be exported to Europe **without duties** or **quotas**.

4 **Investment** in **Infrastructure**

There's been **investment** into **infrastructure** that **supports food production**:

1) **Maintaining** and **building roads** to improve the transport of produce. Between 1995 and 2000 the US funded the construction of 15 000 km of farm-to-market roads.

2) **Increasing electricity supplies** — between 1977 and 2000 over 80 000 irrigation pumps were electrified.

3) **Building flood defences** and **improving water flow** to allow damaging flood water to recede quickly.

5 **Food Aid** is Provided Where it's Needed Most

The government and other organisations operate **schemes** to **provide food**. For example:

1) The '**Food for Work**' programme gives people the opportunity to **work for food** on projects that **improve rural infrastructure** or the **environment**.

2) The '**Food for Education**' programme gives food to families who send their children to school instead of work — **increasing education** and **decreasing child labour**.

These Strategies Have Advantages and Disadvantages

Advantages:

1) Diversification and investment in infrastructure are long-term **sustainable** solutions.

2) Strategies such as "Food for Education" provide **health** and **social benefits**.

3) Diversification would **benefit** the **economy**, providing a wider range of export goods.

Disadvantages:

1) All these strategies cost **money** to initiate.

2) Food imports and food aid are **not sustainable** solutions.

3) Some technologies **damage** the **environment**.

Managing Food Supply — Case Studies

Case Study 2: China — Priority is Self-sufficiency

With 1.3 billion citizens China is the world's **most populated country**. It has had a **history** of **food shortages** so its **goal** is to be **self-sufficient**. It aims to achieve this through focusing agricultural policy on **grain production**. China currently produces 90% of its own grain, despite having only 7% of the planet's arable land and 20% of its population.

Food Supplies are Managed Through a Range of Strategies

1 **State Control** of **Grain Production**

Grain production and **distribution** are **controlled** by the **central government**. Farmers are required to produce at least 50 million tonnes of grain that are sold at **government controlled prices** and 40 million tonnes that are sold to the government at **negotiated prices**. This grain is distributed to **urban areas** and sold at **low prices**.

2 **Incentives** to **Grow Grains**

Provincial governments are responsible for making sure **enough grain** is **produced**. Provinces that **don't produce enough** have to **buy produce** from those that have a **surplus**. **Incentives** put in place by the provinces to encourage grain production vary but include **subsidies**, **guaranteed minimum prices**, **tax exemptions** and **free education**.

3 **Modernisation** of **Agriculture**

There's been **investment** into **modernising agriculture**:

1) **Transportation infrastructure** has been **improved**, speeding up transport of produce (slow distribution has caused famine in the past).
2) **Losses** during **processing** and **distribution** have been **reduced** using Western technology in packing, refrigerating and canning.
3) **Agricultural research** and **development** have become a **priority**. Research into rice breeding, biological pest control and genetic engineering have been funded with the aim of **improving crop yields**.

4 **Domestic Supplies** are **Protected**

China is cautious, **protecting** its **supplies** by:

1) **Stockpiling surplus grain**. In 2008 China held a reserve supply equivalent to 30 to 40% of its annual consumption (the UN regards 17% as a safe minimum).
2) **Limiting grain imports**. This protects the domestic market for home-grown produce.
3) **Reducing grain exports**. In 2007 a global shortage of grain resulted in soaring prices worldwide. Exports to many countries were stopped to protect domestic supplies.

These Strategies Have Advantages and Disadvantages

Advantages:

1) Modernisation of agriculture is a **long-term investment**.
2) Prioritising self-sufficiency leaves **less chance** of **disruption to food supplies** by external events.

Disadvantages:

1) **Urbanisation** is **reducing** the area of **arable land** so food self-sufficiency may **not** be **sustainable** as a policy.
2) The focus on grain **prevents farmers** from **growing high value foods** for export, **increasing rural poverty**.
3) **Reducing grain exports** can **adversely affect food supply** in **countries** that **depend** on **imports**.

Practice Questions

Q1 Why doesn't agricultural production meet demand in Bangladesh?
Q2 What strategies are used in Bangladesh to increase food production?
Q3 How has agriculture been modernised in China?

Exam Questions

Q1 Discuss the sustainability of strategies to manage food supplies in Bangladesh. [10 marks]

Q2 Compare the management of food supply in Bangladesh and China. [15 marks]

Chinese agriculture — just like the good life, but on a slightly larger scale...

These case studies are mega important. Loads of questions ask you to give examples to back up your points and there's tons of specifics here. So pick out some quotable statistics and learn them — then go over them again. And again. And again.

Energy Resources

What with the palaver over climate change and petrol prices energy is a hot topic these days.
So here's a whole section devoted to it, just for you, to help you do stunningly well in your exams.

There are **Different Types** of **Energy**

Energy comes in many different types (e.g. heat, electrical, light, chemical, potential), and although it can't be created or destroyed, it can be **converted** from **one type** to **another**. Energy can be classified as either **primary** or **secondary energy**:

1) **Primary energy** is released from a **direct source**, e.g. heat energy is released from burning coal.

2) When primary energy is **converted into a different form** it becomes **secondary energy**, e.g. when heat energy from burning coal is used to generate electricity.

Primary Energy Resources can be **Renewable** or **Non-renewable**

Renewable Resources

1) A **resource** is **renewable** if it can be **replenished** at a **similar rate** to which it's **used**.

2) Renewable resources are also known as **flow resources**. There's a constant energy transfer occurring, which if balanced will be sustainable.

3) **Tidal energy**, **wind energy** and **solar power** are all renewable resources because you can't use them up.

See pages 92-93 for more on renewable resources.

See pages 90-91 for more on non-renewable resources.

Non-renewable Resources

1) **Non-renewable resources** can **run out** and **can't be replaced** in the **foreseeable future**.

2) They're also known as **stock resources** as the planet has a limited 'stock', which when used up won't be replaced.

3) **Fossil fuels** (**coal**, **oil** and **natural gas**) and **nuclear energy** are non-renewable resources.

Some Resources are only **Renewable** if **Carefully Managed**

Whether a resource is renewable or not depends on **how fast** the resource is being **used compared** to **how fast** it's **replenished**. If the rates are **roughly equal** then it's a **renewable resource**.

1) Some resources are clearly renewable and will be available no matter how much we use, e.g. solar power.

2) Other resources have to be carefully managed if they're to be considered renewable. For example:

- **Wood** — if too much wood is used in a short space of time the natural cycle of replenishment is disrupted and the resource is used up. If wood is managed carefully (using techniques like coppicing and replanting) to ensure that it's replaced at roughly the same rate that it's used, then it can be considered renewable.

- **Geothermal reservoirs** — tectonic heat is used to turn water into steam at geothermal power stations, but if the power station is too large for the site then continually pumping water into the ground will end up cooling the ground. This means the resource is lost, so it's not renewable.

3) Some non-renewable resources can be replaced but aren't considered renewable because of the timescale involved, e.g. fossil fuels. **Fossil fuels are hydrocarbons** that have formed under high temperatures and pressures beneath the Earth's crust. This process hasn't stopped (fossil fuels are still being made), it's just that they take many millions of years to form and we're using them much faster than they are being replaced. So because they can't be replaced in the foreseeable future they're not a renewable energy source.

Energy Resources

The **Primary Energy Mix** Describes the **Sources** of Energy a **Country Uses**

1) Countries need energy for industry and transport, as well as for use in homes.

2) Many countries **aren't able to supply** all of their **energy needs** from **one source**, or they might not want to for energy security reasons. They use a **variety** of sources instead.

3) The **amount** of **each resource used** is called the **energy mix** and it's usually shown as **percentages**.

Solar and wave energy were the ideal mix to satisfy Sam's energy needs.

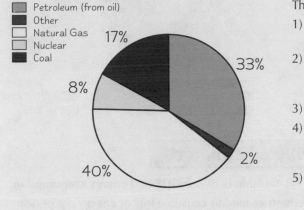

Petroleum (from oil)
Other
Natural Gas
Nuclear
Coal

17%
33%
8%
2%
40%

The pie graph on the left shows the **UK's energy mix** in **2008**.

1) **Over 70%** of the UK's energy supply is provided by **oil and gas**, which makes sense as the UK has **reserves** of both.

2) Since the early 1970s the UK's **consumption of oil increased** due to the discovery of North Sea oil in 1969 and the growing demand for transport fuel.

3) Use of **natural gas** has **increased** by **85%** since 1990.

4) Despite having **large reserves**, use of **coal** has **fallen** by **40%** since 1990, due to closure of mines and the move to using less polluting oil and gas.

5) Use of **renewable resources** has **increased**, as the government aims to move towards a more sustainable energy supply. It's still below the EU average of 6% though.

The pie graph on the right shows **France's energy mix** in **2004**.

1) France has **limited coal and oil reserves** and most of their supplies have to be **imported**. Coal mining stopped completely in France in 2004 so energy production from coal is low. Energy production from oil remains high though, due to the demand for transport fuel.

2) The proportion of **natural gas** that France uses has **increased** by over 50% since 1990, but is still below the EU average of 24%.

3) As it has limited fossil fuel resources France began investing in **nuclear power** in the 1970s in order to **secure energy supplies**. **41%** of France's energy supply now comes from **nuclear power**. It's the biggest producer of nuclear power in the EU, and the second biggest in the world.

4) Most of France's renewable energy comes from **hydropower** and **biomass**.

Petroleum (from oil)
Other
Natural Gas
Nuclear
Coal

5%
33%
41%
6%
15%

Practice Questions

Q1 What is the difference between primary and secondary energy?

Q2 What is a fossil fuel?

Q3 What is meant by 'primary energy mix'?

Exam Questions

Q1 Explain the difference between renewable and non-renewable resources. [6 marks]

Q2 Describe the energy mix of one named country and explain how it has changed recently. [6 marks]

50% pizza, 30% cake, 20% chocolate — the perfect energy mix...

The important thing to learn here is what the words renewable and non-renewable mean and why the boundary between them is a bit blurry. A good way of testing how well you understand this is to try explaining it to someone else. So once you think you know it well, pick a victim and explain away. This also doubles up as a handy way of getting rid of people you don't like.

Global Energy Distribution

With 6.6 billion people in the world, supplying everyone with energy isn't simple.

Global **Energy Production** is **Unevenly Distributed**

The map on the right shows energy produced from fossil fuels, per country 1989-1998.

1) Some countries produce **lots of energy** because they have **large energy reserves** and the **money** to **exploit** them. For example:
   - Iran, Saudi Arabia — large oil reserves.
   - China, Australia — large coal reserves.
   - UK, Russia, Canada — large oil and gas reserves.
   - USA, Indonesia — large coal, oil and gas reserves.

2) Some countries produce **little energy** because they have **few resources** or are **unable** to **exploit** their resources due to lack of **money** or **political instability**.
   - Angola — politically unstable and lack of money.
   - Spain — small fossil fuel reserves.

This map shows the energy produced in each country, not the total reserves of energy.

Energy produced from fossil fuels (BTUs)

■ Over 25.00	■ 5.01 – 10.00	□ 0.00 – 2.50
■ 10.01 – 25.00	■ 2.51 – 5.00	■ no data

Global **Energy Consumption** is also **Unevenly Distributed**

The map below shows the energy consumption per person across the world in 2007.

Energy consumption per person (tonnes oil equivalent)

■ 6.0 and over	■ 3.0 – 4.5	□ 0 – 1.5
■ 4.5 – 6.0	■ 1.5 – 3.0	

There's a **strong relationship** between **GDP** and **energy consumption**:

1) **Wealthy countries** tend to **consume lots of energy** per person because they're wealthy and **can afford to**. **Most people** in these countries have **access** to **electricity** and **heating**, and use **energy-intensive devices** like cars. E.g. **Australia, Sweden, USA**.

2) **Poorer countries consume less energy** per person as they are **less able to afford it**. **Less energy** is **available** and lifestyles are less dependent on high energy consumption than in wealthier countries. E.g. **Burkina Faso, Mongolia**.

Some countries don't consume much energy per person, but consume a lot overall because they have large populations. E.g. Brazil consumes less energy per person than Ireland, but has a higher total energy consumption.

Energy is **Traded Between Countries**

Some countries don't produce much energy but still **consume a lot**, and vice versa. This is possible because **energy** is **traded between countries**.

1) Countries that are able to produce a lot of energy **export** it to those that can't.

2) Canada, Saudi Arabia, United Arab Emirates, Denmark and Venezuela all **export large amounts** of **energy**.

3) Ireland, Italy, Spain and Japan all **import large amounts** of **energy**.

Electricity is traded between neighbouring countries, while coal, oil and natural gas can be transported around the world.

Trans-National Corporations Play an **Important Role** in the **Energy Industry**

Trans-National corporations (**TNCs**) are **companies** that **operate** in **more than one country**. Many TNCs play a **major role** in world **energy production** and **distribution**.

E.g. **ExxonMobil** is an **oil** and **gas TNC** based in the USA. It's the largest company in the world (based on revenue) and **operates** in **over 200 countries** worldwide, **producing 3%** of the **world's oil** and **2%** of its **energy**.

1) **Production:** ExxonMobil **explores** for oil and gas on every continent except Antarctica. When found the oil is **extracted** and sent to ExxonMobil **refineries** (e.g. in the USA, Norway, Thailand or the UK) for **processing**.

2) **Distribution: After processing** ExxonMobil uses its **own transportation system** to **transport products** to **distribution centres**, either its own or independent ones, e.g. Acculube, TrAchem Ltd. These then **sell** to **customers** such as CATERPILLAR® and Singapore Airlines, as well as to individuals for transport fuel.

Global Energy Distribution

The Geopolitics of Energy is a Big Issue

Energy security is an important issue for all governments, for several reasons:

1) All countries are dependent on energy supplies, e.g. for transport, heating, electricity and manufacturing.

2) Global energy use is increasing and fossil fuel reserves are decreasing. Many people believe we're coming to an "energy crisis", so governments are more concerned than ever about how to secure future supplies of energy.

3) To make the situation trickier, the largest reserves of oil and gas are often in areas that are either politically or economically unstable, e.g. Russia, which means that energy supplies are often at risk of being disrupted.

4) So in order to secure supplies, agreements are often reached between exporting and importing regions. For example, the EU will become increasingly dependent on imports as North Sea oil runs out, so it opened talks with Russia in 2000 to try to guarantee access to Russian gas supplies. In return Russia wanted investment into production of fuel and improved access to EU markets.

5) At times agreements can't be reached and concerns over energy security can lead to conflict or the threat of conflict. E.g. the 1980 Carter Doctrine stated that the USA would use military force if necessary to protect its interests in the Middle East and secure the free movement of oil.

6) As energy consumption increases, so does the impact of energy use on the environment (see page 90). International agreements, e.g. the Kyoto Protocol, are drawn up to try to address these problems, but these too can lead to political conflict if environmental protection clashes with other national interests, e.g. economic growth.

Patterns of Energy Production, Consumption and Trade Can Change

Changes in Production

1) Energy production has increased in countries where new reserves have been discovered, e.g. in Nigeria and Algeria.

2) There have also been increases in places that have become more politically stable, e.g. Angola (after the end of the civil war).

3) The production of energy has decreased in other countries as resources are used up, e.g. North Sea oil production has declined since 1999, reducing production in the UK, Norway, Denmark, Germany and the Netherlands.

4) Production often decreases in areas that become more unstable, e.g. Sudan oil production decreased due to civil war between 1983 and 2005.

Changes in Consumption

1) China has the largest population and one of the fastest growing economies in the world. As standards of living and industrial output increase China consumes more and more energy.

2) Other newly industrialised countries, e.g. India, Malaysia and Mexico, are also using more energy as they develop.

Changes in Trade

As production and consumption of energy changes, so does the trade of energy.

1) Exports from ex-Soviet central Asian countries like Kazakhstan are increasing. These countries are attractive as suppliers to the EU, USA and China because the region is more stable than the Middle East and isn't controlled by Russia, reducing dependence on these two areas.

2) Brazil and Denmark were once heavily dependent on imports but are now both energy self-sufficient, due to development of renewable energy and discoveries of domestic oil reserves.

Practice Questions

Q1 Why do wealthy countries consume more energy per person than poorer countries?
Q2 What role do TNCs play in the energy industry?

Exam Question

Q1 Explain why global patterns of energy production, consumption and trade change. [15 marks]

Revision — a serious threat to the energy reserves of sixth formers...

So there you have it — the energy supply of an entire planet on one double page. Doesn't seem too bad to me — some places have loads of energy and some don't have enough, so politicians pal up and shunt it about a bit. Don't see what the fuss is about.

Impacts of Energy Production

Imagine you're running a country — you've got yourself a nice secure supply of energy, you're feeling pretty smug.
Only thing to worry about now is the impact of the energy on your shiny new country.

Fuel Wood Gathering can Damage the Environment...

Although **fossil fuels** supply **87%** of the **world's energy**, a significant proportion of the world's population use **wood** as an **energy source**, usually to provide energy within the home. Wood that's burnt for fuel is called **fuel wood**.
The **gathering** of **fuel wood** can **damage the environment** in several ways:

1) **Deforestation** — most fuel wood gathering isn't regulated and can seriously deplete local woodland.

2) **Habitat loss** — deforestation can damage or destroy the habitats of a wide range of wildlife.

3) **Soil erosion** — tree roots bind soil together. If the trees are removed the soil isn't held together as well and can be washed away by rain or blown away by winds.

| Example | The **Copperbelt** in **Zambia** is a densely populated industrial area that relies heavily on fuel wood. Between **1972** and **2000** an average of **3125** |

hectares of woodland were **cleared** each year for **fuel wood**. Heavy **tropical rains** from November to April resulted in dramatic **erosion of topsoil** as there were fewer trees to hold the soil together. This left much of the land **barren** and **unsuitable for agriculture**, as well as **preventing** the **re-growth** of **woodlands**.

...and so can Using Fossil Fuels

The **extraction** of fossil fuels, e.g. by mining, can damage the environment.
Transportation can also cause environmental damage, e.g. through **oil spills**.
The **use** of fossil fuels has **negative impacts** on the **environment** as well, such as **acid rain** and **global warming**.

1 Acid Rain

Burning fossil fuels releases various **gases**. Some of these **dissolve** in **water vapour** in the atmosphere, which then falls as **acid rain**. Acid rain can:

1) **Kill fish** and other **aquatic life**, which can lead to **reduced biodiversity**.

2) **Kill trees** and other **plant life**, which also **reduces biodiversity**.

3) **Reduce** the **nutrient content** of **soil** so that some species of plants can't grow, or grow more slowly.

4) **Corrode rocks**, e.g. limestone, sandstone.

2 Global Warming

The largest environmental problem created by the use of fossil fuels is **global warming**. Burning fossil fuels **releases** the greenhouse gas **carbon dioxide** into the air. This **enhances** the planet's natural greenhouse effect, **increasing world temperatures** and causing **climate change**. This could lead to:

1) **Rising sea levels** and **increased flooding**.

2) **More frequent** and **severe extreme weather events**, e.g. hurricanes, droughts.

3) **Habitat loss** (which leads to **loss of biodiversity** and the **extinction** of species).

3 Problems Associated with Mining

Coal mining involves disturbing or removing large areas of land, which can lead to:

1) **Wildlife** being **displaced**.

2) **Habitat Loss**.

3) **Reduced air quality** as dust and other particulates are released.

4) **Contamination** of **surface water** with acidic or toxic substances.

4 Oil Spills

Oil spills happen when **pipes**, **oil wells** or **tankers** transporting oil **leak**, dumping oil onto land or into seas or oceans. The effects of oil spills last for a long time and lead to the **death of wildlife**. There are many reasons for this:

1) **Oil reduces** the **ability** of animals to **move freely**, which makes it more difficult for them to swim, fly or forage.

2) **Hypothermia**. When **feathers** and **fur** become **coated in oil** it reduces the animal's ability to control its body temperature.

3) **Consumption of oil**.

The impact of each of these varies depending on the location of the area affected and the severity of the problem.

Impacts of Energy Production

Fossil Fuel Resources Won't Last For Ever

It's **hard to know how long fossil fuel reserves will last**. This is because **new reserves** might be found, or we might find **more efficient ways to use them**. This would **increase** the length of **time** we can **depend on them**.

A 2006 estimation of **proven** reserves suggested that, worldwide, there were:

They might label him a pessimist now, but Rob knew he'd have the last laugh.

- 1000 billion barrels of oil left (enough to last 40 years).
- 150 trillion cubic metres of natural gas left (enough to last 60 years).
- 1000 billion tonnes of coal left (enough to last 250 years).

Eventually **fossil fuels will run out** (or become too difficult to extract) so an **alternative energy source** needs to be found.

Nuclear Power could be an Alternative to Fossil Fuels

In **nuclear power stations heat energy** released from **uranium** or **plutonium** is used to **generate electricity**.
The first commercial nuclear reactor opened in 1956 and there are now 439 reactors in 31 countries around the world.
They supply 15% of the world's electricity, which is 6.3% of the total energy consumption.
There are **advantages** and **disadvantages** of using nuclear power:

Advantages of nuclear power	Disadvantages of nuclear power
1) It has **low carbon dioxide emissions**, so contributes little to global warming.	1) **Nuclear waste** is **highly radioactive** and has to be **stored carefully** for **thousands of years**. This is very **expensive**. Some people argue that as technology improves this problem will be solved, but there's no guarantee of this.
2) **Less toxic waste** is released into the environment than from fossil fuel plants. (Fossil fuel plants release ash containing heavy metals such as mercury, cadmium and lead).	2) **Accidents** causing **radioactive waste** to **leak** into the **environment** can have devastating consequences, e.g. **human, animal** and **plant deaths** and **illnesses, destruction** of the local **environment** and **contamination** of **large areas of land**. The damage lasts for a **long time**. The **explosion** of nuclear power **plants** causes similar problems.
3) **Large amounts of energy** are generated from **small amounts of fuel**.	3) There's only **limited amounts** of **uranium** and **plutonium** so it's a **non-renewable** resource.
4) **Electricity** produced by nuclear power is **cheap**.	4) **Decommissioning** power stations at the end of their life is **very expensive**.

Example: In **France 78%** of **electricity** is produced from **nuclear power**. France has the **cleanest air** of any industrialised country and the **cheapest electricity** in Europe.

Example: The 1986 explosion at the **Chernobyl** nuclear power plant in the Ukraine directly caused **56 deaths** and radiation released caused **thousands** of **deaths** and **illnesses**. **Radioactive material** from the disaster was detected as far away as **Ireland**, a **4 km² area of forest** around Chernobyl **died**, **food supplies** (particularly of fish) were affected in **Scandinavia** for several years after the accident and the Chernobyl area is **still heavily contaminated** today.

Practice Questions

Q1 What is meant by the term fuel wood?
Q2 What environmental problems are associated with coal mining?
Q3 Why is nuclear power a non-renewable source of energy?

Exam Question

Q1 Discuss the advantages and disadvantages of using nuclear power as a replacement for fossil fuels. [10 marks]

Fossil fuels are dwindling — they'll be going, going and then gone

So it's either fossil fuels that damage the environment and will run out soon, or nuclear power, which can also damage the environment and will run out. Guess we'll just have to go back to no electricity and wood fires... No, wait, that damages the environment too. But don't despair. It may seem doomy and gloomy on this page, but there could be a solution. Read on...

Sustainable Energy

Sustainable energy is so important there are four whole pages of it coming your way...

Sustainable Energy Sources are Always Renewable

For **energy production** to be **sustainable** it **musn't deplete resources** or cause any **long term environmental damage**. Energy production using **non-renewable resources isn't sustainable** as it's environmentally damaging and the resource will one day run out. Energy produced from **renewable resources** is **sustainable** as it doesn't usually cause long term environmental damage and the resource won't run out. There are many different types of renewable energy resources:

1. Wind Energy is Harnessed by Wind Turbines

Wind energy is responsible for **1%** of the world's electricity production. **Carbon dioxide** is released during the **production** and **installation** of wind turbines but once that's done **no greenhouse gases** are released and **no fuel** is needed.

1) **Wind turbines** are built in **open exposed areas** where there's a high chance of **strong and regular winds**.

2) The energy of the wind turns the blades of the turbine, **converting wind energy** to **mechanical energy**, which is then converted to **electrical energy** by a **generator**.

3) **Large-scale wind power** involves **wind farms** that may have thousands of turbines. The electricity generated is fed into an **electrical grid** that **transports electricity** to consumers. Wind farms can be **offshore** (out at sea) or **onshore** (on land).

4) **Small-scale wind power** involves small turbines that might be connected to a grid but often just **supply one building**.

EXAMPLE

Denmark has been investing in wind power since the 1970s, establishing **wind farms** onshore and offshore. Families are offered **tax exemptions** for generating their **own electricity**, either by investing in community turbines or by buying their own. By 2004 over 150 000 households had joined this scheme. Denmark now produces **19.7%** of its **electricity from wind power**, the highest proportion in the world.

Disadvantages of wind energy:

1) Wind energy is **unpredictable**. The amount of electricity generated varies with wind strength.

2) **Large numbers of turbines** are needed to produce significant amounts of electricity, which takes up **lots of space**.

3) The **most appropriate places for turbines** are often **protected areas** of natural beauty.

4) Wind farms produce a constant humming **noise**, which some people living nearby don't like.

5) Turbines can **kill** or **injure birds** and **bats**.

2. Biomass is Material That's Burnt for Power or Used to Produce Biofuel

1) **Biomass** is material that **is** or was **recently living**.

2) It includes **wood**, **plants** and **animal waste**.

3) These materials can be **burnt** to release energy.

4) Biomass can also be **processed** to produce **biofuels**, which are then **burnt** to release energy.

5) A common way of producing biofuel is to **ferment sugar cane** to produce **alcohol**, which can then be burnt. **Methane** and **biogas** are also types of **biofuel** produced using fermentation.

6) Using biomass as an energy source can involve a lot of technology (if biofuels are being made), or very little (if biomass is being burnt directly). This means that biomass is a **suitable energy source** for a **wide range of countries**.

7) Biomass energy is released by **burning**, which produces **carbon dioxide**. Biomass **doesn't contribute to global warming** though, as the amount of **carbon released equals** the amount of **carbon taken in** when the material was growing. This means there's **no overall increase** in the amount of **carbon dioxide** in the **atmosphere** from the burning of biomass.

EXAMPLE

Brazil has been running an **ethanol fuel programme** since the 1970s. The ethanol is made by fermenting sugar cane, and any leftover cane is burnt for heating and power. Ethanol supplies **18%** of **transport fuel** and cars either run on **ethanol** or a **petrol and ethanol mix**. This has **decreased** Brazil's **dependence on imported oil**.

Disadvantages of biomass:

1) **Large areas of land** are needed to produce sufficient amounts of biofuels. This **reduces** the **area of land** available to grow **food crops**, which could lead to **food shortages**.

2) Biomass is only a renewable energy resource if it's **carefully managed** (see page 86).

3) **Fossil fuels** are often used to **process** and **transport** biomass.

Sustainable Energy

3. Solar Power Depends on Energy from the Sun

1) **Solar power** comes from the **sun** and can be used in lots of different ways.
2) **Solar water heaters** use **solar energy** to **heat water**, which is then pumped to a storage tank ready for use.
3) **Solar cookers** work by **concentrating sunlight**, converting it to **heat energy** and then trapping it for use in cooking.
4) **Photovoltaic (PV)** cells convert **light energy** into **electrical energy**, which is used in the home or exported to a grid.
5) **Materials** that **absorb** the sun's heat during the day and release it at night can be used to **keep houses warm**.

EXAMPLE

In the Chinese city **Rizhao**, **99%** of buildings have **solar water heaters** (it's now compulsory for new builds), over **6000 households** use **solar cookers** and most **traffic** and **street lights** are powered by **PV cells**.

Disadvantages of solar power:
1) **Carbon dioxide** is released in equipment production.
2) PV cells are **expensive**.
3) **Large areas** of solar panels and **sunny climates** are needed to produce **large amounts** of **electricity**.

4. Tidal Energy is a Reliable Source of Energy

1) **Tidal energy** comes from the movement of tides. It's **less variable** than wind or solar energy as tides are regular, unchangeable events. Tidal energy can be harnessed using **tidal barrages** or **tidal stream systems**.
2) **Tidal barrages** (dams) are built across **estuaries**. As the tide flows in and out water passes through gates in the barrage, turning **turbines** that **generate electricity**. Some turbines are only turned by outgoing tides, some by incoming as well.
3) **Tidal streams** are fast-flowing currents caused by the tide. They turn **turbines** placed in their pathway to **generate electricity**.

EXAMPLE

The **Rance estuary** tidal barrage in Northern **France** began operating in **1967**. It's the **largest** tidal power station in the world, producing enough **electricity** for over **19 000 homes**.

Disadvantages of tidal energy:
1) The equipment is **expensive** and making it releases **carbon dioxide**.
2) Barrages **disrupt ecosystems**, and turbines can **kill aquatic animals**.

5. Wave Energy is Created by Wind Blowing over Water

1) **Wave energy** is harnessed by using a **wave generator** — a chamber with a hole at the top that contains a **turbine**.
2) When a wave flows into the bottom of the chamber, the increased mass of water forces **air** in the chamber upwards and through the hole, which **turns the turbine**.
3) The turbine is connected to a **generator** that **produces electricity**.

EXAMPLE

In 2000 **LIMPET** in Scotland became the world's first device that used **wave energy** on a **commercial scale**. It **generates electricity** for the **national grid**.

Disadvantages of wave energy:
1) Wave energy is **unreliable**, as there aren't always waves.
2) The generators are **expensive** and making them releases **carbon dioxide** into the atmosphere.

6. Hydroelectric Power Uses the Energy of Falling Water

Hydroelectric power (HEP) supplies about **20%** of the world's electricity and is responsible for over 60% of all electricity from renewable sources. Once plants are built they **release no greenhouse gases**.

1) At HEP plants **dams** are built to **trap** large volumes of **water**. Tunnels containing **turbines** are built into the dams.
2) The **pressure of the water** above drives water through the tunnels, **turning the turbines**.
3) **Generators** then convert this energy into **electricity**.

EXAMPLE

The **Nurek Dam** in Tajikistan is the tallest dam in the world and has **nine hydroelectric turbines** in it. In 1994 it supplied **98%** of the country's **electricity**.

Disadvantages of HEP:
1) Creating reservoirs can mean **destruction** of **communities** and **habitats**.
2) If the **dam fails** then large areas of land are likely to be **flooded** rapidly.
3) **Ecosystems** and **fish migratory paths** are **disrupted**.
4) The plants are **expensive** and making them releases **carbon dioxide**.

Sustainable Energy

Keep going...

Appropriate Technology *is Technology That's* **Suitable** *for the* **Area**

1) **Appropriate technologies** are **simple**, **low-cost** technologies.
2) They're **made** and **maintained** using **local knowledge** and **resources** only, so aren't dependent on any outside support, expensive equipment or fuel.

Appropriate Technology *can* **Contribute** *to* **Sustainable Development**

1) Using appropriate technologies to produce energy **isn't always sustainable**, e.g. they could be dependent on local sources of non-renewable energy.
2) Some **appropriate technologies** do produce energy from **renewable sources** though, so it's **sustainable**. Producing energy in a sustainable way contributes to **sustainable development** — growth in a way that doesn't stop future generations getting what they need (i.e. by not depleting resources or permanently damaging the environment).

Example	In mountainous regions of developing countries **clay stoves** have been introduced as an **appropriate technology** that makes **energy use** for **cooking and heating more sustainable**.

1) In **high altitude** areas of **developing countries** many indigenous people rely on **burning biomass** on **open fires** as their main **energy source**.
2) Fuel is usually **straw, crop roots** and **pasture grass**. One family can burn up to 6000 kg a year.
3) At high altitudes the temperature is lower and **plants grow more slowly**, which often means **crops** are **removed faster than they can be replenished**.
4) As energy supplies are depleted there are fewer plant roots in the soil to support it. This causes **soil erosion** and a **decrease** in soil **productivity**.
5) **Burning biomass in this way** is therefore **unsustainable**.

Clay stoves are **more efficient** than open fires and can lead to a **75% reduction in fuel consumption**. This means fuel is **harvested more slowly**, allowing the **crops** to **replenish** themselves. This leads to decreased soil erosion and increased soil productivity. Using a stove rather than an open fire also has **health benefits**, as the smoke from open fires can cause eye and lung diseases.

Clay stoves are an **appropriate technology** as they can be made by **local** craftsmen from metal and clay, providing a source of income for local people. They **reduce** the quantity of **biomass burnt** and therefore help to maintain the **natural cycle of replenishment**. This makes the resource **renewable** (see page 86) and therefore **sustainable**. So, they contribute to sustainable development.

Energy Conservation *is* **Important** *for* **Sustainable Supply**

Energy supply can be made **more sustainable** by **conserving** as much **energy** as possible. By **reducing overall use of energy** fewer resources are used up and the **environmental effects** of energy use are **limited**, e.g. emission of greenhouse gases. **Homes, workplaces** and **transport** can all be **designed** to **conserve energy**:

Buildings *can be made* **more sustainable...**

Energy can be **conserved** in **homes** and **workplaces** in several ways:

1) **Reducing** the amount of energy needed for **heating** by installing **double glazing, draught-proofing, loft insulation** and **cavity wall insulation** to **reduce heat loss**.
2) **Installing energy-efficient boilers**. They're more efficient because a greater proportion of the heat energy they generate is used to heat the water in the boiler and **less energy** is **lost** to the surroundings.
3) Using computers, printers and faxes that **turn themselves off** after a period of time instead of staying on (stand-by mode can consume nearly as much energy as being turned on permanently).
4) Building in **features** that help **absorb** and **retain** the **sun's energy** (e.g. **large south-facing windows**) to provide **heat** as well as **light**.

Iain understood the importance of insulation but this was a step too far. He looked like a fool and he knew it.

Sustainable Energy

5) Using **energy-saving appliances** wherever possible, e.g. **energy-saving light bulbs**.

Example

The **City of Calgary Water Centre** in Canada was designed to conserve energy. Lots of **south-facing windows** let natural light reach all areas, which **reduces the need** for **electric lighting**. The electric lights only come on when they're needed as they're controlled by **light** and **motion sensors**. The **windows** and the **shape** of the building help to **warm the building** in winter, **reducing the need** for **heating**. An **overhanging roof** keeps the heat out in summer so **less energy** is **needed** for **air-conditioning**. A **radiant ceiling slab cooling system** has been built in to **reduce the need for air-conditioning** further. This system draws cold night air through pipes set into concrete, cooling it down. The cooled concrete helps to keep the building cold throughout the next day. These methods have **reduced** annual **energy consumption** by **58%**.

...and so can *Transport*

Energy can be conserved in **transport** by:

1) Changing to **vehicles that don't need any fuel**, e.g. **bicycles**. Employers receive tax exemptions for loaning or selling bicycles to employees as part of the **Cycle to Work** scheme. This encourages people to switch cars for more sustainable bicycles.

2) Establishing out-of-town **park-and-ride schemes** and **investing in public transport**. This **reduces fuel consumption** by reducing the number of vehicles on the road.

3) Introducing **congestion charges**. This **encourages public transport use** and is used in London, Singapore, Rome and Stockholm.

Example

The **London congestion charge** was **introduced in 2003**. It charges drivers for entering a central zone of the city during normal working hours. It aims to reduce congestion and raise money for public transport improvements. Since the scheme started the **number of vehicles** within the zone has **decreased** by **21%** (70 000 fewer cars each day) and **carbon dioxide emissions** have **decreased** by **20%**. In 2007/2008 **£137 million** was raised, which was **invested in public transport**. **Bicycle use** has **increased** by **12%** since 2003, and use of **public buses** has **increased** by **6%**. There's been an **increase in congestion** in the area **surrounding the central zone** though and some small businesses within the zone (e.g. shops and restaurants) claim that the charge has **reduced trade**.

Transport can also be made more sustainable by using **technologies** that run off **sustainable energy sources**:

- **Hydrogen fuel cell buses** run on electricity produced from **hydrogen**. The hydrogen that fuels the bus is **made from water**. The process **uses electricity**. So, for hydrogen fuel cells to be sustainable this initial electricity must be produced from **renewable resources**.

- **Electric buses**, e.g. the **Islay Wave Bus** runs off **wave power generated electricity** from LIMPET (see page 93).

- Using **hybrid fuel vehicles** (vehicles that run off a mixture of two fuels). If one fuel is from a **renewable** source then the vehicle is **more sustainable**, e.g. use of **ethanol-petrol hybrid fuel cars** in Brazil (see page 92).

Practice Questions

Q1 How is wind energy harnessed?
Q2 Give three examples of biomass.
Q3 What are the disadvantages of solar power?
Q4 What does HEP stand for?
Q5 What are appropriate technologies?

Exam Questions

Q1	Explain what biomass is and how it's used as an energy source.	[4 marks]
Q2	Compare wave energy and tidal energy.	[6 marks]
Q3	Explain how energy use in the home can be made more sustainable.	[8 marks]
Q4	Describe and explain how transport can be made more sustainable.	[10 marks]

Brain chargers and memory plugs — now they're appropriate technologies...

Well done — you made it. I know there's loads to learn here and I'm guessing you're not too happy about it, but I've not put it in for the good of my health (you do need to know all about sustainable energy for the exam). Don't forget to learn the examples as well — the examiners will expect you to be able to spew some up for any questions they ask on this topic. They're evil like that.

Managing Energy — Case Studies

So, you know the different sources and impacts of energy, you're crammed full of interesting facts and impressive knowledge. You just need to make a tiny bit of space in that grey blob for these case studies...

Chad has Very Low Energy Consumption per Person

Chad is a **developing country** in **North Africa**. It's very **unstable politically** and is one of the **poorest** and **most corrupt countries** in the world. Despite having **large reserves of oil**, annual **energy consumption** is very **low** at only **0.005 tonnes of oil equivalent** per person (average consumption in the EU is 3.8 tonnes). **80%** of the **population** live **below** the **poverty line**.

Chad's Main Energy Resources are Oil and Biomass

Chad is an oil exporter...

1) Chad has **large reserves of oil**.

2) **TNCs** like ExxonMobil, Chevron and Petronas began **exploiting the oil** in 2003.

3) It's **exported** via a **pipeline through Cameroon** to the Atlantic coast. The pipeline was **part funded** by the **World Bank** on the condition that **80% of the revenue** from the oil was **spent on projects to reduce poverty**.

4) The Chadian government **didn't keep to this agreement**.

5) So although oil is an **important source of income** for Chad and **could** help **improve economic** and **social conditions** for Chadians, the **corruption** and **political instability** in the country at the moment mean that **it doesn't**.

...and also an oil importer

1) Chad **can't use its own oil** because it doesn't have any way of **refining** it.

2) Instead, it has to **rely on imports** of refined oil from **Cameroon** and **Nigeria** to supply its only major power station.

3) The cost of doing this means that the **electricity** generated is **very expensive**, and most Chadians **can't afford it** (only 2% of the population have access to electricity).

4) Also, **delivery problems** caused by the **poor transport system** can lead to **shortages**.

5) So importing oil is **expensive**, **unreliable** and **doesn't support** the **energy needs** of most of the population.

Most Energy is supplied by Biomass

90% of Chad's **total energy** and **98%** of **household energy** is supplied by **wood**. There's no control over wood production or use, so it's **overexploited**. In 1998 the **World Bank** and the **Chadian government** jointly funded the **Household Energy Project** to address this problem by:

1) Using **non-governmental organisations (NGOs)** to **educate** local people about the **need for conservation**.

2) Setting up **village resource management schemes** that **limit** the amount of **wood cut down**. This can involve **charging** people for **collecting wood**.

3) **Giving villages ownership** of the local **resources**. This allows them to **make money** from wood, so makes it a **more valuable resource** to them and **worth conserving**.

4) **Improving energy use in homes** by introducing **more efficient cooking stoves** that use less fuel than open fires (see page 94).

The Household Energy Project **only operates on a small scale** at the moment though (about 100 villages near the capital city).

1) At the moment Chad's **energy supply isn't sustainable**.

2) Chad's oil policy doesn't help it meet its energy needs, and as oil is **non-renewable** it's **unsustainable** anyway.

3) Most energy is provided by **biomass**, which has the **potential to be sustainable** if it's **managed properly**.

4) The **Household Energy Project** could help to make the supply of biomass sustainable but **needs to be implemented more widely**, which takes time and money.

5) There is the potential to do this using money from exporting oil, but political corruption and instability could be a barrier to this.

Practice Questions

Q1 What are Chad's main energy resources?

Q2 Why does Chad have to import oil?

Exam Question

Q1 Discuss the potential for Chad's energy supply to become sustainable. [15 marks]

Managing Energy — Case Studies

Norway has High Energy Consumption per Person

Norway is a **wealthy, developed country** in **Northern Europe**. **Energy consumption** is **high** in Norway, at **6.2 tonnes of oil equivalent** per person, and **electricity consumption** per person is the **highest in the world**. It has **large reserves of oil** and **gas** (located under the North Sea) and utilises its **high potential for hydroelectricity**, with **99%** of **electricity** being generated from hydroelectric plants. Overall, **39%** of its **energy** comes from **fossil fuels** and **61%** from **renewables**.

Norway's Main Energy Resources are Oil, Gas and Hydroelectricity

Norway is an oil and gas exporter

1) Norway is the **5th largest exporter of oil** and the **3rd largest exporter of gas** in the world.

2) These **fossil fuels** are an **important source of income** for the country, with oil alone providing about **25%** of **GDP**.

3) Despite being oil-rich, Norwegian **fuel prices** are among the **highest in Europe** due to **high taxation**. This fits in with Norway's energy policy of increasing the proportion of their energy supply that comes from renewable sources by **discouraging** the **use of oil**.

4) Almost **all** of Norway's **gas** supplies are **exported** as it's not used much domestically.

5) So, like Chad, Norway **exports most of its fossil fuel** resources, but for different reasons. Chad needs the income from exports and can't exploit the resources itself, whereas Norway **chooses to use other sources of energy** and actively discourages the use of oil.

Most electricity is supplied by hydropower

1) With **natural lakes** at **high altitudes** and **lots of rain** Norway is able to generate **99%** of its **electricity** and **50%** of its **total energy** from **HEP**.

2) This makes it the **6th largest producer** of hydropower in the world and the **largest in Europe**.

3) As many lakes are natural the plants have **less impact on the environment** than **artificially created** reservoirs.

4) Whilst Chad's main source of energy (biomass) has the potential to be renewable if it's managed carefully, **Norway's main source** (hydropower) **is renewable** by nature, and is therefore **sustainable**.

Norway is investing in renewable energy

1) One of Norway's energy aims is to **reduce its dependency** on **hydroelectric power** by using a **wider range** of **renewable resources**.

2) This is needed to cope with any future rise in energy consumption, as **almost all potential HEP sites** have been **exploited**.

3) **€2.5 billion** was invested in **developing renewable energy** and **energy efficiency** in **2006**. One of the main projects is to **triple wind power capacity**.

4) Research into **solar power** aims to **increase the percentage** of the Sun's energy that can be converted **into electricity** from **17%** to **50%**.

5) The state also provides **funding** for companies to **research and develop biofuels** to use for transport instead of oil, e.g. producing biodiesel from salmon waste.

6) As a **wealthy nation** (unlike Chad), Norway is able to **invest in research** in order to develop a **sustainable energy supply**.

1) Norway is **energy-rich** so doesn't have to worry about **energy security** in the short term.

2) It can concentrate on developing a **long-term sustainable energy supply**.

3) **Some aspects are already sustainable**, e.g. using hydropower for electricity generation, but **others aren't**, e.g. relying on oil for transport.

4) Policies such as **investing in energy efficiency** and **renewables**, and putting **high taxes on oil**, **promote sustainability**.

5) The **political stability** and **wealth** of the country allow it to pursue **energy sustainability**.

Practice Questions

Q1   What are Norway's main energy resources?

Q2   Why is Norway particularly suited to using hydroelectric power?

Exam Question

Q1   Describe how Norway's energy supply is becoming more sustainable.   [15 marks]

My energy resources are running a bit low after all that...

So that's energy done. Learn these two pages and you'll be all set for the exam. As long as you can still remember the other pages that is... You might want to look back over them to check... well OK, you might not want to but you should do it anyway.

Global Patterns of Health, Disease and Death

This section's all about global health issues. Where you live in the world affects your health in many different ways.

Health is Better in Wealthier Countries

1) **Health** is defined as your **physical**, **mental** and **social well-being**, and the **absence of disease**.

2) Health **varies** between different parts of the world.

3) Health is **difficult** to **measure**, which makes it pretty difficult to **compare** the health of people in two places. There are things you **can measure** that **indicate health** though (they're called health indicators... imaginative).

4) An example of a health indicator is **healthy life expectancy** (**HLE**) — this is the **number** of **years** a newborn child can **expect** to **live** in **full health** without major disease. The **global pattern** of HLE is shown on the map below:

Global pattern of healthy life expectancy (2002)

Units = years

No data
29 to 38.2
38.2 to 47.4
47.4 to 56.6
56.6 to 65.8
65.8 to 75

- The map shows **HLE** is **highest** in **wealthier countries** such as the **UK**, **USA** and **Australia**.
- **HLE** is **lowest** in **poorer countries** such as those in **sub-Saharan Africa**.

Sub-Saharan Africa includes all the countries south of the Sahara Desert.

5) How **healthy** a country is **depends** on how much **disease** there is in the country, and what **types** of **diseases** there are.

Global Morbidity Patterns are Different Depending on the Type of Disease

1) **Morbidity** means **illness**.

2) Morbidity **indicators** include:
   - **prevalence** — the **total** number of **cases** in a **population** at a **particular time**.
   - **incidence** — the number of **new cases** in a **population** during a **particular time period**.

3) You can use these indicators to **compare global patterns of illness**.

4) **Global patterns** of morbidity **differ** depending on the **type** of **disease** you're looking at:

   - **Infectious diseases** (e.g. malaria, HIV/AIDS) — these are often **more common** in **poorer countries**.
   - **Non-communicable diseases** (e.g. cancer, heart disease) — these are often **more common** in **wealthier countries**.

'Non-communicable' means the disease can't be caught from someone else.

① Morbidity pattern of infectious diseases

- The map shows the **global morbidity pattern** of the **infectious** disease **tuberculosis** (**TB**).
- There's **high TB morbidity** in **poorer** countries, e.g. countries in **sub-Saharan Africa**.
- There's **low TB morbidity** in **wealthier** countries, e.g. the **UK**, **USA** and **Australia**.

Global morbidity pattern of tuberculosis (TB) (2005)

Units = new cases per 100 000 of the population

No data
0 to 24
25 to 49
50 to 99
100 to 299
>300

The **reasons** for **high infectious disease morbidity** in **poorer** countries include:

1) **Malnutrition** (due to **poor food availability** and **periodic famines**) — **reduces** the body's **ability** to **fight** disease.

2) **Lack** of **clean water** and **sanitation** — **increases** the **spread** of **infectious** diseases.

3) **Overcrowded** conditions in **urban** areas — **increases** the **spread** of **infectious** diseases.

4) **Poor access** to **health care** — people **can't** access drugs to **treat** and **prevent** infectious diseases.

5) **Limited health education** — people **aren't well-informed** about how they can **avoid** infectious diseases.

6) **Disease vectors** (organisms that spread disease) — these are often **more common** in poorer countries, e.g. the **mosquitoes** that spread **malaria** are more common in **tropical** regions of **Africa**.

Global Patterns of Health, Disease and Death

② Morbidity pattern of non-communicable diseases

- The map shows the **global morbidity pattern** of the **non-communicable** disease **breast cancer**.
- There's **high breast cancer morbidity** in **wealthier** countries, e.g. the **UK**, **USA** and **Australia**.
- There's **low breast cancer morbidity** in **poorer** countries, e.g. countries in **Africa** and **Asia**.

The **reasons** for **high non-communicable disease morbidity** in **wealthier** countries include:

1) **Higher proportion** of **older people** (due to higher life expectancy) — if there are more old people **more** people are **likely** to suffer from **diseases** associated with **old age**, e.g. **cancer** and **heart disease**.

2) **Unhealthy lifestyle** — the **risk** of getting **some diseases** (e.g. cancer, heart disease) **increases** if you're **overweight** or **obese**, eat **unhealthy food** and don't do enough **exercise**. These **factors** are **more common** in **wealthier** countries.

Global morbidity pattern of breast cancer (2003)

Units = cases per 100 000 of the population

- ☐ No data
- ☐ <19.3
- ☐ 19.3 to <26.1
- ☐ 26.1 to <36.0
- ☐ 36.0 to <54.2
- ■ 54.2 to <91.6

Mortality Patterns Depend on Morbidity and the Ability to Treat Morbidity

1) **Mortality** means **death**. In general, **high morbidity** causes **high mortality**.

2) The **mortality rate** is how many people **die** in a **population** over a **period of time**. You use mortality rates to **compare global patterns of death**.

- The table on the right shows that **wealthier** areas, such as **Northern America** and **Australia**, have a **high mortality** rate for **cancer** (caused by a **high incidence** of the disease). But only a **low percentage** of **cases** result in **death**.
- The **mortality rate** from **cancer** is **lower** in **poorer** areas, such as **Middle** and **Eastern Africa** (caused by a **low incidence** of the disease), but the **percentage** of cases **resulting in death** is **much higher**.

The **risk** of **dying** from a disease is **much higher** in **poorer countries** because of:

1) **Malnutrition** — **reduces** the body's **ability** to **fight** disease.

2) **Poor access** to **health care** — people **can't access** the drugs they need to **treat** the disease.

Global incidence and mortality rates from all forms of cancer (2002)

Area of the world	Incidence rate (cases per 100 000)	Mortality rate (deaths per 100 000)	% of cases resulting in death
Middle Africa	125	105	83
Eastern Africa	152	123	81
Northern Africa	87	70	80
Southern Africa	174	122	70
Central America	144	89	62
Northern America	331	125	38
Northern Europe	252	132	52
Southern Europe	237	122	51
Western Europe	267	131	49
Australia/ New Zealand	299	120	40

Health and Disease are World Issues

1) **Infectious diseases** can **spread** to **other countries** and can even **spread** around the **world** (e.g. **HIV/AIDS** now **affects** people in **all countries**).

2) This means **countries** need to **work together** to help **improve global health** and **prevent diseases spreading**.

3) **Organisations** like the **WHO (World Health Organisation) work** with **most governments** and in **most countries** to help **eradicate** and **prevent disease**. For example, they run a **programme** of **vaccinations** (**paid** for by **wealthy** countries) to **eradicate polio** (an **infectious disease** mainly found in **poorer countries**).

Practice Questions

Q1 Define health.

Q2 Give an example of how you can measure health.

Q3 What is morbidity?

Exam Question

Q1 Measles is an infectious disease spread by close contact. Use the map to outline the global pattern of measles morbidity. [10 marks]

Global measles morbidity in 2003

Units = incidence per 100 000 of the population

- ☐ No data
- ☐ <1
- ☐ 1 to <5
- ☐ 5 to <10
- ■ 10 to <50
- ■ ≥50

Disease — it's morbid stuff...

This isn't the cheeriest of sections, I know, but that doesn't mean you can get away with not learning it. Sorry. It doesn't help when they make morbidity and mortality such similar words but with different meanings — that's just asking for trouble. So just remember — morbidity means illness and mortality means death. So what are you waiting for, get on and learn it...

Health Care Approaches

Poor health affects millions of people, both rich and poor. There are lots of ideas for how to improve health, but no easy fix...

Lack of Money Makes it Difficult to Improve Health in Poorer Countries

Health in **poorer countries** isn't great, mainly because **infectious diseases** are **common** and **spread easily** (because of issues like **lack** of **clean water** and **poor sanitation**). Helping people become healthier isn't easy — the **key barriers** to improving health include a **lack of money** to provide **effective health care** and **difficulties** in getting health care to **remote populations**.

Health Care in Poorer Countries Focuses on Treating Disease

1) In **poorer** countries the **national income** is **low**, so **spending** on **health** tends to be **low** too.

2) A **large proportion** of the **money** that's available for health care is often spent on **treating** large numbers of patients with **diseases**. This leaves **little money** available for **preventative care** (like **vaccinations**) and **health education**.

3) **Preventing disease** is often a **more effective** way to **improve health** than just treating disease.

4) Some poorer countries **rely heavily** on **foreign aid** to help with **health care**, e.g. grants and loans, donated medicines and medical equipment, and volunteer doctors and nurses.

5) **Foreign aid** can help poorer countries **improve health care services** in the short-term, but **longer-term solutions** are needed so countries can become **self-reliant**.

Local Health Care Training Can Improve Health in Remote Populations

1) A **key health care issue** in poorer countries is the **lack** of **medical services** in **remote rural populations**.

2) One solution is to **train local people** in **basic health care** and **employ** them to provide basic health care **services** to their **local communities**. Services include **first aid**, **treating common diseases**, providing **medicines** and **vaccinations**, **pregnancy support** and **midwifery**, and **health education**.

3) There are **advantages** and **disadvantages** to training local basic health care workers:

Advantages
1) It's a relatively **inexpensive** way of **improving health care** and **health education** in **rural** areas.
2) It **creates jobs** for **local** people.
3) It **increases** the **self-reliance** of communities.
4) Local basic health care workers are **unlikely** to **leave** (professionals, e.g. doctors, often migrate to wealthier countries where pay is better).

Disadvantage
Basic health care workers **can't replace** fully trained **medical professionals**. So **long-term solutions** must improve access to **proper medical facilities** and **fully trained staff**.

Case Study: Local Health Care Workers in Ethiopia

ETHIOPIA

Problem
Ethiopia, in Eastern Africa, is one of the world's **poorest** countries. There's widespread **poor health**, e.g. **life expectancy** is only **52 years** and **infant mortality** is around **8%**. People have **poor nutrition**, **poor sanitation** and **unclean water**. **Infectious diseases** are very common. There's a **shortage** of **medical professionals** and **health facilities**, especially in **remote rural** areas — in some places there are only **three doctors** per **100 000 people**.

Solutions

1) Ethiopia's government receives **foreign aid** to improve **health**, **sanitation** and access to **clean water**. Some of the money's spent on **preventative health care** such as **vaccinations** and **contraceptives**.

2) Foreign aid funds the **Health Extension Programme**, which **trains local health care workers** in **rural** areas. Workers deliver **basic health care** (vaccinations, malaria treatments and maternity care) and **health education** (teaching about family planning, prevention of HIV/AIDS, hygiene and nutrition). But **more** health workers are **still needed** by many communities.

3) **Money** is being used to **prevent disease**. E.g. since 2005, millions of **insecticide-treated bed nets** have been given out — a **cost-effective** way of **preventing** the spread of **malaria** by **mosquitoes**. In **one year**, the number of new **malaria** cases **fell** by **20%**.

Health Care Approaches

Ignoring Advice Makes it Difficult to Improve Health in Wealthier Countries

1) **Health** in **wealthier countries** isn't that good either, partly because of **ageing populations**. This is when there's a **higher proportion** of **older people** in the population — often due to a **high life expectancy** and **low birth rate**.

2) **More people** suffer from **age-related illnesses**, such as cancer and heart disease. This can put a **big strain** on **health services**.

3) **Lifestyle choices** also affect health. Choosing to **eat healthily**, **exercise**, **not smoke** and **reduce alcohol** consumption can **improve** your **health**.

4) The **key barrier** to improving health in **wealthier** countries is people **ignoring advice** on **lifestyle changes** that would **reduce** their chance of **developing disease**.

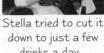

Stella tried to cut it down to just a few drinks a day...

Health Care in Wealthier Countries Includes Preventing Disease

In **wealthier** countries a great deal of **money** is spent on **preventative health care**, such as:

1) Providing **vaccinations against diseases** (e.g. measles, mumps, meningitis).

2) **Health awareness campaigns** to **promote good lifestyle choices** (e.g. eating healthily and taking regular exercise).

3) **Providing support services** to help people **improve** their **health** (e.g. services to help people stop smoking).

4) **Early diagnosis** (e.g. cancer screening, antenatal screening and screening for heart conditions).

Case Study: Preventing Cervical Cancer in England

| Problem | Nearly **3000 women** are diagnosed with **cervical cancer** each year in **England**, which can cause **death** if left **untreated**. **99%** of all **cervical cancers** are **caused** by a virus called **HPV** (human papillomavirus). |

| Solutions | 1) | Some forms of cervical cancer are **preventable** by **stopping infection** with **HPV**. An **HPV vaccine** is now offered to **all girls** aged **12-13** in **England**. |

| | 2) | **Cervical screening** (a **smear test**) is offered to **all women over 25** in **England**. **Unusual cells** (signs of cancer) can be **detected early**, allowing **treatment** to **prevent cancer**. **Death rates** from cervical cancer have **decreased** by nearly **70% since screening** began. |

Practice Questions

Q1 What are the main barriers to improving health in poorer countries?

Q2 What are the advantages of training local people in basic health care in rural areas of poorer countries?

Q3 Why does an ageing population contribute to a country's poor health?

Q4 Give four examples of preventative health care that wealthier countries spend money on.

Exam Question

Q1 The graph shows global differences in public health spending per person.

a) Describe the pattern of public health spending shown by the graph. [2 marks]

b) The amount of money available for public health services can affect the health care approach countries use. With reference to one or more schemes, describe the contrasting health care approaches used in wealthy and poor countries. [10 marks]

Annual spending on public health services per person (US$): 2000, 1600, 1200, 800, 400, 0 — Central Africa, South-eastern Africa, Northern Africa, Southern Asia, Asia Pacific, Middle East, Eastern Asia, South America, Eastern Europe, North America, Western Europe, Japan

Prevention is the best cure — or so my mum says...

It's not easy to improve the health of populations, in poor or rich countries — you can't just throw money at people. Well, you can, but that'll only help in the short-term. Long-term solutions need to tackle ways of preventing diseases. It's vital that people are educated — this helps people to help themselves. Whether they'll listen or not is another matter...

The Geography of Disease

Different diseases affect different countries — but they all have a big impact...

Diseases Affect Health, Economic Development and Lifestyle

The **cost** of a **disease** to any country includes the following:

HEALTH	**Increased poor health** in the population and in some cases **permanent disability** and **death**.
ECONOMIC DEVELOPMENT	**Slow economic development** due to **increasing death rates** (so **fewer taxes** go to the government), **decreasing productivity** (due to **days lost** from **work**) and **increasing health care costs**.
LIFESTYLE	**Increased poverty** (due to **days lost** from **work** and **health care costs**), **impaired learning** (due to **days lost** at **school**) and a **downward spiral** as the poorest families are **trapped in poverty**.

Malaria is Common in Tropical Regions such as Sub-Saharan Africa

1) Malaria is an **infectious disease** caused by **parasites**, which are transmitted by **mosquitoes**.

2) Malaria can be **cured** with **anti-malarial drugs**, but **without treatment** it can quickly become **life-threatening**.

3) Malaria can be **prevented** by using **bed nets** and **insecticides** (which kill the mosquitoes that carry the disease).

Distribution of malaria CASES

Most **cases** of **malaria** are found in **tropical** areas, e.g. **sub-Saharan Africa**. In **2006** there were nearly **250 million global cases** of malaria and **86%** occurred in the **poorest** countries in **Africa**. **Reasons** include:

- **Climate** — **mosquitoes** that carry **malaria** can only **survive** in **warm countries** like those in **Africa**.

- **Limited health education** — people **aren't informed** about how to **avoid malaria** (e.g. by using **bed nets**).

- **Poor health care** — people with malaria are **less likely** to be **treated**. This means there are **more infected people** and so **more sources** of the **parasite** for mosquitoes to pick up and transmit.

Distribution of malaria DEATHS

In **2006**, **91%** of **global deaths** from **malaria** were in **sub-Saharan Africa**. **Reasons** include:

- **High number** of **cases**.

- **Poor health care** — **anti-malarial drugs aren't affordable** or **available**, especially to people living in **remote rural populations**.

- **Poor health** and **nutrition** — reduces the body's **ability** to **fight infections**.

HIV/AIDS is Very Common Across Africa but Quite Common Elsewhere

1) **HIV** (Human Immunodeficiency Virus) is a virus that **destroys** the **immune system**. It eventually causes **AIDS** (Acquired Immunodeficiency Syndrome), which causes **death**.

2) HIV is transmitted by **sexual contact**, **sharing needles**, **blood transfusions** and **contaminated medical equipment**.

3) There's **no cure** for AIDS but you can **slow** the **development** of **HIV to AIDS** by using **antiviral drugs**. HIV can be **prevented** by practising **safe sex**, **screening blood donors** and by using **sterile medical equipment**.

Distribution of HIV/AIDS CASES

66% of the **population** (and **90%** of **children**) living with **HIV/AIDS** are in **sub-Saharan Africa**. **Reasons** include:

- **Society** — people are more **reluctant** to get **tested** for **HIV/AIDS**.

- **Gender inequality** — in some African countries men are **socially dominant**, which makes **women** less likely to insist on **condom** use, and so they're **more vulnerable** to **HIV/AIDS**.

- **Limited health** and **sex education** — people **aren't aware** of what HIV is and **aren't informed** of how they can **avoid it** (e.g. by using **condoms** and **sterile medical equipment**).

- **Limited health care** — people with HIV/AIDS are **less likely** to be **diagnosed**, so they're more likely to **pass on** the disease.

HIV infection in adults (2005)

- No data
- <0.1%
- 0.1-<0.5%
- 0.5-<1%
- 1-<5%
- 5-34%

Distribution of HIV/AIDS DEATHS

Over **70%** of **global deaths** from **HIV/AIDS** occur in **sub-Saharan Africa**. **Reasons** include:

- **High number** of **cases**.

- **Poor health care** — **antiviral drugs** that prolong life **aren't affordable** or **available**.

- **Poor health**, **nutrition** and **hygiene** — **increase** the **risk** of other **infections** that can be **fatal** because HIV **destroys** the **immune system**.

The Geography of Disease

Coronary Heart Disease is Becoming More Common in Poorer Countries

1) **Coronary heart disease** (**CHD**) is a disease where the heart doesn't get enough blood. It can lead to a **heart attack**.

2) **CHD** has **no cure** but it can be **controlled** with **treatment** (e.g. **aspirin**, or **surgery** such as a heart bypass operation). **Early diagnosis** and access to **health care** can **increase life expectancy**.

3) The **risk** of developing CHD can be **reduced** by **lifestyle changes** such as **eating healthily**, **exercising** and **not smoking**.

Distribution of CHD CASES

CHD is a **non-communicable disease** — it's **more common** in **wealthier** countries, e.g. the **UK** and the **USA**. **Reasons** include:

- **Ageing populations** — your **risk** of developing CHD **increases** as you get **older**.
- **Lifestyle factors** — an **unhealthy lifestyle** and being **obese** or **overweight increases** your **risk** of developing CHD.

Cases of CHD are **increasing** in **poor** and **newly-industrialised countries** though (e.g. countries in **sub-Saharan Africa** and **India**), as their **wealth increases**. **Reasons** include:

- **Increasing life expectancy** — **more people** suffer from **CHD** because of **ageing populations**.
- **Social**, **economic** and **cultural changes** — people are adopting **Western diets** and **lifestyles**, e.g. smoking.

Distribution of CHD DEATHS

CHD is one of the **world's biggest killers**. It caused **14%** of **global deaths** in **1997**. Over **80%** of deaths occur in **poor** and **newly-industrialised** areas, e.g. **sub-Saharan Africa** and **India**. **Reasons** include:

- **Poor health care** — **treatments** (e.g. **surgery**) **aren't affordable** or **available**.
- **Limited health education** — people **aren't aware** of the **effects** of **lifestyle changes** (e.g. **smoking** and **eating fatty foods**).

Death rates are **falling** in **wealthier** countries though, because of **improvements** in **diagnosing** people **at risk** of CHD, developing **effective treatments**, and **awareness campaigns** to **prevent** the disease.

Cancer is Becoming More Common in Poorer Countries

CHD and cancer are non-communicable diseases, see p. 98.

1) **Cancer** is the **uncontrollable growth** and **spread** of **abnormal cells** in the body.

2) If **detected early** enough, many cancers can be **cured** or **controlled** with **treatment** (e.g. surgery). Many cancers are **detected early** through **awareness** of **symptoms** and **regular screening**, e.g. detecting breast cancer lumps.

3) The **risk** of getting cancer can be **reduced** with **lifestyle changes**, such as **eating healthily**, **exercising more** and **not smoking**. Some forms of **cervical cancer** can be **prevented** by having a **vaccination**.

Distribution of cancer CASES

Cancer is another **non-communicable disease** — it's **more common** in **wealthier** countries, e.g. the **UK** and USA. The **most common** types are **prostate**, **breast** and **colon cancer**. **Reasons** include: →

- **Ageing populations**.
- **Lifestyle factors**.

Cancer is becoming **increasingly common** in poor and newly-industrialised countries — especially **liver**, **stomach** and **cervical cancer**. **Reasons** include:

- **Increasing life expectancy**.
- **Social**, **economic** and **cultural changes** (adoption of a more **Western lifestyle**).

Distribution of cancer DEATHS

Cancer is the **world's second biggest killer**, causing **13%** of **deaths** in **2007**. **75%** of those **deaths** were in **poor** and **newly-industrialised** countries. **Reasons** include:

- **Poor health care**.
- **Limited health education**.

Death rates are **falling** in **wealthier** countries though, because of **improvements** in **diagnosis**, **treatment** and **awareness**.

Practice Questions

Q1 Describe the impact of disease on economic development.

Q2 What measures can help prevent the spread of HIV/AIDS?

Q3 Describe the global distribution of coronary heart disease.

Exam Question

Q1 Describe and explain the reasons for the global distribution of malaria and discuss its impact.   [10 marks]

Diseases affect the poor and wealthy — but death rates are very uneven...

Irritatingly, any one of these diseases could come up in your exam, so I'm afraid you have to learn them all.
But hey — at least some of the points are similar for the examples of poor and wealthy diseases...

Health and Globalisation

The distribution of disease is affected by some companies, which sounds a bit weird, but it's true (Scout's honour).
A lot of these companies now operate at a global level (globalisation) so they have an impact on global health —
in both good and bad ways...

Trans-National Corporations can Improve Health or Add to Health Problems

Trans-National corporations (TNCs) are companies that operate in **more than one country**. Some TNCs are **very large**, with **huge budgets** and **powerful political influence**. TNCs affect global health by their **actions**:

1) How they **treat employees** — the **wages** they **pay**, their **safety standards** and the **health care** they provide.

   > **Example** | **Namdeb diamond corporation** runs an **HIV/AIDS awareness programme** in **Namibia** and provides its **HIV-positive employees** with **drug treatment**.

2) How they **market products** — such as **tobacco, fatty foods** and **breast milk substitutes**.

   > **Example** | There are **concerns** that aiming **fast-food advertising** at **children** may **contribute** to long-term **unhealthy eating** choices and **obesity**.

3) How they **sell products** (such as **tobacco, medical drugs** and **medical supplies**) and **how much they charge** for them.

   > **Example** | Many **African** countries have to **rely** on the **generosity** of **overseas governments** and **pharmaceutical companies** to **subsidise drugs** because they **can't afford them**.

4) Which **products** they choose to **research and develop** — such as **healthy foods** and **medicines**.

   > **Example** | **Kraft Foods** are **developing** a **new food** that **kills intestinal worms**. It's aimed at **rural** Africa, Asia and South America, where **intestinal worms** are a **big health problem**.

Pharmaceutical Companies Affect Global Health

Pharmaceutical companies **research, develop, produce** and **distribute drugs** to treat disease.
They affect **world health** because they can choose **which drugs** to develop and what **prices** to charge.

Research and Production

1) There's **more money** in **wealthier countries** so pharmaceutical companies often choose to **research and produce** drugs for diseases that **mainly** affect wealthier countries (e.g. drugs for impotency). This leads to **improved health** in **wealthier countries**.

2) Some pharmaceutical companies use the **profits** they make in wealthier countries to **subsidise research** into diseases that affect **poorer countries** (e.g. malaria vaccines). This leads to **improved health** in **poorer countries**.

Distribution and Sales

1) Drugs cost **a lot of money** to research and develop, which companies get back from the **sale** of their drugs.

2) Pharmaceutical companies have **exclusive rights** for **20 years** to produce new drugs they've developed. This means they can set **any price** for them because you can't get them **anywhere else**.

3) This affects **global health** because some **poorer countries** may not be able to **afford** the drugs they need.

4) Some pharmaceutical companies, often through **deals** with wealthier countries, provide **free or cheaper drugs** for poorer countries (e.g. anti-HIV drugs).

Case Study: GlaxoSmithKline (GSK)

GSK is one of the **world's largest pharmaceutical companies**.
It **produces** many different **drugs** and **health products**.

Research and Production

1) GSK produces almost **four billion** packs of **medicines** and health care products **each year**, including **one-quarter** of the **world's vaccines**.

2) It produces products for **wealthy countries** (e.g. Pravastatin-RL™, a drug for CHD), and for **poorer countries** (e.g. polio vaccines).

Distribution and Sales

1) GSK makes a **large profit** from drug sales but also **donates** some drugs to poorer countries for **free**. For example, GSK's donated **750 million albendazole tablets** to treat over **130 million people** with **elephantiasis** (an infectious inflammatory disease).

2) GSK also **invests** a large amount of its profit in **community programmes** to help people in need — **3.8%** of their pre-tax **profits** (**£282 million**) in 2007.

Health and Globalisation

Tobacco Companies Also Affect Global Health

1) About a **third** of the **world's population over** the **age** of **15 smokes**. Although **wealthier countries** are starting to **smoke less**, it's becoming a **huge problem** elsewhere — **80%** of **smokers** live in **poorer countries**.

2) Almost **four million** people **die each year** from **tobacco-related illnesses**, such as **lung cancer** and **heart disease**. **Death rates** are **rising** because most **tobacco-related illnesses** take years or decades to develop.

3) Because tobacco-related illnesses take a long time to develop, they're **traditionally** a health problem associated with **wealthier countries** (because people **live long enough** for the disease to develop).

4) As poorer countries develop and **life expectancy increases**, tobacco-related illnesses are becoming **more common**.

5) In **2003**, the **World Health Organisation** (**WHO**) developed a **treaty** called the '**Framework Convention on Tobacco Control**'. The treaty **protects public health** by **restricting tobacco advertising**, **regulating** the **contents** of **tobacco products**, making sure they're **packaged** and **labelled correctly** and **regulating** who they're **sold to**.

Some people thought tobacco restrictions had gone too far this time.

6) It's hoped these measures will help to **reduce** the number of global **smokers**, **reducing** the number of **tobacco-related illnesses** worldwide.

7) There are **concerns** that some **tobacco companies** are **targeting** countries that **haven't signed** the **WHO treaty**, so have **fewer restrictions**. Companies are accused of **aggressive marketing** to **target vulnerable populations** (e.g. young people), and **exploiting** people's **lack of knowledge** about tobacco's **health effects**.

8) This could result in **increased tobacco-related illnesses** in these countries.

Case Study: Philip Morris International (PMI)

PMI is the **world's largest tobacco company** and **owns** the **world's top selling brand**.

Research and Production

1) PMI **sells** a lot of **tobacco products**. In **2005** it **sold 805 billion cigarettes** worldwide.

2) But PMI does **research** and **develop** some potentially **less harmful tobacco products**, e.g. **cigarettes** that might **reduce** the **exposure** of the **smoker** to **toxic chemical compounds**. These measures could help to **reduce** the number of **tobacco-related illnesses** worldwide.

Distribution and Sales

1) PMI does stick to the '**Framework Convention on Tobacco Control**' in the **countries** that **have signed** it. But it uses a different range of **advertising** and **marketing strategies** in countries that haven't signed up. E.g. PMI offers adult **smokers free samples** of cigarettes where it's **legal** to do so.

2) PMI does have a '**responsible marketing policy**'. It's **agreed not** to **market products** to **children** and to put **health warnings** on all **marketing materials** and all **packaging**.

Practice Questions

Q1 Briefly describe how research carried out by pharmaceutical companies can affect global health.

Q2 Briefly describe how the distribution and sale of drugs by pharmaceutical companies can affect global health.

Q3 Give one possible reason why the number of tobacco-related illnesses is rising.

Exam Question

Q1 With reference to one or more specific examples, explain how transnational corporations can affect global health. [10 marks]

TNC — aren't they a girl band...

Some of the largest TNCs are wealthier than some of the world's poorest countries — seems a little unfair, doesn't it.
People have divided opinions about how much these companies should be doing to improve world health. But don't worry,
you don't have to come up with the answer to that problem — you just have to get learning these wonderful pages.

The Geography of Health in the UK

Health isn't just different between countries, it's different within countries too. Take the UK for example...

Health *is* Better *in* Southern England *than in* Northern England *and* Scotland

There are **big differences** in **health** across the **UK**. **Life expectancy** from birth (a measure of health) for **males** born between 2004-2006 is shown on the map.

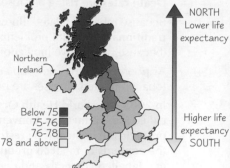

1) The **general health trend** for the UK is a **North-South divide** — people living in the **South** of England are **healthier** than people living in the **North** of England and in **Scotland**.

2) The **highest life expectancy** at birth for **males** (1991-2001) was in **North Dorset**, South-west England (**79 years**) and the **lowest** was in **Glasgow** (**69 years**).

3) The **trend** of morbidity (illness) also **varies** — it has a **similar pattern** to **life expectancy**. E.g. **lung cancer** is **more common** in women living in **Scotland** (about **50% higher** than the rest of the UK) and **less common** in women living in **South-west England** (about **40% lower** than the rest of the UK).

Income *Affects* Health Patterns *in the* UK...

There's a **strong link between** how much **money** you earn and how **healthy** you are. In general, **wealthier people** tend to be **healthier** because they have **better access** to **exercise facilities** and **health care**, and are **more educated** about **health issues**. The **pattern** of **household income** in the **UK** broadly **matches** the **pattern** of **life expectancy** (above).

For example, average **household income** (2003/04 to 2005/06) was **highest** in **South-east England** (**£91** a week **higher** than the UK average) and **lowest** in **North-east England** (**£141** a week **lower** than the UK average).

...and so Do Age Structure, Occupation Type, Education *and* Environment

1 Age structure

1) **Older people** are **more likely** to **suffer** from **age-related diseases**, e.g. **cancer** and **heart disease**.

2) **All regions** of the **UK** have an **ageing population**, due to **low birth rates** and **increasing life expectancy**.

3) But, **some areas** have a **higher proportion** of old people than others because **more retired people** choose to live there, e.g. **rural** and **coastal areas** like **Devon**.

2 Occupation type

1) If you do a **manual job** (e.g. a **labourer** or a **cleaner**) then you're up to **three times more likely** to suffer from **poor health** than if you do a **non-manual job** (e.g. a **doctor** or an **accountant**). Reasons for this include a **higher risk** of **accidents** and **exposure** to **hazardous substances**, e.g. asbestos.

2) **More people** do **manual jobs** in the **North** of England, which may contribute to the **higher levels** of **poor health**.

3) People doing **non-manual jobs** are **more likely** to suffer from **stress** and **mental health problems**. For example, **London** has the **highest proportion** of **people** in **non-manual jobs** and the **highest level** of **self-reported stress**.

3 Education

1) The **better educated** you are, the **more likely** you are to **choose a healthier lifestyle** — such as **eating healthy foods, exercising regularly** and **not smoking**.

2) This could be because **poor education** means **poor knowledge** of how to stay healthy.

3) In 2003, **18.8%** of the working-age population in **North-east England** had **no educational qualifications**. Only **10.7%** of the working-age population in **South-west England** had **no educational qualifications**. This might contribute to the **difference** in **health** between the two areas.

Some of these factors are linked together, e.g. people with a poor education are more likely to do manual jobs.

4 Environment and pollution

1) If you live in a **polluted area**, like a **big city** or near a **major road**, then you're **more likely** to suffer from **poor health**.

2) For example, **London** has a particularly **high mortality** rate from **respiratory diseases**, thought to be **caused** by the **poor air quality** in the city.

3) In contrast, **Devon** and **Cornwall** in **South-west England** are **countryside areas** with much **less pollution**. This may contribute to the **better health** there.

The Geography of Health in the UK

Gender Influences Health Too

Women tend to **live longer** than men but they're **twice as likely** to have **higher morbidity** from **chronic illnesses**, such as **arthritis**, and are **three times more likely** to suffer from **migraines**. **Women** are also **less likely** to take part in **sports** than men (**18.5%** compared with **23.7%**). Some **leisure facilities** have introduced 'ladies only' sessions to **encourage participation**.

Health Care Provision is Affected by Ageing Populations

An **ageing population** requires **more money** to be **allocated** to **certain health care services**, for example:

1) **Specialised wards** — to **care** for the **growing population** of **elderly people** who have **ill health**.

2) **Increased screening** for **age-related diseases** (e.g. cancer and heart disease).

3) **More residential care homes** and **carers**.

4) **More mobile health care services** — to **cope** with the **increasing immobilised elderly population**, especially those in **rural areas** without family support.

> **More older people** in a population means **more people** are **retired** and **fewer people** are **working** — this can result in a **declining tax base** to **pay** for **health** and **social services**.

Case Study: Health in South-west England

The **South-west** of **England** has the oldest population structure in the UK — in **2001**, **21%** of the **South-west's** population was pension age or over (60+ for women and 65+ for men). This compares to **19%** in **England** and **14%** in **London**. This will **increase** as **more people** are reaching **retirement age** and are choosing to **live in rural** and **coastal** areas.

An **ageing population** affects the **general health** of the area and the provision of **health care**:

1) **Higher rates** of diseases associated with **age** — in the South-west in **2003**, the rate of **breast cancer** was **7% above** UK average, and the rate of **prostate cancer** was **14% above** the UK average.

2) More **carers** and **health workers** are needed — in **2001**, **11%** of the working population of the South-west worked in the **social and health sectors**, compared to **10%** in **London**.

3) More **care homes** are required — **14%** of care homes in England are located in the **South-west** (only 10% are located in London).

1% extra might not seem like a lot but it's over 22 000 people.

Pumping money into **health care services** might **not** be the **best way** to **improve health** in the South-west:

1) Although the **South-west** has the **oldest population structure**, it's still the **healthiest region in the UK** — which **suggests that age isn't** the **most important factor** in **poor health**. There's **evidence** in the **South-west** that **low income is strongly linked** to **poor health**.

2) **Inland Revenue** figures show that **older people** have **lower personal incomes** than average, so it could be their **low income**, rather than age, that's **mostly affecting** their health. So the **most effective way** of **improving health** in the region could be to **focus** on **reducing** the number of **people** living on a **low income**.

3) For example, the **government** provides people **over 60** years old with a **heating allowance** — grants of up to **£4000** to **insulate homes** and make **heating improvements**. This is especially important in the **South-west** because this area has the **highest proportion** of **energy-inefficient homes** in England. The **heating allowance improves health** in the **South-west** because it helps **reduce illness** and **speeds recovery** in the **elderly population**.

Practice Questions

Q1 Describe the general health trend for the UK.

Q2 Why are wealthier people more likely to live healthier lives?

Q3 Name two factors that affect health in the UK.

Exam Question

Q1 Describe how an ageing population in the UK is likely to affect the provision of health care services. [6 marks]

Repeat after me — wealthier means healthier...

So, your health depends on many things but it seems like income's the major factor. Of course, they're all linked — it's hard to afford gym membership and a house by the coast on a low income. Still, there's just no excuse for deep-fried Mars Bars...

Exam Structure and Answering Questions

And now onto the unpleasant topic of exams (sorry, I had to mention them sooner or later).

You Have to Sit Two Exam Papers

UNIT 1 EXAM – PHYSICAL AND HUMAN GEOGRAPHY

1) It's **2 hrs** long and there are **120 marks** to be had (worth 70% of your AS grade).
2) It tests **all** the topics you've studied.
3) There are **two section**s — **A** and **B**.
4) Both sections have the **same structure**:

For both exams you have roughly 1 minute per mark — so if a question's worth 10 marks you should spend about 10 minutes answering it.

- You have to **answer the FIRST question** and **ONE other** (on the **optional topic** that you've studied) in each section.
- For each question there are a couple of **short-answer parts** — some test your **knowledge** of the topic and some test your **understanding** by getting you to **interpret** a **photo**, **diagram**, **map** etc.
- The **last part** of each question is an **'essay' question**, which often needs **case study** material (see next page).

UNIT 2 EXAM – GEOGRAPHICAL SKILLS

1) It's **1 hr** long and there are **50 marks** in total (worth 30% of your AS grade).
2) This paper tests your **investigative**, **map-reading**, **graph-reading**, **statistical** and **fieldwork skills** (see pages 113-118).
3) The questions will be based on stuff you've learnt **throughout** the **year** (i.e. on any topic).

Make Sure You Read the Question Properly

It's dead easy to **misread** the question and spend ages writing about the **wrong thing**. **Four** simple tips can help you avoid this:

1) Figure out if it's a **case study question** — if the question wording includes 'using **named examples**' or 'with reference to **one named area**' you **need** to include a case study.

2) <u>Underline</u> the **command words** in the question (the ones that tell you **what to do**):

Answers to questions with 'explain' in them often include the word **'because'** (or **'due to'**).
E.g. for the question 'Explain how vegetation affects a river's lag time', your answer would include '...more vegetation decreases lag time because it increases interception...'.

'Assess', 'Evaluate' and 'Discuss' all mean pretty much the **same thing**. They're all about **weighing something up**, e.g. the **success** of a coastal management scheme, or the **role** of people in causing desertification in the Sahel.

Command word	Means write about...
Describe	what it's **like**
Explain	**why** it's like that (i.e. give **reasons**)
Compare	the **similarities AND differences**
Contrast	the **differences**
Distinguish	the **differences**
Assess	the **advantages** and **disadvantages OR** the **arguments for** and **against**
Evaluate	
Discuss	
Examine	describe **AND** explain
Outline	describe **AND** explain
Define	the **meaning** of the word

If a question asks you to describe a **pattern** (e.g. from a map or graph), make sure you identify the **general pattern**, then refer to any **anomalies** (things that **don't** fit the general pattern).

When writing about differences, **'whereas'** is a good word to use in your answers, e.g. 'Employment in north-east England in 2007 was 6.1% whereas it was 4.1% in the south-west'.

'Examine' and 'Outline' are pretty similar. The main difference is that you do **more explaining** for '**Examine**' and **more describing** for '**Outline**'.

3) <u>Underline</u> the **key words** (the ones that tell you **what it's about**), e.g. rivers, population, social impacts etc.

4) **Re-read** the question and your answer **when you've finished**, just to check that your answer really does address **all parts** of the question being asked. A **common mistake** is to **miss a bit out** — like when questions say 'use data from the graph in your answer' or 'use evidence from the map'.

Don't Forget to Do These Things

1) For any **longer answers**, you need to think carefully about how to **structure** your answer **before you start**. Jot down the **order** you're going to cover things in under the question. **Label** your **plan** and **answer** clearly so the examiner knows which is which.

2) Use the **proper geography words** for things, e.g. say 'tributary' rather than 'small river'.

Q1 Describe the <u>physical</u> and <u>human</u> factors that can affect <u>river discharge</u>.
<u>PLAN</u>
1. *Intro — define 'discharge' and say it's affected by human and physical factors.*
2. *Physical — drainage basin characteristics, weather, rock and soil type, vegetation.*
3. *Human — impermeable surfaces, drainage systems.*
<u>ANSWER</u>
River discharge is the volume of water...

Answering Case Study Questions

Geography examiners are even keener on case study questions than they are on tweed jackets with fetching elbow patches...

Don't Forget the **Three Tips** When Answering **Case Study Questions**

1) For **every question** you need to do the following three things:

① **Read** the **question properly**.
② **Figure out** your **structure before** you **start**.
③ **Include** relevant **geographical terms**.

2) But for case study questions you also **need to**:

Include **PLENTY** of **RELEVANT DETAILS**

3) This includes things like **place names**, **dates**, **statistics**, **names** of **organisations** or **companies**.

4) Don't forget that they need to be **relevant** though — it's no good including the exact number of people killed in a flood when the question is about the causes of a flood.

5) For many case study questions, a great way to show your specific knowledge is to learn an **annotated map** and re-draw it in the exam (e.g. the Blackwater Estuary map on page 33) — but take care to only include labels relevant to the specific question being asked.

Jeremy's case study revealed very few relevant details... black, handle, smells a bit funny...

Here's an **Example Answer** to a Case Study Question

'With reference to one named area' means you **have to include** a **case study**.

Whenever you write about **causes** it's a really good idea to split them up into **physical** and **human**.

Include **relevant details**, e.g. if the coast is made from an easily eroded rock type, say exactly **what rock type** it is.

Use relevant **geographical terms**, e.g. **corrasion** and **slumping**.

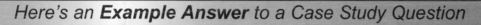

Q1   With reference to one named area <u>describe</u> and <u>explain</u> the <u>causes</u> of <u>coastal erosion</u>.   [15 marks]

PLAN
1. Introduce Holderness
2. Describe the physical causes of erosion — rock type, narrow beaches, powerful waves
3. Describe the human causes of erosion — sea defences

ANSWER
Holderness is a 61 km long stretch of coastline in East Yorkshire. It's eroding at an average rate of 1.8 m/year, and in some places, e.g. at Great Cowden, the rate of erosion is over 10 m/year.

There are many physical causes of the high rate of erosion. There is a long fetch (from the Arctic Ocean), which means that waves that hit the coastline have a lot of energy and so a lot of erosive power. The coastline also faces the dominant wind and wave direction (from the north-east). This also increases the energy of the waves (and so increases their erosive power). Another important physical factor is that the coastline is made from till, which is an easily eroded rock type. As well as being susceptible to corrasion it is prone to slumping when wet. The presence of Flamborough Head also increases erosion along holderness. The longshore drift runs from north to south along the coastline, so Flamborough Head traps sediment from the north. This means that the beach material eroded along Holderness is not replenished. Flamborough head is also made from chalk, which does not produce beach material when eroded (the chalk dissolves rather than forms sand). This means that the beaches along Holderness are quite narrow. Beaches slow the waves, reducing their erosive power. Narrower beaches protect the coast from erosion less than wider beaches.

Humans are contributing to the high rate of erosion. This is mainly through the building of sea defences, e.g. at Mappleton. Sea defences trap sediment and starve down-drift beaches of sediment. The thinner beaches don't protect the cliffs as well as wider beaches do.

CHALK

Flamborough Head traps sediment from the north, reducing beach width. Erosion of the chalk produces little beach material.

Sea defences at Mappleton trap sediment, making beaches down drift narrower.

Mappleton

Longshore drift

BOULDER CLAY

Humber Estuary

Don't think 'Ah, this is about the bit of coast I've studied' and then write everything you know about a particular coastline.
The key words are 'causes' and 'coastal erosion' and the command words are 'describe' and 'explain', so you need to write about the causes of erosion along a specific coastline (but not about the impacts of erosion).

You can't always include an **annotated map** in case study answers, but for this question including one **helps you illustrate** how **Flamborough Head** and **sea defences at Mappleton** increase erosion at Holderness.

Answering Resource Interpretation Questions

In the exam you're going to get some questions where you have to interpret a resource.
The following pages show you the kind of thing that might crop up. Knock yourself out...

You Might Get a Question Based on an **OS Map**...

Q1   Below is a map showing Cockermouth. <u>Describe</u> what the <u>social</u> and <u>economic impacts</u> of <u>flooding</u> in Cockermouth might be.   [18 marks]

© Crown copyright all rights reserved, License no. 100034841

> See page 116 for how to read OS® maps and give grid references.

The question only mentions **social** and **economic** impacts, so you **shouldn't** write about any possible **environmental** impacts. This makes your structure pretty simple.

When you're talking about somewhere specific on the map always **give the grid reference**.

Include relevant **details**, e.g. if there's a road that might flood, say what **road number** it is.

PLAN
1. Describe the possible social impacts — hospital, houses, roads
2. Describe the possible economic impacts — brewery, roads, campsite, farms

ANSWER

Possible social impacts of a flood in Cockermouth include loss of life, inconvenience and disruption to people's lives. The hospital at grid reference 125 321 is very close to the river so could be flooded. The lives of patients could be at risk if it floods.

There are lots of homes close to the river which would be affected if the river flooded (e.g. grid reference 1231). This could put lives at risk. It could also lead to the damage or loss of household goods and personal possessions. This is also an economic impact as they cost money to repair or replace.

Some roads run very close to the river at some points (e.g. the A5086 at grid reference 116 318). If these flood it would disrupt local traffic, which could cause congestion. It may also prevent people from reaching businesses, which would decrease trade.

The brewery at grid reference 125 317 is also close to the river so could flood. This would have economic consequences, as production could be stopped, reducing revenue. Equipment could be damaged and have to be replaced, which would also be expensive.

The campsite at grid reference 129 304 could be flooded. As well as disrupting holidays this would cause economic problems. The campsite owners would lose income whilst the ground was unusable for camping, and any facilities damaged by flooding would need repairing or replacing.

There is farmland near to the river, e.g. Green Bank Farm land (grid reference 125 297). If this farmland was flooded it could damage crops or kill livestock. This would be expensive for the farmer to replace.

Answering Resource Interpretation Questions

...or a Photo

The best thing to do first is write a list of the landforms you can see (just so you don't miss any out when writing your answer).

The command words in the question are 'describe' and 'explain' so you need to say what each landform is like and give reasons for its formation.

Q1   Describe and explain the landforms shown in the photo on the right.   [8 marks]

PLAN
Describe and then explain how each landform is formed — arête, corrie, tarn, ribbon lake.

ANSWER
There are four main glacial landforms present in the photo.

There is an arête in the centre-left of the photograph. An arête is a steep-sided ridge. It's formed when two glaciers flow in parallel valleys. The glaciers erode the sides of the valleys, which sharpens the mountain ridge between.

There is a corrie on the right of the photo. A corrie is a bowl-shaped hollow. Glaciers form when snow accumulates in a hollow and turns to ice. Basal sliding, along with abrasion and plucking, deepens the hollow into a corrie. When there is enough ice the glacier starts to move downhill. Frost shattering and plucking steepen the back wall of the corrie.

There is also a tarn. Tarns are lakes that form in corries after glaciers have retreated. There is a ribbon lake at the top of the photo. Ribbon lakes are long, thin lakes that form after a glacier retreats. They form in dips caused by the erosion of bands of less resistant rocks, or behind dams of debris left by the glacier.

You need to scour the photo to make sure that you've got everything — it'd be really easy to miss the ribbon lake at the top of this photo if you hadn't looked properly.

Include diagrams where they help illustrate your answer.

Cross-section of a corrie forming

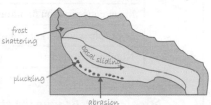
frost shattering
basal sliding
plucking
abrasion

...or a Graph

The command word is 'examine' so you need to describe the trends on the graph and give reasons for them.

As well as describing general trends, describe specific details, e.g. energy production in Country B increased in the period shown, but you also need to say it increased rapidly between 1980 and 1990.

Q1   Examine the graph of energy production in two countries.   [8 marks]

PLAN
1. Describe the trend in energy production for country A, then describe the trend for country B.
2. Give possible reasons for the trend for country A, then give possible reasons for the trend for country B.

ANSWER
The amount of energy produced by Country A was high and roughly constant between 1950 and 1980, at around 95 mtoe. After 1980 energy production started to decrease slowly (to approximately 75 mtoe in 2000). The amount of energy produced by Country B increased between 1950 and 2000, apart from a small dip around 1970. It increased very rapidly between 1980 and 1990 (from approximately 30 mtoe in 1980 to 90 mtoe in 1990). By 1990, country B produced more energy than country A.

Country A may have produced a lot of energy up to 1980 because it had large energy reserves and the money to exploit these reserves. The decrease in energy production from 1980 may have been caused by the energy resources, e.g. oil reserves, running out. Country B may have produced little energy up to 1980 because it didn't have the money to exploit the resources it had. The small dip around 1970 could have been caused by a period of political instability in the country, e.g. civil war. The rapid increase in energy production from 1980 to 1990 could have been caused by the discovery of new energy reserves, greater political stability in the country or investment to exploit energy resources.

Energy production for two countries between 1950 and 2000

million tonnes of oil equivalent (mtoe)

100
75
50
25

Country A
Country B

1950 1960 1970 1980 1990 2000
Year

Use evidence from the graph to back up your points (to get accurate figures from the graph it often helps to draw working lines on with a ruler).

Answering Resource Interpretation Questions

...or Some Data

Q1 Outline the trend in <u>health</u> between two regions of a developed country, using information in the table below. [10 marks]

Measure	East	West
Number of visits to a doctor per 100 people per year	306	512
Population	4 265 429	4 375 642
Average income	£25 225	£20 100
% people with degree level qualifications	24	15
% people over 65 years old	30	35
Mean concentration of nitrogen dioxide (μgm^{-3})	42	20
% people who work in non-manual jobs	53	36
Number of schools	1789	2111

PLAN

1. Describe the trend in number of visits to a doctor (and so health) in the country.
2. Give reasons for the trend in health — income, education, age structure, occupation type.
3. Mention any anomalies — air pollution.

The command word is 'outline' so you need to describe the trend in health and give reasons for the trend.

ANSWER

Always quote data from the table to back up your points.

People in the East of the country visit the doctor less frequently than people in the West (306 visits per 100 people per year, compared to 512 visits). This suggests that the people in the East are healthier than the people in the West.

Try to manipulate data from the table where appropriate, e.g. instead of giving the average income for each area, give the difference between them.

The difference in health could be caused by the difference in average income between the two areas. People living in the East have an average income of approximately £5000 more than people in the West. Wealthier people tend to be healthier because they have better access to exercise facilities (e.g. membership of gyms) and healthcare (e.g. private hospitals), and are usually more educated about health issues.

People could be healthier in the East because they are better educated (24% of the people in the East have degree level qualifications, whereas it's only 15% in the West). People with a better education are more likely to choose a healthier lifestyle, e.g. eating healthy foods, exercising regularly and not smoking.

Make sure you only include the relevant data from the table, e.g. '% people with degree level qualifications' shows how educated people in an area are, but 'number of schools' doesn't so shouldn't be included.

The difference in health could also be due to the fact that the East has a different age structure from the West (30% of the population in the East is over 65 years old compared to 35% of the population in the West). The fact that the West has a higher proportion of older people means that there are likely to be more people suffering from age-related diseases (e.g. cancer) in that area, which decreases the health of the population.

Another possible reason for the poorer health of the population in the West is their occupation type. More people in the West do manual jobs than in the East (64% compared to 47%). People who do manual jobs are more likely to suffer from poor health, e.g. because they have a higher risk of accidents and exposure to hazardous substances such as asbestos.

The environment also affects people's health, e.g. people living in an area with worse air quality are likely to have poorer health due to more respiratory illnesses. The data in the table does not show this because the people in the East are healthier despite having 42 μgm^{-3} of nitrogen dioxide in the air compared to only 20 μgm^{-3} in the West. However, the detrimental effect of air pollution in the East may be offset by the high income and education level of the population.

Investigative Skills

Whether you consider yourself a modern-day Poirot or not, you need to know this basic stuff about investigating things through fieldwork and research.

You Need to Have an **Aim** and a **Hypothesis**

1) When you're doing fieldwork and research you won't get very far without an **aim**, and a **hypothesis** to **test**.

2) An aim is **what you want to find out**, e.g. 'To see if coastal defences at Holderness affect the rate of erosion of the coastline'.

3) A hypothesis is a **specific testable statement**, e.g. 'Coastal defences at Holderness increase the rate of erosion downdrift of the defences'.

4) Both your aim and hypothesis should be '**developed**' — this just means that they have to be **really specific**. E.g. the above aim is better than 'To see if coastal defences affect erosion', and the hypothesis above is better than 'Coastal defences do affect erosion'.

Herman's hypothesis that large brown bears could drive German police cars was very specific (and seemed to be correct).

You Need to **Select** Your **Sites Carefully**

1) When you're investigating an urban area, river or coast you **can't study** the **whole thing**, so you have to **select sites** to investigate instead.

2) Selecting sites can be **tricky** though — you need places that are **easy to get to** (e.g. places with **footpath access**) and **not too far** from a **parking place** (if you've got **heavy equipment** to carry you don't want to be walking for miles). But you also need sites that are a **good representation** of all the things you want to study, e.g. if you're studying how **channel characteristics** change along the **course** of a **river** it's no good selecting three sites at the **top** of the river (sites near the **source only**) — this would be a **biased sample**. You need to select sites at **different stages** along the course of the river, **from source to mouth**.

3) **Systematic sampling** is often used to select sites in geography fieldwork — this involves selecting sites in a **regular, structured way**, e.g. **every 2 km** along a coastline, or **every third shop** on the high street. Doing it this way means you should be able to **cover** the **whole area** in an unbiased way.

4) You can also use **random sampling** — e.g. using a **random number table** to find the distance of a site from the source of a river. As long as you're using a big enough sample this should **remove** any **bias**.

You Need to **Collect Data**

1) You'll **collect data** when you're doing your **fieldwork** and when doing your **research**.

2) There are two types of data — **primary** and **secondary**:

- **Primary** data is data you **collect yourself** (i.e. the data you get from your **fieldwork**).
- **Secondary** data is data **someone else** has **collected** (i.e. the data you get from your **research**).

3) You might have to **describe** how you collected your data **in detail** in the **exam**. This includes mentioning things like what type of **equipment** you used (e.g. a velocity meter), **how you did it** (e.g. you conducted a questionnaire containing 10 questions) or **what source** it came from (e.g. 2001 census data from www.statistics.gov.uk).

4) Also, point out any **limitations** of the **data**, e.g. whether it could be **biased** due to the collection method.

You Need to Know About **Risk Assessment**

1) When you're out and about doing your **fieldwork** you need to be **pretty careful**.

2) You need to **identify** any **risks** there might be and **take action** to reduce the risks.

3) Risks basically include any way you could **get hurt**.

4) Here are a few examples:

Area	Risk	Action
City	Being run over	Cross roads using pedestrian crossings where possible.
City	Abuse (verbal and physical)	Be polite.
City	Abuse (verbal and physical)	If you're asking people questions make sure you introduce what you're doing and give them an opportunity to refuse to answer.
River	Drowning	Don't go into deep water (e.g. past knee height) or water that's fast flowing.
River	Drowning	Don't tread on slippy rocks (e.g. ones with moss on them).
Coast	Rock falls from cliffs	Where possible, keep away from cliff faces.
Coast	Drowning	See above. Also, make sure you're aware of when the tide's coming in.

Graph and Map Skills

As sure as death and taxes, there'll be graphs and maps in your exam. So make sure you know all the different types...

There are Loads of **Different Types** of **Graphs** and **Maps**

1) There are some types of graphs and maps that you'll have come across lots of times before. These include **line graphs**, **bar charts**, **pie charts**, **scatter graphs**, **atlas maps** and **sketch maps**.

2) Some graphs and maps are trickier than others, so the next three pages are full of tips to help you interpret the tougher ones.

3) When you're **interpreting** graphs and maps you need to remember to **read** the **scale** or **key really carefully**.

4) If you have to read from a graph **draw working lines on** to help you get an accurate figure.

Triangular Graphs Show **Percentages** Split into **Three Categories**

1) To read a triangular graph start by **finding the point** you want on the graph.

2) **Follow** the **line** that goes **down** from the **point** to the **lowest end** of the **scale** and record the percentage.

3) Then **turn the graph around** so that the next axis is at **the bottom, follow** the **line** down to the lower end of the scale and record that percentage.

4) Do the same for the **third axis**.

5) The three readings should **add up** to **100%**.

6) The graph on the right shows the age distribution of three populations. There are **three age groups** so a triangular graph can be used. **Each point** represents **one population**.

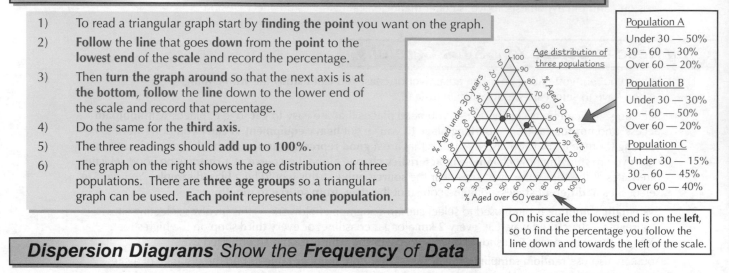

Population A
Under 30 — 50%
30 – 60 — 30%
Over 60 — 20%

Population B
Under 30 — 30%
30 – 60 — 50%
Over 60 — 20%

Population C
Under 30 — 15%
30 – 60 — 45%
Over 60 — 40%

On this scale the lowest end is on the **left**, so to find the percentage you follow the line down and towards the left of the scale.

Dispersion Diagrams Show the **Frequency of Data**

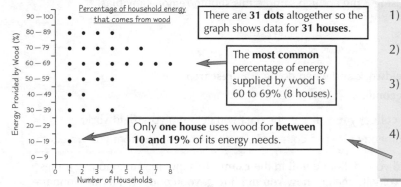

There are **31 dots** altogether so the graph shows data for **31 houses**.

The **most common** percentage of energy supplied by wood is 60 to 69% (8 houses).

Only **one house** uses wood for **between 10 and 19%** of its energy needs.

1) Dispersion diagrams are a bit like a cross between a **tally chart** and a **bar chart**.

2) The **range of data that's measured** goes on one axis. **Frequency** goes on the other axis.

3) **Each dot** represents **one piece** of **information** — the **more dots** there are in a particular category, the **more frequently** that event has happened.

4) The dispersion diagram on the left shows the **percentage** of **household energy** that comes from **wood** for **houses** in a **particular village**.

Logarithmic Scales are Used When the **Data Range** is **Large**

1) The **intervals** on logarithmic scales are **not fixed amounts** (e.g. they don't go up by 5 every time).

2) Instead, the **intervals** get **increasingly larger** at the top end of the scale (e.g. 10, 20, 40, 80).

3) This lets you fit a **very wide range** of **data** onto one **axis** without having to draw an enormous graph.

4) The graph on the right uses a **logarithmic scale** on the **vertical axis** to show how the world's population changed between 1950 and 2000.

This interval represents **1.28 billion** people.

This interval represents **20 million** people.

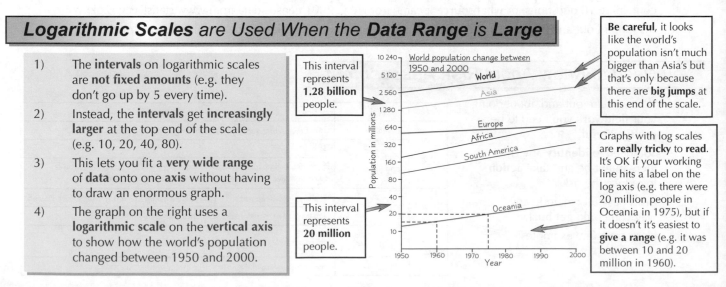

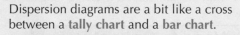

Be careful, it looks like the world's population isn't much bigger than Asia's but that's only because there are **big jumps** at this end of the scale.

Graphs with log scales are **really tricky** to **read**. It's OK if your working line hits a label on the log axis (e.g. there were 20 million people in Oceania in 1975), but if it doesn't it's easiest to **give a range** (e.g. it was between 10 and 20 million in 1960).

Graph and Map Skills

Choropleth Maps Show Information Using Colours and Patterns

1) Choropleth maps show how something **varies** between **different areas** using **colours** or **patterns**.

2) The maps in exams often use **cross-hatched lines** and **dots**.

3) They're straightforward to read but it's **easy to make mistakes** with them as the patterns can be very similar.

4) If you're asked to talk about all the parts of the map with a **certain type of hatching**, look at the map carefully and put a **big tick** on each part with that hatching, to make them all **stand out**.

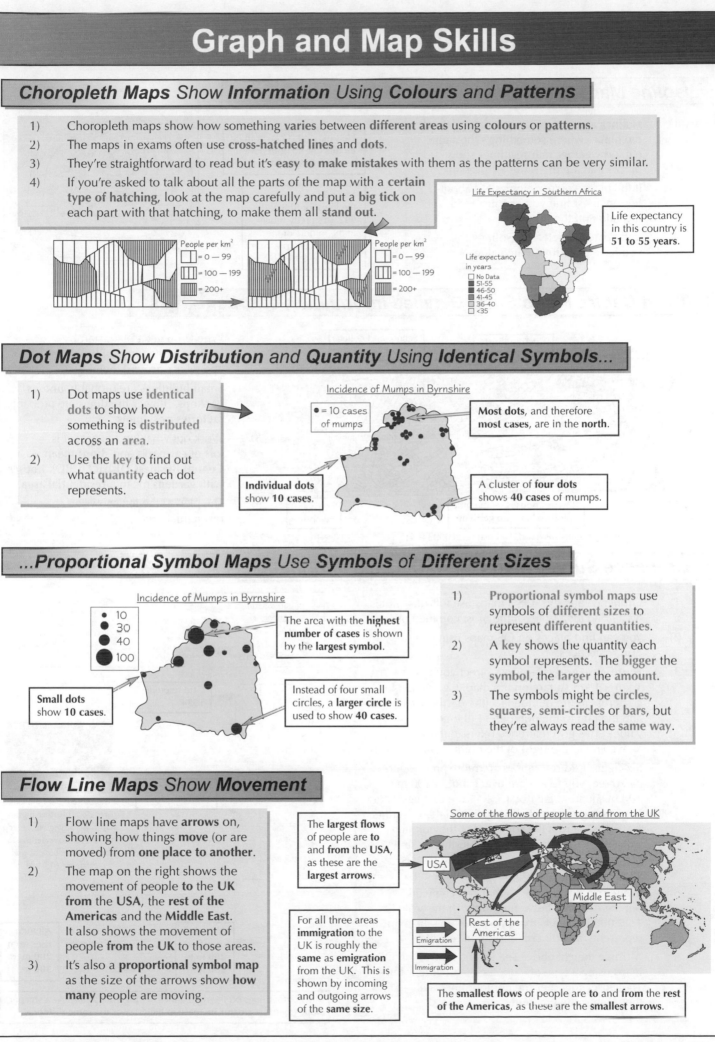

Life Expectancy in Southern Africa

Life expectancy in this country is **51 to 55 years**.

Life expectancy in years
- No Data
- 51-55
- 46-50
- 41-45
- 36-40
- <35

People per km²
- = 0 — 99
- = 100 — 199
- = 200+

Dot Maps Show Distribution and Quantity Using Identical Symbols...

1) Dot maps use **identical dots** to show how something is **distributed** across an **area**.

2) Use the **key** to find out what **quantity** each dot represents.

Incidence of Mumps in Byrnshire

● = 10 cases of mumps

Most dots, and therefore **most cases**, are in the **north**.

Individual dots show **10 cases**.

A cluster of **four dots** shows **40 cases** of mumps.

...Proportional Symbol Maps Use Symbols of Different Sizes

Incidence of Mumps in Byrnshire

- 10
- 30
- 40
- 100

The area with the **highest number of cases** is shown by the **largest symbol**.

Small dots show **10 cases**.

Instead of four small circles, a **larger circle is used** to show **40 cases**.

1) **Proportional symbol maps** use symbols of **different sizes** to represent **different quantities**.

2) A **key** shows the quantity each symbol represents. The **bigger** the symbol, the **larger the amount**.

3) The symbols might be **circles, squares, semi-circles or bars**, but they're always read the **same way**.

Flow Line Maps Show Movement

1) Flow line maps have **arrows** on, showing how things **move** (or are moved) from **one place to another**.

2) The map on the right shows the movement of people **to the UK from** the USA, the **rest of the Americas** and the **Middle East**. It also shows the movement of people **from the UK** to those areas.

3) It's also a **proportional symbol map** as the size of the arrows show **how many** people are moving.

The **largest flows** of people are **to** and **from** the **USA**, as these are the **largest arrows**.

For all three areas **immigration** to the UK is roughly the **same** as **emigration** from the UK. This is shown by incoming and outgoing arrows of the **same size**.

Emigration
Immigration

Some of the flows of people to and from the UK

USA
Middle East
Rest of the Americas

The **smallest flows** of people are **to** and **from** the **rest of the Americas**, as these are the **smallest arrows**.

Graph and Map Skills

Isoline Maps *Show Where* **Conditions** *are the* **Same**

1) **Isolines** are lines on a map **linking** up all the **places** where something's the **same**, e.g. on **weather maps** isolines show places that are the **same air pressure**.

2) If the place you're being asked about lies **on** an isoline you can just **read** the value off the line.

3) If the place is **between** isolines you have to **estimate** the value.

Helsinki and Lecce both lie **on** this line so both have a pressure of **996 mb**.

Madrid lies **between** the lines for **988** and **992**. It's pretty much in the middle of the lines, so has a pressure of roughly **990 mb**.

Map of low pressure system

Town Centre Plans *Show* **Detailed Information** *of* **Urban Areas**

1) When you get a plan, start by looking at the **types of buildings** and what's **around** them.

2) **Small buildings** are probably **houses** or **shops**. **Bigger buildings** are probably **factories** or **schools**.

3) Work out what kind of **area** it is — lots of **car parks** and **shops** mean it's a **Central Business District** (CBD), **houses with gardens** mean a **residential area**.

4) The plan to the left shows a **residential area**.

Roads

Park (obviously)

School and college (also obvious)

Railway track

Rows of **houses** — the little plots of land are **gardens**

Fields and woods

© Crown copyright all rights reserved, License no. 100034841

Ordnance Survey Maps *Show* **Detailed Information** *of* **All Areas**

1) Ordnance Survey® (OS®) maps use lots of **symbols**. It's a good idea to **learn** the most common ones.

2) You can find places on OS maps using **grid references**.

3) **Four-figure grid references** direct you to a 1 km × 1 km **square** on the map, e.g. for **1534** go **across** to the number 15 (the **eastings** value) and then **up** to the number 34 (the **northings** value). This grid reference refers to the **square above** and to the **right** of the point 1534.

4) **Six-figure grid references** are more precise and can direct you to a more **exact spot** (a 100 m × 100 m square). E.g. for **155341** the eastings value is 155, so go across to 15 again and then a further **5 "tenths"** across the square. For the northings value of 341 go up to 34 and a further **1 "tenth"** of that square. The spot you're looking for is where the easting and northing values **cross**.

5) Every map has a **scale** so that you can work out the **distance between points**. If the scale is **1:25 000**, it means that every **1 cm** on the map represents **25 000 cm** (250 m) in real life.

6) **Altitude** (height above sea level) is shown on OS maps using a type of isoline called **contour lines**. The **closer together** the contour lines are, the **steeper the gradient** is.

Common OS Map Symbols
— Railway
▢ Building
+ Place of worship
⯗ Place of worship, with a tower
⯗ Church with a spire, minaret or dome
— Motorway
— Main (A) road
— Secondary (B) road
● Bus station
PO Post office
PH Pub
-·-·- County boundary
=== National Park boundary
------- Footpath

Grid reference: 1534

Grid reference: 155341

The contour lines did look very close together on the map, but nothing would stop Chaz and Dave getting to the Public House at grid reference 613 574.

Altitude rises from **200 m** to **250 m**.

Altitude rises from **200 m** to **300 m**.

The contour lines on the right are closer together and show a **steeper slope** (there's a **greater increase in height** over the **same distance**).

Statistical Skills

As if knowing about loads of weird graphs and maps wasn't enough, you also need to be pretty familiar with statistics. These next two pages cover the ones you need to know.

There are **Different Ways** of Finding the **Average** Value of a Set of Data

1) The **mean**, **median** and **mode** are different ways of finding the **average** value of a set of data.

2) You find the **mean** by **adding up** all the numbers in a set of data, then **dividing** by the number of **sample points**, **n**.

Take a look at the data in this table:

Location	1	2	3	4	5	6	7	8	9	10	11
Temperature in °C	3	7	4	3	7	9	9	5	5	7	6

n = 11, so the mean temperature is: $\dfrac{3+7+4+3+7+9+9+5+5+7+6}{11}$ = **5.9 °C**.

3) The **median** is the **middle value** in an ordered set of data. So you need to **sort the numbers into order**, then work out which one is in the middle. So for the data above the median is **6 °C**.

$$3 \quad 3 \quad 4 \quad 5 \quad 5 \; (6) \; 7 \quad 7 \quad 7 \quad 9 \quad 9$$

If there are an even number of sample points the median is the mean of the middle two numbers.

4) The **mode** is the **most common value** in a set of data. So for the data above the mode is **7 °C**.

$$3 \quad 3 \quad 4 \quad 5 \quad 5 \quad 6 \; (7 \quad 7 \quad 7) \; 9 \quad 9$$

Sometimes there isn't a mode, and sometimes there's more than one.

The **Interquartile Range** is a **Measure of Dispersion**...

1) The **interquartile range** (**IQR**) is the range of values covered by the **middle 50%** of a set of data.

2) To find the interquartile range you first need to find the median of the values **to the left** of the median. This is called the **lower quartile** (**LQ**). Next find the median of the values **to the right** of the median. This is the **upper quartile** (**UQ**). Then you just **subtract** the **LQ from the UQ** to give you the **IQR**.

3) So, for the data above, the **LQ** is **4** and the **UQ** is **7**, and the interquartile range is UQ – LQ = 7 – 4 = **3 °C**.

$$3 \quad 3 \; (4) \; 5 \quad 5 \; (6) \; 7 \quad 7 \; (7) \; 9 \quad 9$$

LQ ⟶ Median ⟶ UQ, IQR

4) The interquartile range tells you about the **spread** of data **around** the **median**. If it's a **big** number, it shows that the numbers are pretty **spread out**. And yep, you've guessed it — a **small** number means that a lot of the data is pretty **close** to the **median**.

...and so is **Standard Deviation**

1) The **standard deviation** is a bit trickier to calculate than the IQR, but it's often a **more reliable** measure of dispersion (spread). The symbol for it is σ.

The formula is $\sigma = \sqrt{\dfrac{\sum(x - \bar{x})^2}{n}}$

Σ just means 'sum of', and $\bar{x}$ is just a way of writing 'mean'.

2) To calculate it, it's easiest to **work out** the **individual bits** in the formula **first**, e.g. the mean. It's a good idea to **draw** a **table** to help you. Below is a simple example for the set: 5, 9, 10, 11, 14.

- For these numbers, the **mean** is (5 + 9 + 10 + 11 + 14) ÷ 5 = **9.8**. This is shown in the 2nd column in the table.

- For each number, **calculate** x – $\bar{x}$ (3rd column in the table).

- Then **square** each of those values (4th column) — remember that the square of a **negative number** is always **positive**.

- Then **add up** all the squared numbers you've just worked out — this will give you $\sum(x - \bar{x})^2$.

- Now just **divide** your total by **n**, then take the **square root**.

- In this example, n = 5, so $\sigma = \sqrt{\dfrac{42.8}{5}}$ = **2.93** (2 d.p.)

x	$\bar{x}$	x – $\bar{x}$	$(x - \bar{x})^2$
5	9.8	−4.8	23.04
9	9.8	−0.8	0.64
10	9.8	0.2	0.04
11	9.8	1.2	1.44
14	9.8	4.2	17.64
		Σ	42.8

*Standard deviation can be represented by σ or **s**.*

3) If the standard deviation is **large**, the numbers in the set of data are **spread out** around the **mean**. If it's **small**, the numbers are **bunched** closely around the mean.

Statistical Skills

Make Sure You Know How to Find Spearman's Rank Correlation Coefficient

The Spearman's Rank correlation coefficient is a handy way to find out whether two sets of numbers are **correlated** (there's a **relationship** between them). The example below uses the test to see if **river discharge** (m³/s) and **rainfall** (mm) are correlated.

1) The bad news is that it's a bit of a pain to calculate. The first step is to give a **rank** to each number in both sets of data. The **highest** number is given rank **1**, the second highest is given rank 2... you get the idea. ⟶

2) Then you **calculate 'd'**, the **difference** between the ranks for each item, e.g. if the ranks for River F are 4 and 6, the difference is –2. ⟶

3) Next you **square 'd'** and **add up** the **d² values**.

4) Finally you need to work out the **Spearman's Rank Correlation Coefficient** (known as r_s).

The formula is: $r_s = 1 - \dfrac{6\sum d^2}{n^3 - n}$

River	Discharge	Discharge rank	Rainfall	Rainfall rank	d	d²
A	14	5	28	5	0	0
B	19	4	27	6	2	4
C	9	9	15	8	–1	1
D	6	11	9	11	0	0
E	21	3	35	3	0	0
F	13	6	30	4	–2	4
G	22	2	36	2	0	0
H	35	1	38	1	0	0
I	5	12	6	12	0	0
J	7	10	14	9	–1	1
K	11	8	10	10	2	4
L	12	7	20	7	0	0

$\sum d^2$ | 14

5) So for the example above, $\sum d^2 = 14$ and n = 12. So $r_s = 1 - \dfrac{6 \times 14}{12^3 - 12} = 1 - \dfrac{84}{1716} = 1 - 0.05 = \textbf{0.95}$.

6) The number you get is always **between –1** and **+1**.

7) A **positive number** means the variables are **positively correlated** — as one variable **increases** so does the **other**. The **closer** the number is to 1 the **stronger** the correlation. ⟶

8) A **negative number** means that the two sets of variables are **negatively correlated** — as one variable **increases** the other **decreases**. The **closer** the number is to –1 the **stronger** the correlation. ⟶

9) If the coefficient is **0**, or near 0, there probably isn't much of a relationship between the figures.

10) The value of r_s in the example above was **0.95**, which is **close to 1**, so there's a **strong positive correlation** between the **data** for river discharge and rainfall.

Strong positive correlation   Weak positive correlation

Strong negative correlation   Weak negative correlation

You Have To Check the Correlation Is Significant Though

1) A **Spearman's Rank correlation coefficient** might tell you that **two sets of numbers** are **correlated**. But you need to check whether this is evidence for a **genuine link** between the two quantities you're looking at. (You sometimes get correlations between sets of data **by chance**, even if there's no underlying relationship. For example, there **is** a correlation between river discharge and rainfall **for the data shown above**, but this might have been a fluke and there might be **no real relationship** between the two things.)

2) You can check whether it's evidence for a genuine link by looking at the **probability** that a correlation would happen by chance. If there's a 5% (or higher) probability that a correlation is because of chance then it's **not significant** evidence for a link. If there's a **0.1% or less** chance, then it's **very significant** evidence for a link. (This is what's meant by the **significance level** of a statistical test — it's a kind of 'cut-off' probability.)

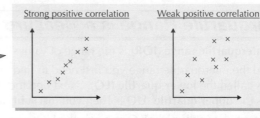

Probabilities of Spearman's Rank correlation coefficients (assuming no relationship between variables

3) To test whether the value of r_s is evidence for a relationship between discharge and rainfall, you'll need a **graph** like the one on the right. You'll also need to know the **degrees of freedom** (this is just n – 2, so in the example above degrees of freedom = 12 – 2 = **10**). Since $r_s = \textbf{0.95}$, you can use the graph to find that this correlation has a **less than 0.1%** probability of being due to chance. This means you have **very significant** evidence for a **relationship** between river discharge and rainfall.

Answers

Section 1 — Rivers, Floods and Management

Page 3 — The Hydrological Cycle

1 Maximum of 4 marks available.
In wet seasons, precipitation exceeds evapotranspiration, creating a water surplus — ground stores fill with water as there's more surface runoff and higher discharge, so river levels rise [1 mark]. In drier seasons, precipitation is lower than evapotranspiration — ground stores are depleted as some water is used by plants and humans and some flows into the river channel, but isn't replaced by precipitation [1 mark]. At the end of a dry season, there's a deficit (shortage) of water in the ground [1 mark]. This has to be paid back in the next wet season (ground store recharge) [1 mark].

Page 5 — River Discharge

1a) Maximum of 2 marks available.
Lag time = 12 hours [1 mark].
Peak discharge = 35 cumecs [1 mark].
 b) Maximum of 4 marks available.
Vegetation intercepts precipitation and slows its movement to the river channel, increasing lag time [1 mark].
So deforestation will reduce interception, resulting in a decreased lag time [1 mark]. The more vegetation there is in a basin, the more water is lost through transpiration and evaporation directly from the vegetation before it reaches the river channel, reducing peak discharge [1 mark].
So deforestation will reduce transpiration and evaporation, causing an increase in peak discharge [1 mark].

Page 7 — River Processes

1 Maximum of 5 marks available.
Erosion by hydraulic action happens as the pressure of the water breaks rock particles away from the bed and banks [1 mark]. Abrasion (corrasion) occurs when eroded pieces of rock in the water scrape and rub against the bed and banks, removing material [1 mark]. Attrition is when eroded rocks smash into each other and break into smaller fragments [1 mark]. Erosion by cavitation occurs as air bubbles in turbulent stretches of water implode causing shockwaves that break pieces of rock off the banks and bed [1 mark]. Corrosion erosion (solution) is the dissolving of rock by chemical processes [1 mark].

2 Maximum of 6 marks available. This question is level marked.
   HINTS:
   • Start off by defining what the critical erosion velocity curve shows, e.g. 'The critical erosion velocity curve shows the minimum velocity needed to pick up and transport particles of different sizes'.
   • Then you need to describe how it's different for different particle sizes, e.g. 'It's lowest for sand (particles between 0.1 mm and 1 mm), but it's higher for particles that are both larger (e.g. gravel, pebbles and boulders) and smaller (e.g. clay and silt)'.

   • Finally explain why clay and silt require a faster velocity to be picked up and transported than sand (they tend to stick together more, so it takes more energy (velocity) to erode them), and do the same for larger particles (they require more velocity as they're heavier).

Page 9 — The Long Profile and Channel Characteristics

1 Maximum of 3 marks available.
A river's hydraulic radius is a measure of how efficient the river is [1 mark]. It's calculated by dividing the river's cross-section area [1 mark] by the length of its wetted perimeter (the total length of the banks and bed that are in contact with the water) [1 mark].

2 Maximum of 6 marks available. This question is level marked.
   HINTS:
   • It's fairly easy to structure your answer to this question. You can either talk about each stage of the river in turn and describe how the processes change. Or you can talk about each process in turn and describe how it changes as you go down the river.
   • The questions says 'outline' so you need to describe what's happening and explain why, e.g. 'In the lower stage of a river, there's less erosion because turbulence is lower and sediment particle size is reduced (reducing erosion due to abrasion)'.

Page 11 — River Landforms

1 Maximum of 4 marks available.
Levees are natural, raised embankments formed when a river overflows its banks [1 mark]. During a flood, material is deposited across the whole flood plain as the river loses velocity and energy due to increased friction [1 mark]. The heaviest material (e.g. sand and gravel) is dropped first, closest to the river channel [1 mark]. Over time, this material builds up on the river bank, creating a levee [1 mark].

Page 13 — Causes and Impacts of Flooding

1 Maximum of 6 marks available. This question is level marked.
   HINTS:
   • The question asks you to 'outline' — this means describe the physical characteristics and explain why they would increase the risk of flooding.
   • Focus on one characteristic at a time and give a full explanation, e.g. 'Drainage basins with impermeable ground (such as clay soils) don't allow infiltration of surface water. This increases surface runoff, which increases river discharge and increases the risk of flooding'.
   • Cover a range of physical characteristics in detail, e.g. sparse vegetation, high drainage density, circular basin, steep slopes, etc.

Answers

2 Maximum of 5 marks available.
   Urban areas have large areas of impermeable tarmac and concrete *[1 mark]*, so when it rains, surface runoff is very rapid *[1 mark]*. Urban areas also have gutters and drains, which quickly take runoff to the rivers *[1 mark]*. Both of these reduce lag time *[1 mark]*, which increases discharge and so increases the risk of flooding *[1 mark]*.

Page 15 — Causes and Impacts of Flooding — Case Studies

1 Maximum of 10 marks available.
   This question is level marked.
   HINTS:
   • Focus your answer on the <u>impacts</u> of flooding — write about the <u>effect</u> flooding has on society, the economy and the environment.
   • The question asks you to use two named examples, so use <u>two case studies</u> you've learnt (e.g. the South Asia flood and the Carlisle flood).
   • '<u>Compare</u>' means you should describe the impacts that are <u>similar</u> in poor and wealthy countries, and those that are <u>different</u>. For example, 'When South Asia was flooded in 2007 over 2000 people died, but only three people died in the Carlisle floods of 2005. The death toll in South Asia was high for many reasons, e.g. because many people living there rely on agriculture, so were reluctant to evacuate and leave their land and livestock unattended. Also, many children couldn't swim so they drowned in the floods'.

Page 17 — Flood Management Strategies

1 Maximum of 8 marks available. This question is level marked.
   HINTS:
   • This is a sneaky one — to answer the question you need to know that most <u>soft engineering defences</u> don't use man-made structures.
   • <u>Explain</u> how flooding can be reduced using soft engineering defences, and <u>explain</u> how each defence works. For example, 'Flooding can be reduced by restoring the river to its natural state, e.g. by removing man-made levees. This allows the river to flood naturally. The water spreads out over the flood plain, which reduces river discharge and so decreases flooding downstream'.
   • You don't need to include weather forecasts and flood warnings, as these don't actually reduce flooding (they only reduce the impacts of flooding).

Page 19 — Flood Management Strategies — Case Studies

1 Maximum of 10 marks available.
   This question is level marked.
   HINTS:
   • The question asks you to refer to 'named example<u>s</u>', so you need to write about at least <u>two case studies</u> (e.g. the different approaches used on the Yangtze River and in Abingdon).

• Start off by describing <u>what type of defences</u> have been implemented in each place, e.g. 'Hard engineering defences, such as dams and levees, have been used along the Yangtze river in China'.
• Next write about the <u>success</u> of the schemes — say whether they have reduced flooding and describe any <u>problems</u> they have caused. For example, 'The Three Gorges Dam on the Yangtze River is thought to have successfully reduced major flooding from once every 10 years to once every 100 years. However, it has had many negative impacts, e.g. people have had to relocate as the reservoir behind the dam builds up. It's thought that between 1.3 and 2 million people will have been forced to relocate by the time the reservoir is full'.
• Don't forget to stuff your answer full of <u>specific details</u> about the case studies, e.g. 'There are 3600 km of levees along the middle and lower parts of the Yangtze'.

Section 2 — Coastal Environments

Page 21 — Introduction to Coastal Environments

1 Maximum of 4 marks available.
   2 marks available for characteristics of constructive waves, from any of the following points: Constructive waves are flat and gentle *[1 mark]*. They have a low frequency *[1 mark]* of about 6-8 waves per minute *[1 mark]*. Their swash is greater than their backwash *[1 mark]* which carries material up the beach and deposits it *[1 mark]*. 2 marks available for characteristics of destructive waves, from any of the following points: Destructive waves are tall and steep *[1 mark]*. They have a high frequency *[1 mark]* of about 10-14 waves per minute *[1 mark]*. Their backwash is greater than their swash *[1 mark]* and removes beach material *[1 mark]*.

2 Maximum of 6 marks available. This question is level marked.
   HINTS:
   • 'Outline' means <u>describe</u> and <u>explain</u>, so first you need to list the erosion processes that affect cliffs — these include abrasion/corrasion, hydraulic action, quarrying and corrosion/solution.
   • Don't write about attrition — it's not a type of erosion that affects cliffs (it's the erosion of rocks in the water by smashing together).
   • Then for each type of erosion you need to <u>explain how</u> it erodes cliffs, e.g. 'Hydraulic action is where air in cracks in cliffs is compressed by waves. The pressure exerted by the compressed air breaks bits of rock off the cliff'.
   • For top marks you also need to explain how <u>sub-aerial weathering</u> makes cliffs more vulnerable to erosion, e.g. 'Freeze-thaw weathering weakens cliffs and so makes them more vulnerable to erosion'.

Answers

Page 24 — Coastal Landforms

1   Maximum of 5 marks available.
Weathering and wave erosion forms a notch in a cliff **[1 mark]** at the high water mark **[1 mark]**. This eventually develops into a cave **[1 mark]**. Rock above the cave is unsupported and so collapses **[1 mark]**. As this process is repeated the cliff retreats, leaving behind a flat wave-cut platform **[1 mark]**.

2   Maximum of 6 marks available. This question is level marked.
    HINTS:
    • Spits are formed by <u>longshore drift</u> — to get top level marks you'll need to describe the process.
    • Describe <u>where</u> spits are likely to form, e.g. 'Spits tend to form where the coast suddenly changes direction, such as across a river mouth'.
    • Explain what a <u>recurved end</u> is, and how it's formed.
    • Make sure you include what happens <u>behind</u> the spit, e.g. 'The area behind the spit is sheltered from the sea and often forms salt marshes'.
    • Include a <u>diagram</u> (or a series of diagrams, like on page 23) to illustrate the formation.

Page 25 — Coastal Erosion — Case Study

1   Maximum of 15 marks available.
This question is level marked.
See page 109 for a full worked answer to this question.

Page 27 — Sea Level Changes

1   Maximum of 8 marks available. This question is level marked.
    HINTS:
    • The question asks for <u>possible</u> impacts, so you need to write about what the impacts might be in the <u>future</u>.
    • Make sure you include all the main impacts — more frequent and more severe flooding, submergence of low-lying islands and changes in the coastline.
    • For each impact describe what could happen and <u>give an example</u> to back up your point if possible, e.g. 'Low-lying coastal islands may be submerged if sea level rises, e.g. if it rises 0.5 m, most of the Maldives would be submerged'.
    • Don't forget to include that the main impacts have <u>further impacts</u>, e.g. decrease in tourism, damage to infrastructure etc.

2   Maximum of 8 marks available. This question is level marked.
    HINTS:
    • The question asks about <u>coastal submergence</u>, so you need to explain how it happens, e.g. 'Coastal submergence happens when the sea level rises relative to the land'.
    • Then you need to explain <u>how</u> the rise in sea level may occur, and the difference between eustatic and isostatic change.
    • The question also asks for a <u>range</u> of landforms, so make sure you talk about more than one (e.g. cover rias, fjords and Dalmatian coastlines).
    • For each landform, describe <u>how it's formed</u> and its <u>main features</u>, e.g. 'Rias are drowned river valleys. They are wide and deep at the mouth, becoming narrower and shallower further inland'.

Page 29 — Coastal Flooding

1   Maximum of 10 marks available.
This question is level marked.
    HINTS:
    • The question says a <u>named coastal area</u>. It might sound obvious, but remember to write about a <u>case study</u>, not just the general causes and effects of flooding.
    • Talk about both the <u>physical</u> and <u>human</u> causes of the flooding, e.g. 'Coastal areas in south-east Asia were flooded by a tsunami that was caused by a submarine earthquake measuring about 9.0 on the Richter scale off the coast of Indonesia. However, human activity, such as destruction of mangrove forests in Thailand to make way for fish farms, and coral mining in the Indian Ocean, meant that a lot of the coasts' natural protection was missing. This made the effects of flooding worse'.
    • Make sure you know whether each effect is <u>social</u>, <u>economic</u> or <u>environmental</u> because you <u>might not always</u> get asked for <u>all three</u>.
    • Include plenty of <u>facts</u> and <u>figures</u> and make plenty of <u>place-specific statements</u> to show that you really know the case study, e.g. 'A quarter of hotels in southern Thailand were forced to close for at least 6 months because of damage from the flooding'.

Page 31 — Coastal Management

1   Maximum of 6 marks available. This question is level marked.
    HINTS:
    • First you need to <u>describe</u> what hard engineering defences and soft engineering defences are and give a couple of <u>examples</u>. E.g. 'Hard engineering defences are built structures, e.g. revetments, groynes and sea walls'.
    • Then go on to explain <u>why</u> soft engineering defences are <u>more sustainable</u>, e.g. 'Soft engineering defences usually require much less time and money to maintain than hard engineering defences. They also create habitats like dunes and marshland, e.g. coastal realignment leads to the formation of marshland. Hard engineering defences often disrupt natural processes'.
    • Finish up with a <u>conclusion</u>, e.g. 'Soft engineering schemes have a lower environmental impact and a lower economic cost than hard engineering schemes, so are more sustainable'.

Answers

Page 33 — Coastal Management — Case Studies

1 Maximum of 15 marks available.
This question is level marked.
HINTS:
- The command word in this question is _evaluate_, so you need to talk about the costs _and_ benefits of your chosen scheme.
- The question doesn't specify whether you need to write about a _hard_ or _soft_ engineering scheme, so the choice is yours. Make sure you pick one that you _know loads about_, so you can get plenty of _detail_ in your answer.
- Whatever scheme you choose, the _benefits_ are likely to be things like saving land, housing, transport routes, and industry, and preserving natural habitats. The _costs_ will include things like the price of setting up and maintaining the defences, the appearance of the defences and the possible effects on adjacent areas of the coast.
- Examiners love '_specific and detailed reference_' to the case study, so it's always good to have some _numbers_ to back up your points, e.g. '£2 million was spent on two rock groynes and 500 m of revetment at Mappleton in 1991'.
- But don't just scribble down all facts — you need to explain _why_ these measures were used and the _effect_ that they've had, e.g. 'They were built to protect the village and the B1242 road. The scheme has successfully protected these areas, but the groynes have starved down-drift beaches of sediment, which has caused increased erosion of the cliffs south of Mappleton'.

Section 3 — Cold Environments

Page 35 — Distribution of Cold Environments

1 Maximum of 15 marks available. This question is level marked.
HINTS:
- The question only mentions _glacial_ and _periglacial_ environments, so don't write about alpine or polar environments.
- Start by _defining_ each environment, e.g. 'Glacial environments are areas of land covered by ice (either glaciers or ice sheets)'.
- Then _describe where_ each environment is found (i.e. its _distribution_). Don't forget to _include examples_. E.g. 'Glacial environments are found at high latitudes, e.g. the Antarctic Ice Sheet is above 60°, and at high altitudes, e.g. there are glaciers in the Himalayan mountains (the highest mountain range in the world)'.
- Then _explain why_ they're found there. E.g. 'Glaciers and ice sheets only form where it's really cold. High latitude areas are really cold because they receive little solar radiation. The Sun's energy hits the Earth at more of an angle at high latitudes, so it's spread out over a larger area'.
- For extra marks explain why glacial environments aren't found on low altitude land in the middle of continents.

Page 37 — Glaciers

1 Maximum of 3 marks available.
A glacial budget is the balance between accumulation (the input of snow and ice into a glacier) and ablation (the output of water from a glacier) over a year _[1 mark]_. If the glacial budget is positive, accumulation is exceeding ablation, and the glacier is advancing _[1 mark]_. If the glacial budget is negative, ablation is exceeding accumulation, and the glacier is retreating _[1 mark]_.

2 Maximum of 5 marks available.
In warm-based glaciers, the base temperature is warmer than the melting point of ice, so melting occurs. The meltwater acts as a lubricant, making it easier for the glacier to move downhill _[1 mark]_. Ice at the surface also melts if the temperature reaches 0 °C. Meltwater moves down through the glacier and lubricates it even more _[1 mark]_. In cold-based glaciers the base is cold, so there's very little melting at the bottom of the glacier. The ice is frozen to the valley floor _[1 mark]_. So warm-based glaciers move faster than cold-based glaciers _[1 mark]_, which means they erode the landscape more _[1 mark]_.

Page 39 — Glacial Processes

1 Maximum of 4 marks available.
At the head of a glacier the valley is steep, so there's a strong gravitational force pulling the ice downwards _[1 mark]_. This makes the ice move quickly _[1 mark]_. The tension created causes the ice to crack into layers, which slip downwards over each other _[1 mark]_. This is called extensional flow _[1 mark]_.

2 Maximum of 4 marks available.
Glaciers pick up debris by plucking _[1 mark]_ and abrasion _[1 mark]_. Plucking is when ice thaws and then refreezes around rocks. When the glacier moves forward, it plucks the rocks from the valley floor or wall _[1 mark]_. Abrasion is when debris carried by the glacier scrapes material off the valley walls and floor _[1 mark]_.

Page 41 — Glacial Landforms

1 Maximum of 8 marks available. This question is level marked. See page 111 for a full worked answer to this question.

2 Maximum of 3 marks available.
Lateral moraine is deposited where the sides of the glacier were _[1 mark]_. Medial moraine is deposited in the centre of the valley where two glaciers converge _[1 mark]_. Terminal moraine is deposited as semicircular hillocks at the end of the glacier _[1 mark]_.

Answers

Page 43 — Fluvioglacial Processes and Landforms

1   Maximum of 2 marks available.
    Kame terraces are piles of sorted deposits that run along the valley walls *[1 mark]*. They're deposited by meltwater streams that run between the glacier and the valley sides *[1 mark]*.

2   Maximum of 4 marks available.
    Delta kames are formed when meltwater streams flow into a proglacial lake *[1 mark]*. When they flow into a proglacial lake, they slow down and deposit the sediment they're carrying on the ice *[1 mark]*. These deposits are known as deltas *[1 mark]*. After the ice has melted the deltas are deposited on the valley floor, forming delta kames *[1 mark]*.

Page 45 — Periglacial Processes and Landforms

1   Maximum of 6 marks available. This question is level marked.
    HINTS:
    • Start by _explaining_ what's meant by patterned ground.
    • _State_ the _two_ ways that patterned ground is formed — by frost heave and frost contraction.
    • _Explain_ how each process causes stones to form patterns on the surface of the ground, e.g. 'Frost contraction occurs when temperatures drop very low in winter — the ground contracts, causing polygon shaped cracks to form in the permafrost. The cracks get filled in with stones forming polygon patterns on the surface'.

Page 47 — Issues in Cold Environments

1   Maximum of 6 marks available. This question is level marked.
    HINTS:
    • The main types of development in cold environments are mining, fishing, oil extraction, tourism and hydroelectric power production.
    • For each type of development, _describe how_ it can damage the environment and give an _example_. E.g. 'Oil spilt when it's being transported can lead to the death of birds and marine life. For example, when the Exxon Valdez tanker crashed off the coast of Alaska over 40 million litres of oil were spilt, which killed over 250 000 birds and fish'.
    • Include that cold environments have _fragile ecosystems_, which means that they struggle to recover from damage.

2   Maximum of 6 marks available. This question is level marked.
    HINTS:
    • Start by describing the _traditional way of life_ of native tribes, i.e. what their lifestyle was like _before_ development of tundra areas.
    • Then say what development has taken place, e.g. whaling, sealing and fishing by newcomers.
    • Finally, explain how this development has _affected_ the native tribes, e.g. by bringing diseases and depleting their resources.

• Include any relevant _facts_ you can remember, e.g. 'When newcomers arrived in Canada in the late 19th century and early 20th century, they brought diseases like tuberculosis, which killed 90% of the Inuvialuit tribe'.

Page 49 — Issues in Cold Environments — Case Study

1   Maximum of 15 marks available.
    This question is level marked.
    HINTS:
    • Start off by describing what resources are found in the Antarctic and what type of development they attract.
    • Then explain how the Antarctic is being protected by the Antarctic Treaty — i.e. it _bans some development_ and _controls other activities_.
    • _Describe_ which activities are _banned_ (mining, oil extraction and whaling) and _explain why_ they're banned — the possible environmental impact of mining and oil extraction could be huge, and the whale population has decreased due to whaling. Don't forget to include the _names of the protocols_ that ban them.
    • Then say which activities are _allowed_ but controlled (tourism, scientific research, fishing). Explain how they're controlled and how the measures reduce their environmental impact and make them _more sustainable_.
    • Finish off by talking about _any issues_, e.g. illegal fishing.

Section 4 — Hot Desert Environments

Page 51 — Desert and Desert Margin Characteristics

1a) Maximum of 6 marks available. This part is level marked.
    HINTS:
    • Start by describing what the _rainfall_ is like — say which months have no rainfall, which months do, and which month has the highest rainfall, e.g. 'Riyadh receives no rainfall from June to September. It typically rains from October until May, with most rain falling in April (average 29 mm)'.
    • You get higher marks if you _manipulate the data_, so count up the total rainfall for the year and say if Riyadh has an arid or semi-arid climate, e.g. 'The total rainfall in Riyadh is about 100 mm per year, which is less than 250 mm per year, so it has an arid climate and is classed as a desert'.
    • Next describe the _temperature_ throughout the year.
    • Remember to _quote data from the graph_ to back up your points.

Answers

b) Maximum of 5 marks available. This part is level marked.
HINTS:
- First, say that if it's 25° north of the equator it's located in an area of circulating air known as a Hadley cell.
- Then you need to explain how the circulating air leads to low precipitation, e.g. 'As air rises at the equator, the moisture that it holds condenses and falls as rain. The dry air descends over Riyadh, creating an area of high pressure. Winds blow outwards from this area, meaning no moisture can be brought in, so there's very little precipitation'.

c) Maximum of 4 marks available.
The total amount of vegetation in Riyadh will be low **[1 mark]** because the lack of water makes it difficult for plants to grow **[1 mark]**. Any vegetation present will be specialised to collect, store and conserve water **[1 mark]**. Vegetation is likely to include shrubs, grasses and cacti **[1 mark]**.

Page 53 — Processes in Hot Desert Environments

1 Maximum of 8 marks available. This question is level marked.
HINTS:
- To get full marks you need to describe all four types of mechanical weathering that occur in hot desert environments — thermal fracture, frost shattering, wetting and drying, and salt weathering.
- Write a brief paragraph about each type of weathering, e.g. 'Thermal fracture is caused by the large daily temperature variations in hot desert environments. Rocks expand during the day (when it's hot) and contract at night (when it's cold). Sometimes outer layers of rock flake off because they warm up and cool down more quickly than the inner layers (exfoliation). Individual grains can also fall off because different minerals within the rock expand and contract at different rates (granular disintegration)'.
- Include diagrams to help you explain the processes involved.

2a) Maximum of 3 marks available.
Exogenous rivers have a source outside the desert margin and they flow throughout the year despite evaporation reducing their volume **[1 mark]**. Endoreic rivers terminate inland in the form of an inland sea or delta **[1 mark]**. Ephemeral rivers flow intermittently or seasonally after rainstorms **[1 mark]**.

b) Maximum of 6 marks available. This part is level marked.
HINTS:
- Start your answer by describing what flash floods and sheet floods are.
- Then describe how both types of flood transport material. Make sure you point out that flash floods have more energy and so can carry larger pieces of rock.
- Be specific in your answer — don't just say, 'Flash floods carry large pieces of rock', instead say, 'Flash floods carry large pieces of desert rock by traction'.
- The question asks about erosion — so make sure your answer includes how both types of floods erode the desert surface by abrasion and attrition.

Page 55 — Landforms in Hot Desert Environments

1 Maximum of 7 marks available. This question is level marked.
HINTS:
- You need to describe and explain the formation of both yardangs and zeugen to get full marks. Make sure you don't get them confused.
- First explain what yardangs are and how they're formed, e.g. 'Yardangs are narrow, streamlined ridges. Strong winds (blowing in one direction) carry sand in suspension, which erodes rocks by abrasion. Softer rock is eroded faster than harder rock, so ridges of hard rock are created'.
- Then do the same for zeugen.
- You could include diagrams of each to help explain how they're formed. For example, draw one like this for yardangs:

2a) Maximum of 3 marks available.
Landform A is a sand dune/barchan/crescent-shaped sand dune **[1 mark]**. Landform B is an alluvial fan **[1 mark]**. Landform C is a wadi **[1 mark]**.

b) Maximum of 4 marks available.
A mesa is an isolated, flat-topped, steep-sided landform found only in arid places **[1 mark]**. It's a type of inselberg **[1 mark]** made of hard rock that's more resistant to erosion than the surrounding rock **[1 mark]**. It's formed when the surrounding softer rock is eroded away by wind or water, leaving the harder rock mesa standing out **[1 mark]**.

c) Maximum of 4 marks available.
Feature E could be a salt lake or a salt pan **[1 mark]**. Salt lakes form when desert rivers are endoreic/terminate inland **[1 mark]**. The water can't leave the lake and evaporation is high, resulting in a lake with a high salt content **[1 mark]**. Some salt lakes are ephemeral — evaporation is so high that they dry up at certain times of the year, leaving the salt behind to form salt pans **[1 mark]**.

Page 57 — Desertification

1 Maximum of 10 marks available.
This question is level marked.
HINTS:
- Split your answer into two — first cover the physical causes, then the human causes.
- For each cause, explain how it leads to desertification, e.g. 'Climate change is causing an increase in temperature in some areas. This increases the rate of evapotranspiration, which dries soils out and lowers surface water levels. Vegetation dies due to lack of water and so there are fewer roots to hold the soil together. This leads to an increase in soil erosion'.
- Make sure you explicitly say how each one leads to either soil erosion or the land being less fertile (e.g. because the salt content has increased).
- Don't forget that there are a number of ways that irrigation leads to desertification.
- As a final point, include how an increase in population can increase overgrazing, overcultivation and deforestation.

Answers

Page 59 — Desertification Case Study — The Sahel

1   Maximum of 15 marks available.
    This question is level marked.
    HINTS:
    • This question asks you to <u>evaluate</u> the strategies, so you need to say if they <u>worked</u>, if they caused any <u>problems</u> and if they had any <u>extra benefits</u>, e.g. 'Jatropha curcas is being grown around crops in Mali to protect them from wind erosion. The strategy has reduced erosion in the area and has also reduced rural poverty, as oil from the plant can be sold'.
    • Include whether each strategy is <u>sustainable</u> or not.
    • As always with case study questions include plenty of <u>relevant details</u>, e.g. 'Yields of some crops increased 40% in Burkina Faso as a result of contour bunding'.

Page 61 — Desertification Case Study — Southern Spain

1   Maximum of 15 marks available.
    This question is level marked.
    HINTS:
    • The question asks you to <u>compare</u> strategies, so you need to write about the <u>similarities</u> and <u>differences</u> between the strategies used to tackle desertification in Spain and the Sahel.
    • Start off by describing the <u>similarities</u> in the strategies used in the Sahel and Spain, e.g. 'Both the Sahel and Spain are implementing strategies to increase the level of vegetation, as loss of vegetation is a major cause of desertification in both areas'.
    • Then explain the <u>differences</u> in the strategies used, e.g. 'In Spain lots of money is being spent on transferring water from one place to another, whilst in the Sahel the focus is on working with what little water they have, by conserving rainwater (using contour bunding) and growing plants that are suited to drought conditions'.

Section 5 — Population Change

Page 63 — Population Change Basics and the DTM

1   Maximum of 10 marks available.
    This question is level marked.
    HINTS:
    • Write an introduction briefly explaining what the DTM is, e.g. 'The Demographic Transition Model (DTM) shows how the population of a country changes over time through five stages. The model shows birth rate, death rate and total population'.
    • The question asks you to <u>refer to the DTM</u>, so you can use this to <u>structure</u> your answer — start by explaining what stage of the DTM the country was in in 1600. E.g. 'In 1600 the birth rate and death rate were very high (38 and 37 respectively) and the population was low (2 million). The country was in Stage 1 of the DTM. Birth rate was high because there was no birth control or family planning, and education was poor. Also, infant mortality was high, so people had more children to replace those who'd died. The death rate was high because of poor health care, sanitation and diet, which led to disease and starvation'.
    • Next, <u>describe</u> how the data <u>changes</u> and relate the changes to the stages of the DTM, e.g. 'Between 1600 and 1800, the death rate decreased (from 37 to 18 per 1000 per year) and the population had more than tripled, from 2 million to 7 million. The birth rate had dropped very slightly from 38 to 35 per 1000 per year. The country had reached Stage 2 of the DTM'. Don't forget to <u>give reasons</u> for the changes.
    • Make sure you <u>use data</u> from the table in your answer.

Page 65 — Applying the DTM

1   Maximum of 15 marks available.
    This question is level marked.
    HINTS:
    • Start with an <u>introduction</u> briefly <u>explaining</u> the DTM.
    • The question asks you to <u>discuss</u> the <u>uses</u> and <u>limitations</u>, so you need to talk about the <u>advantages</u> and <u>disadvantages</u>.
    • Write a section on what the DTM can be used for and why it's <u>useful</u> (the advantages), e.g. 'The DTM can be used to forecast how a population may change, which can help governments decide on policies such as one-child limits or immigration laws'.
    • Then <u>explain</u> each <u>limitation</u> of the DTM (the disadvantages), e.g. 'The original data used to create the DTM was from more developed, richer countries (e.g. European countries, Japan and the USA). This means it might not be a valid model worldwide — what happened in these countries might not be the same as what's happening in others, e.g. countries in Asia or Africa'.

Answers

Page 67 — Population Structure and Migration

1   Maximum of 4 marks available.
Push factors are the things that make people want to move out of the place they're in *[1 mark]*. They're negative factors about the place they're leaving, e.g. lack of jobs or poor living conditions and services, fear of political persecution *[1 mark]*. Pull factors attract people to a new place *[1 mark]*. They're positive factors about the place they're moving to, e.g. better jobs and more job opportunities, better living conditions and services *[1 mark]*.

Page 69 — Impacts and Management of Population Change

1   Maximum of 15 marks available.
This question is level marked.
HINTS:
- First, briefly *explain* what an ageing population is, e.g. 'An ageing population is a population where the proportion of older people (over 65) is increasing'.
- Then write a section *describing* and *explaining* each social effect. E.g. 'An ageing population means there's increased pressure on public services such as hospitals and hospices. More people are needed to care for the elderly, so more carers and nurses will need training'.
- Next write about the *economic effects*, e.g. 'There could be increased taxes for the working population. Pensions and services are paid for by taxes, so if there's a greater proportion of older people claiming pensions and support, there'll be higher taxes for the working population'.

Page 71 — Managing Populations — Case Studies

1   Maximum of 10 marks available.
This question is level marked.
HINTS:
- Remember, *evaluate* means you need to talk about whether the strategies have been *successful* or not.
- Introduce the named example, and say briefly how the population has been changing, e.g. 'Uganda has a youthful population — in 2007, 50% of the population were under 15 and only 3% were over 65. The youthful population is increasing because the birth rate is high — 48 babies are born for every 1000 people each year'.
- Next talk about any strategies that have been used to manage the population change, e.g. 'The use of contraceptives and family planning has been encouraged in Uganda to try to slow the increase in the youthful population, e.g. the government has brought in free contraceptives like condoms'.
- Finally, *assess* the strategy, e.g. 'Family planning clinics aren't widespread, so many people don't have easy access to birth control. This may explain why the strategy has been unsuccessful — since 1991 the birth rate has increased'.

Page 73 — Urban and Rural Characteristics

1   Maximum of 6 marks available. This question is level marked.
HINTS:
- Cover one characteristic at a time and for each one explain how population change and migration can affect it, e.g. 'As young, wealthy professionals move to redeveloped urban areas, they increase the wealth of those areas. This can improve inner city areas, but can also mean that the younger original residents can't afford to live in these areas any more'.
- Remember that the question says 'explain', so you need to say *why* population change and migration can affect the character of urban areas, e.g. 'Younger people could migrate into urban areas to look for work, which would affect the population structure of the area. This could also affect the provision of services, as younger people (of reproductive age) require more schools and childcare services'.
- The question only asks you about the character of *urban* areas, so don't start talking about how rural areas are affected.

Page 75 — Urban and Rural Characteristics — Case Study

1   Maximum of 15 marks available.
This question is level marked.
HINTS:
- Start by naming your region and the two areas you've chosen, and describe and compare their characteristics. E.g. 'The wards of Fishwick (inner city area) and Lea (rural/urban fringe) can be found in Preston, a city in the North-west of England. Fishwick has lots of high-density, 19th century housing, whereas Lea has large detached and semi-detached houses with gardens and driveways'.
- Then for each of the different characteristics, describe and explain any effects they have on the social welfare of the residents in your chosen areas, e.g. '74% of people in Lea (rural/urban fringe) described their general health in the 12 months leading up to the 2001 census as 'good'. This was only 64% for Fishwick. This may be because a higher percentage of people in Fishwick live in houses that are likely to be cold and damp due to a lack of central heating — 17.5% of houses in Fishwick have no central heating, compared to 5.6% in Lea'.
- *Include data* from the table on p. 74 in your answer, and don't forget to use appropriate terms such as suburban area, occupancy rate, professional sector.

Answers

Section 6 — Food Supply Issues

Page 77 — Global Food Distribution

1   Maximum of 5 marks available.
Intensive farming produces as much as possible from the
land *[1 mark]*. It has a high input of capital or labour relative
to land area *[1 mark]*. Extensive farming has a low input of
capital and labour relative to land area *[1 mark]*.
Extensive farming produces less food from the land than
intensive farming *[1 mark]*, but has less environmental impact
and offers better animal welfare *[1 mark]*.

2   Maximum of 8 marks available. This question is level marked.
HINTS:
   * Start by *describing the role* of TNCs in the global food
     industry, e.g. in production, processing and distribution.
   * To get full marks you need to discuss at least three
     advantages *and* three disadvantages of the involvement
     of TNCs.
   * Give *specific examples* where possible, e.g. 'Cargill™ employs
     local people to trade and distribute their produce in Pakistan,
     which benefits the local economy'.
   * *Discuss* points from *different angles*, e.g. 'Although some local
     people benefit from the job opportunities that TNCs provide,
     local companies that can't compete with the TNCs often go
     bankrupt, and this causes unemployment in the area'.
   * *Link* points together, e.g. '...and this causes unemployment in
     the area. Another effect of smaller companies going bankrupt
     is delocalisation of food supplies'.

Page 79 — Changes in Demand

1   Maximum of 4 marks available.
The demand for high value food exports from developing
countries has increased *[1 mark]*. The demand for seasonal
products all year round has also increased *[1 mark]*. 1 mark
for each reason up to a maximum of two marks. Reasons
include: rising incomes *[1 mark]*, an increasing culture of high
consumption *[1 mark]*, increased demand for exotic products
in developed countries *[1 mark]*.

2   Maximum of 8 marks available. This question is level marked.
HINTS:
   * To get full marks you need to describe a *range* of
     environmental issues relating to the globalisation of the food
     industry (e.g. deforestation, damaging effects of intensive
     farming, transporting food / food miles).
   * Write a paragraph for each environmental issue, covering the
     negative environmental impacts. For example, 'Transporting
     food releases carbon dioxide into the atmosphere.
     Carbon dioxide is a greenhouse gas, which contributes to
     climate change'.

Page 81 — Increasing Food Production

1   Maximum of 6 marks available. This question is level marked.
HINTS:
   * To get full marks you need to *describe* what the technologies
     and methods are and *give their disadvantages*,
     e.g. 'Mechanisation brought in by the green revolution involves
     the use of expensive machines. Farms that can't afford
     these machines could go bankrupt, leading to unemployment
     and food shortages'.

Page 83 — Controlling Food Production and Supply

1   Maximum of 15 marks available.
This question is level marked.
HINTS:
   * This question is about EU *market policies* so don't write about
     non-market policies.
   * EU market policies include: subsidies, tariffs, intervention
     (including pricing) and quotas.
   * To get full marks you need to cover at least three EU
     market policies.
   * For each policy you need to describe *what it is*, then *explain
     how* it controls the level and nature of agricultural production,
     e.g. 'Subsidies are payments made to farmers. They can
     control production by encouraging farmers to produce
     particular products'.
   * Quote facts and give real-life examples where possible,
     e.g. 'In 2006 EU farmers were paid €1 billion to produce dairy
     products' and 'Tariffs of 18-28% are applied to imported
     beef products'.

Page 85 — Managing Food Supply — Case Studies

1   Maximum of 10 marks available.
This question is level marked.
HINTS:
   * First *describe* the strategies used to manage food supplies
     in Bangladesh.
   * Strategies include: investment in green revolution
     technologies, investment in improving infrastructure,
     diversification, free market policies and food aid.
   * Then discuss the sustainability of each strategy you describe,
     e.g. 'Investment in green revolution technologies is not
     sustainable because of the high cost and the environmental
     impact (falling water tables and soil salinisation due to
     irrigation, water pollution from agrochemicals, and soil
     degradation due to overcultivation)'.
   * Quote facts and give real-life examples where possible,
     e.g. 'Between 1974 and 2000 the use of high yielding rice
     seeds, increased irrigation and increased use of agrochemicals
     increased rice production from 11.7 to 23.1 million tonnes'.

Answers

2 Maximum of 15 marks available.
   This question is level marked.
   HINTS:
   • To 'compare' the management of food supplies in the two countries you need to look at the similarities and differences between them.
   • Start by describing and explaining the aim of food supply management in Bangladesh and China, e.g. 'Food supply management in Bangladesh aims to provide enough food for the population, as there isn't enough at the moment. Chinese management is focused on producing enough food within the country to be self-sufficient, as it has a history of food shortages'.
   • Next, describe and explain the similarities in the management of food supply in China and Bangladesh, e.g. 'Both China and Bangladesh have invested in transportation infrastructure to improve the transport of produce around the country'.
   • Then describe and explain the differences between the two countries, e.g. 'Bangladesh has removed subsidies, eliminated quotas and reduced import tariffs to encourage food imports as this increases the amount of food available to feed the population. In contrast, China limits imports in order to protect the market for local produce, encourage production and improve food security'.
   • Discuss the sustainability of the contrasting strategies, e.g. 'Self-sufficiency may not be a realistic and sustainable strategy in China as the limited amount of arable land available is being reduced as the country becomes increasingly urbanised. Free market policies in Bangladesh may not be sustainable because they increase susceptibility to rising food prices, and maintain reliance on food imports – more sustainable solutions may involve improving local production and reducing imports'.

Section 7 — Energy Issues

Page 87 — Energy Resources

1 Maximum of 6 marks available. This question is level marked.
   HINTS:
   • Start off by describing what renewable and non-renewable resources are.
   • Include examples of renewable and non-renewable resources.
   • Explain why it can be difficult to classify resources as renewable or non-renewable (because some resources are only renewable if carefully managed).

2 Maximum of 6 marks available. This question is level marked.
   HINTS:
   • Start off by explaining what the term 'energy mix' means.
   • Then describe the energy mix of a particular country, e.g. 'In 2008 the UK got 33% of its energy from petroleum (oil), 40% from natural gas, 17% from coal, 8% from nuclear and 2% from other sources'.
   • Finally describe how the amount an energy source contributes has changed and give reasons for the change, e.g. 'The use of coal has fallen 40% since 1990. This is due to the closure of coal mines in the UK and a move to less polluting oil and gas'.

Page 89 — Global Energy Distribution

1 Maximum of 15 marks available.
   This question is level marked.
   HINTS:
   • Start off by explaining why the amount of energy that a country produces could increase or decrease.
   • Then explain why the amount of energy a country consumes could change.
   • Go on to energy trading next. Explain what energy trading is and why it's needed.
   • Describe how the amount of energy that a country needs to import (or is able to export) could change and how this would affect trade, e.g. 'After Brazil discovered new supplies of oil it was able to become energy self-sufficient and no longer needed to import energy'.
   • Explain why some countries might decide to change their energy supplier, e.g. to reduce their dependence on a particular country or to receive imports from a more stable and therefore more reliable region.

Page 91 — Impacts of Energy Production

1 Maximum of 10 marks available.
   This question is level marked.
   HINTS:
   • Start off by describing why a replacement for fossil fuels needs to be found, i.e. fossil fuel use is environmentally damaging and they will run out.
   • Describe the advantages and disadvantages of nuclear power in relation to fossil fuels, e.g. 'Accidents at nuclear power plants can cause more serious environmental damage than accidents at fossil fuel plants, as radioactive material can be released into the environment. However, if accidents are avoided fossil fuels cause the more serious environmental problems as burning them leads to global warming and climate change, whereas the environmental impacts of nuclear energy are much smaller'.
   • Using your arguments for and against nuclear power, come to a conclusion on whether it's a suitable replacement for fossil fuels. It doesn't matter whether you think that nuclear power is a good replacement for fossil fuels or not, as long as you can give reasons for your choice.

Page 95 — Sustainable Energy

1 Maximum of 4 marks available.
   Biomass is material that is or was recently living [1 mark].
   It can be burnt directly to release energy [1 mark].
   Biomass can also be used to produce biofuels like ethanol [1 mark], which are burnt to release energy [1 mark].

Answers

2 Maximum of 6 marks available. This question is level marked.
HINTS:
- 'Compare' means talk about the similarities and differences.
- Start off by describing the similarities between wave energy and tidal energy, e.g. they both rely on seas/oceans, they both involve the use of turbines to convert the energy into electricity.
- Then describe the differences between them, e.g. 'Although both wave and wind energy use turbines to generate electricity, tidal energy is a reliable and constant source of energy (as tides are regular events), but wave energy isn't. If there's no wind no waves are produced and that means electricity can't be generated. This is a big disadvantage of wave energy'.

3 Maximum of 8 marks available. This question is level marked.
HINTS:
- Start off by explaining why energy use isn't sustainable (i.e. the energy that we use comes from unsustainable sources), but that there are things that can be done to make energy use more sustainable.
- Then explain that energy use can be made more sustainable by conserving as much energy as possible.
- Describe the different strategies that conserve energy in the home, e.g. insulation, energy-efficient boilers, features that absorb the Sun's energy.

4 Maximum of 10 marks available.
This question is level marked.
HINTS:
- Start by explaining why transport isn't sustainable at the moment, e.g. using oil for transport depletes non-renewable resources and releases greenhouse gases.
- Explain that energy conservation can make transport more sustainable and describe strategies that can conserve energy, e.g. park-and-ride schemes and congestion charging.
- Then explain how technologies that run off sustainable energy sources can improve sustainability of transport. Describe at least two and explain why they improve sustainability of transport, e.g. 'Hybrid fuel vehicles use more than one source of fuel. If a vehicle runs on an ethanol and petrol mix then less fossil fuels are used and less greenhouse gases are emitted, making the vehicle more sustainable than those that just run on petrol'.
- Technologies include hydrogen fuel cell vehicles, hybrid fuel vehicles and vehicles that run off other renewable energies, e.g. wave power.

Page 96 — Managing Energy — Case Studies

1 Maximum of 15 marks available.
This question is level marked.
HINTS:
- Start by describing Chad's energy resources and its energy mix.
- Explain which aspects of Chad's energy supply aren't sustainable, e.g. 'Currently, oil is used to generate electricity. This is unsustainable as oil will run out one day and its use contributes to global warming. If Chad is to generate electricity in a more sustainable manner, a different energy source must be used'.

- Describe aspects of Chad's current energy supply that are sustainable or have the potential to be sustainable, e.g. '90% of Chad's energy is supplied by biomass. This has the potential to be a renewable resource, but at the moment it's overexploited, making it unsustainable'.
- Then explain how supplies could be made sustainable, e.g. 'If the Household Energy Project was successfully implemented over a larger area, more of the country's biomass resources would be better managed, becoming renewable and therefore sustainable'.
- Include details of any aspects of Chad's energy supply that are a barrier to sustainability, e.g. 'The revenue from Chad's oil exports could be invested in projects to improve the sustainability of energy supplies, e.g. the Household Energy Project. This doesn't happen though, due to the high level of corruption in Chad, which is a serious barrier to sustainability'.

Page 97 — Managing Energy — Case Studies

1 Maximum of 15 marks available.
This question is level marked.
HINTS:
- Start by describing Norway's current energy supply and briefly explain which aspects of it are sustainable, e.g. '50% of Norway's energy is supplied by HEP which is a renewable source of energy and (once established) is sustainable'.
- Then explain which aspects of Norway's energy supply are unsustainable and what methods are being used to improve their sustainability, e.g. 'Norway relies on oil for transport, which as a non-renewable resource is unsustainable. Biofuels are being developed to replace oil. This will make energy supply for transport more sustainable as long as the sources of materials used to produce the biofuels are managed properly'.
- Other methods that Norway is pursuing to improve sustainability include development of wind power and development of solar power.

Section 8 — Health Issues

Page 99 — Global Patterns of Health, Disease and Death

1 Maximum of 10 marks available.
This question is level marked.
HINTS:
- Take your time to study any maps or graphs you get — look carefully at the title, key and units.
- The map shows the global pattern of measles morbidity (measles cases) — don't get this confused with measles mortality (deaths due to measles).
- The question asks you to 'outline' the pattern — in other words, you should 'describe and explain' it.
- When describing the pattern, say what the map shows and quote relevant data for the most and least affected countries. E.g. 'The countries most affected by measles are mostly in Africa — some countries had over 50 cases per 100 000 of the population in 2003. Measles morbidity is low

Answers

in North America, South America and Australia, which had less than 1 case per 100 000 of the population in 2003'.

- Give <u>reasons why</u> the pattern is like this, e.g. 'The countries mostly affected by measles are those in poorer areas of the world. There's limited health education in Africa so many people aren't informed about how they can avoid infectious diseases, like measles. Also, overcrowded conditions in urban areas of poorer countries means that measles is more likely to spread to other people'.
- Remember, the general trend is that <u>poorer countries</u> have <u>higher mortality</u> and <u>morbidity</u> than wealthier countries — but always point out any <u>exceptions</u> to the rule. E.g. 'The map shows that measles also affects wealthier countries like Italy'.

Page 101 — Health Care Approaches

1a) Maximum of 2 marks available.
   Public health spending is high in Western Europe, North America and Japan **[1 mark]** and particularly low in Africa, Asia and South America **[1 mark]**.
b) Maximum of 10 marks available.
   This question is level marked.
   <u>HINTS:</u>
   - To get <u>full marks</u>, you need to <u>describe</u> the <u>differences</u> in health care approaches used in poor <u>and</u> wealthy countries — and refer to at least one scheme (<u>case study</u>).
   - Start with the <u>main difference</u> — e.g. 'Poor countries have less money, which is mainly spent on treating diseases, whereas wealthier countries have more money to spend on treatments, prevention and awareness of diseases'.
   - Give <u>examples</u> of the main approaches to health care used in poor and wealthy countries, and <u>describe</u> at least one <u>specific scheme</u> you've studied. E.g. 'Many people live in remote rural areas in sub-Saharan Africa, so have limited access to health care and medical services. One inexpensive health care approach is to train local people as basic health care workers. For example, the Health Extension Programme in Ethiopia trains people who live in remote rural areas as local health care workers. Workers can then deliver basic health care and education to people in their local communities'.
   - Use <u>statistics</u> where relevant, e.g. 'Insecticide-treated bed nets helped the number of malaria cases to fall by 20% in just one year'.
   - The question <u>doesn't</u> ask you to discuss or evaluate, so don't go on about advantages or disadvantages.

Page 103 — The Geography of Disease

1 Maximum of 10 marks available.
   This question is level marked.
   <u>HINTS:</u>
   - Start off by <u>describing</u> the global distribution of malaria — the main countries affected by malaria (with a <u>statistic</u>) and those least affected.
   - Give <u>reasons</u> for the uneven distribution of malaria cases and explain each reason, e.g. 'Mosquitoes that carry malaria can only survive in tropical climates, such as those found in sub-Saharan Africa'.

- '<u>Discuss its impact</u>' means you should <u>explain</u> a range of <u>effects</u> that malaria has on a country's health, economic development and lifestyle. E.g. 'Malaria has a big impact on a country's economic development because of the number of people dying, decreasing productivity due to days lost from work, and increasing health care costs'.

Page 105 — Health and Globalisation

1 Maximum of 10 marks available.
   This question is level marked.
   <u>HINTS:</u>
   - Start off by <u>describing</u> what is meant by a Trans-National Corporation (TNC).
   - <u>Explain</u> how TNCs can <u>improve</u> global health and how they can <u>add</u> to global health problems. E.g. 'Pharmaceutical companies can improve health in wealthier countries by choosing to research and produce drugs for diseases that mainly affect wealthier countries, such as drugs for impotency. However, this can add to health problems in poorer countries because money isn't being spent on life-saving drugs for diseases such as malaria and HIV/AIDS'.
   - To get <u>full marks</u>, you need to give a <u>range of examples</u> of how specific TNCs (like GSK or PMI) affect global health. E.g. 'The pharmaceutical company GSK helps to improve global health by investing a large amount of their profit (e.g. £282 million in 2007) in community programmes to help people in need'.
   - You can take a <u>mixture of examples</u> from different case studies if you want, as long as each example backs up whatever point you're making and doesn't just repeat points you've already made.

Page 107 — The Geography of Health in the UK

1 Maximum of 6 marks available. This question is level marked.
   <u>HINTS:</u>
   - Start off by <u>describing</u> what's meant by the term 'ageing population'.
   - To <u>describe</u> how ageing populations will affect the provision of health care services, you need to cover <u>examples</u> of <u>services</u> needed by the elderly. For example, 'An ageing population has different health needs, such as the need for more mobile health care services to cope with the increasing immobilised elderly population. This is a particularly important way of providing health care to elderly people in rural areas who don't have family support'.

Acknowledgements

Page 24 — Sand dune and salt marsh photos © iStockphoto.com.

Page 26 — Graph adapted from Climate Change 2001: The Scientific Basis. Contribution of Working Group I to the Third Assessment Report of the Intergovernmental Panel on Climate Change. Figure 5. Cambridge University Press.

Page 29 — All three photos © iStockphoto.com

Page 35 — Antarctic diagram reproduced from 'Fundamentals of the Physical Environment' by Peter Smithson, Ken Addison and Ken Atkinson, Third edition June 2002, Chapter 24, Polar Environments, Fig. 24.2. © 2007, Routledge, member of the Taylor & Francis Group.

Page 51 — Data used to construct the Riyadh climate graph from: http://www.climate-charts.com/Locations/s/SD40438.php © Climate-Charts.com

Page 56 and 60 — World map of desertification risk and vulnerability to desertification map of Spain reproduced from U.S. Department of Agriculture: National Resources Conservation Service, Soil Survey Division, World Soil Resource, Washington, D.C.

Page 70 — Data used to construct the UK population pyramids reproduced with kind permission from National Statistics online. Reproduced under the terms of the Click-Use license.

Page 71 — Data used to construct the population pyramid for Uganda, source: U.S. Census Bureau.

Page 74 — Data used to compile the table on Preston, source: National Statistics website: www.statistics.gov.uk. Crown copyright material is reproduced with the permission of the Controller Office of Public Sector Information (OPSI).

Page 76 — Barley production map reproduced with kind permission from the Food and Agriculture Organization of the United Nations, http://oregonstate.edu/instruct/css/330/five/BarleyOverview.htm with data from FAOSTAT, http://faostat.fao.org/default.aspx.

Page 76 — Data used to construct the daily calorie intake map, source: Food and Agriculture Organisation of the United Nations, FAO Statistical Yearbook 05/06, http://www.fao.org/docrep/009/a0490m/PDF/a0490m01d.pdf

Page 87 — UK energy mix pie chart © Crown copyright reproduced under the terms of the Click-Use license.

Page 87 — France's energy mix pie chart reproduced with kind permission from Obeservatoire de l'énergie.

Page 88 — Map of world energy production and consumption of energy, source: Map projection, Buckminster Fuller Institute and Dymaxion Map Design, Santa Barbara, CA. The word Dymaxion and the Fuller Projection Dymaxion™ Map design are trademarks of the Buckminster Fuller Institute, Santa Barbara, California, ©1938, 1967 & 1992. All rights reserved.

Page 88 — Global Energy Consumption map © BP Statistical Review of World Energy 2008, BP p.l.c.

Page 98 — Healthy Life Expectancy map reproduced from UNEP/DEWA/GRID-Europe, GEO Data Portal, Healthy Life Expectancy (HALE), 2002, United Nations Environment Programme.

Page 98 — TB map © WHO, 2008. All rights reserved. World Health Organisation, http://www.who.int/ith/maps/tuberculosis_2008.jpg

Page 99 — Breast cancer map reproduced with thanks to WHO © International Agency for Research on Cancer, March 2003. Data from Stewart B. W. and Kleihues P. (Eds): World Cancer Report. IARCPress. Lyon 2003. http://www.who.int/bookorders/anglais/detart1.jsp?sesslan=1&codlan=1&codcol=76&codcch=16#

Page 99 — Cancer table, Cancer Research UK: http://info.cancerresearchuk.org/cancerstats/geographic/world. November 2008.

Page 99 — Global measles map reproduced with thanks to WHO, from the WHO/IVB database, 2004 © WHO 2004. All rights reserved. http://www.who.int/vaccines-surveillance/graphics/NY_graphics/glob_inc_measles_map.jpg

Page 101 — Graph © Copyright 2006 SASI Group (University of Sheffield) and Mark Newman (University of Michigan), www.worldmapper.org

Page 102 — HIV map © WHO, 2008. All rights reserved. World Health Organisation, http://www.who.int/ith/maps/HIV_infection2005_en.gif

Page 106 — Data used to construct the UK life expectancy map reproduced with kind permission from National Statistics website: www.statistics.gov.uk. Crown copyright material is reproduced with the permission of the Controller Office of Public Sector Information (OPSI). Reproduced under the terms of the Click-Use license.

Page 110 and 116 — Mapping data reproduced by permission of Ordnance Survey® on behalf of HMSO © Crown copyright (2009). All rights reserved. Ordnance Survey® Licence No. 100034841.

Page 114 — World populations graph, data from World Population Prospects: 2008 Population Database © United Nations, 2009. Reproduced with permission.

Page 115 — Movement map source: International Passenger Survey, Office for National Statistics © Crown copyright reproduced under the terms of the Click-Use License.

Every effort has been made to locate copyright holders and obtain permission to reproduce sources. For those sources where it has been difficult to trace the originator of the work, we would be grateful for information. If any copyright holder would like us to make an amendment to the acknowledgements, please notify us and we will gladly update the book at the next reprint. Thank you.

Index

Index

Index